Rethinking Wesley's Theology
for
Contemporary Methodism

Rethinking Wesley's Theology
for
Contemporary Methodism

Edited by
Randy L. Maddox

 KINGSWOOD BOOKS
An Imprint of Abingdon Press
Nashville, Tennessee

Library of Congress Cataloging-in-Publication Data

Re-thinking Wesley's theology for contemporary Methodism / edited by
Randy L. Maddox.
       p.   cm.
    Festschrift in honor of Theodore Runyon.
    Includes bibliographical references.
    ISBN 0-687-06045-1 (alk. paper)
    1. Wesley, John, 1703–1791. 2. Methodist Church—Doctrines.
3. Theology, Doctrinal. I. Maddox, Randy L. II. Runyon, Theodore.
BX8495.W5R45 1998
230'.7'092—dc20

           98-6005
           CIP

For

Theodore Hubert Runyon Jr.

Contents

Foreword: Homage to a Friend

Jürgen Moltmann

I heard about Ted Runyon long before I met him personally. It happened during my student days at Göttingen, when my *Doktorvater* Professor Otto Weber told me that an American had come to him and asked to write a dissertation under his supervision on Weber's colleague Friedrich Gogarten. In those early years after World War II Gogarten was still a controversial figure. In the 1920s Gogarten had joined Karl Barth in launching what was called "Dialectical Theology." In the early 1930s he had turned to a kind of neoconservativism (Armin Mohler's "conservative revolution"). After the war, Gogarten stepped forward as the first German theologian of the modern world; his "Theology of Secularity" was the first original protestant theology of modernity. As this itinerary might suggest, Gogarten was somewhat of a theological chameleon, taking on the colors of his shifting political and cultural environment. However, he was always an inspiring teacher and original thinker. Ted expanded his dissertation to include Paul Tillich, focusing on Tillich's interpretation of history. This provided him greater distance from Gogarten's thought, so that he did not become a "Gogärtner" (as we called the disciples of Gogarten—Dorothee Sölle was one), but under the stimulus of Gogarten's insights Ted provided fresh American and Methodist perspectives. And so a Lutheran teacher produced an excellent Methodist scholar. Ted's dissertation was well received by the theological faculty at Göttingen and was designated *magna cum laude*.

I first met Ted Runyon in person in the fall of 1967 at Duke University. My late friend Fred Herzog had brought me over from Tübingen to serve as a guest lecturer for two semesters at this Methodist school in North Carolina. My family and I were faced with the challenge of making ourselves at home in this foreign country. Our transition was eased by Ted's brief visit to Duke. I noticed that I

9

understood Ted's way of thinking and lecturing immediately. As children of the same *Doktorvater* in Göttingen, we found the basis of an enduring friendship in all we had in common. We spent some prized time during that visit talking about the good old days at Göttingen in Sarah Duke's Memorial Park.

I returned the favor of Ted's visit to Duke with a guest lecture at Emory University in 1968. Here Ted and his colleague Manfred Hoffmann introduced me to Southern theology, while my wife, Elisabeth, was introduced to Southern life and hospitality by a gracious older lady who took her on a tour of the famous Cyclorama (portraying the battle of Atlanta) and explained Sherman's infamous march through the South. This visit to Emory came at a time when Thomas Altizer (another of Ted's colleagues at Emory) was the center of public attention with his "Death-of-God Theology," and I well remember Altizer sitting in the front row as I spoke about the Christian-Marxist dialogue in Prague, arguing that for Vitezslav Gardavsky "God is not yet dead." My memory of how Manfred Hoffmann's theological concern at the time differed in focus from my own is connected to a more scenic event. Hoffmann was in his existentialist phase, and when he took me on the cable car ride to the top of Stone Mountain (a large granite outcropping turned into a Confederate memorial to the Civil War) I recall that he was fascinated by the abyss below us while I was looking forward "in hope" to the top of the mountain! During this visit I also began to sense the quiet but persistent influence of Ted Runyon at Emory's Candler School of Theology. While the concern to articulate an authentic contemporary Wesleyan or Methodist theology was not yet in vogue, it was clear that the core of such a theology provided the sustaining convictions beneath the coming and going fads at Candler. The health of this core owed much to Ted's nurturing.

After that first visit I returned to Atlanta whenever I could. Together with Jim Waits (whom I now considered "my Dean"), Ted and his wife, Cindy, were my hosts every time. For example, in 1978 I was present for Candler's Ministers' Week, which was devoted to the topic "A Theology of Hope and Parish Practice." My lectures for this event were gathered with those of Douglas Meeks, Rodney Hunter, James Fowler, and Noel Erskine in the book *Hope for the Church*, which Ted edited. Ted's connections to Korean Methodism led to a Korean translation of this book four years later.

I returned to spend a guest semester at Candler in the fall of 1983, with Elisabeth joining me partway through. I was seriously attracted to moving from Tübingen to Atlanta during this visit, feeling already "almost a Methodist." It was only for family reasons that I resisted this temptation. Ted and I gave a joint seminar during this semester—and gathered with the students at Jagger's (a popular pub) for long dialogues afterwards. I came to value the theological and personal discussions that I shared with such colleagues as Ted, Jim Waits, Ted Weber, and Walt Lowe at Candler. Ted also helped me with translations, paper work, and the rest; Elisabeth and I were even guests at the Runyon home for a big Thanksgiving dinner. I fell in love with Stone Mountain during this visit, and made it my habit to climb up to the top the first morning after every arrival in Atlanta (not to view the Confederate flags there, but to look out on the beautiful landscape of Georgia). I do not think that Ted ever chose to accompany me on these climbs, but this would prove to be the only area in which our passions differed. In particular, slowly but not without success, Ted introduced me to John Wesley's theology and Charles Wesley's hymns, which we sang in Cannon Chapel and Glenn Memorial United Methodist Church.

Elisabeth and I returned to Atlanta most recently in 1995, when we were invited to present together the lectures for Ministers' Week at Candler. Through the Runyons and our many other friends we felt like old members of the Candler community. It was always a kind of "heart-warming experience" to return and be embraced by that community.

The impact of Ted Runyon upon my life reached far beyond this personal level; it has enriched my theological perspective. Thus in 1989 when working on *The Spirit of Life*, I decided it was time to try bringing a new understanding of sanctification and holiness into the theological discourse in Germany, where we normally stop after the "justification of the godless." I do hope that my chapter on the "Sanctification of Life" (with the report of the Wesley-Zinzendorf encounter) finds some favor in Methodist eyes. In preparing it, I once again turned to Ted for help with Wesley's sermons. His unobtrusive and gracious way of making suggestions drew me more and more into the unique offerings of the Methodist tradition, without trying to force me into a Methodist denominational identity. In this Ted was being true to both the "catholic spirit" of Wesley himself and the ecumenical commitment of Methodist movement in the twentieth century. This reinforced my own ecumenical conviction. I have always said "Whatever confessional or denominational origin I may have—the one, ecumenical church is my future!"

Looking back on my theological journey, I have discovered with surprise how much Ted Runyon must have been the mastermind in the background of at least the American side of my life. And wherever I discern his hidden hand I am grateful for his guidance and rejoice in our friendship. Now both of us are old, and no longer "young, promising theologians." Queen Sabbath is coming to the retirees and we may enjoy her peace looking back on a long life as a long grace of the Lord, and a very rare gift in these decades of change since 1968. Ted was always a "man of peace," while my heart is still a little restless. I shall learn true peace of heart from him, whenever my restless heart brings me back to Atlanta again. *Ad multos annos,* my friend!

Introduction

Randy L. Maddox

In 1995 John B. Cobb Jr. published *Grace and Responsibility: A Wesleyan Theology for Today*. He noted in the preface to this book that he had become aware of a "back to Wesley" movement in Methodist circles and had originally resisted it because he feared it was a merely reactionary agenda. However, further consideration persuaded him that contemporary Methodist theologians needed to reappraise Wesley's work and the relevance of his thought for our time.[1] Thus Cobb—one of the most prominent current United Methodist theologians—joined the growing ranks of Methodist theologians who are self-consciously engaging John Wesley and finding his theological precedent instructive for their own theological work.

Such a broad and purposeful engagement of Wesley *as a theologian* by Methodist theologians is unique in this century, and much rarer in the previous century than is popularly believed (see chapter 14). The purpose of the present volume is to collect a set of original essays that are representative of this new engagement around the globe, thus allowing the reader to evaluate the potential contribution of rethinking Wesley's theology for contemporary Methodism.

This volume is dedicated to Theodore Hubert Runyon Jr. (or "Ted" as we all know him) on the occasion of his retirement after forty years of teaching theology at Candler School of Theology, Emory University. But the volume honors more than just these years of faithful service; it specifically honors as well the vital role that Ted has played in fostering the renewed engagement with Wesley's theology by Methodist theologians. While figures such as Frank Baker, Albert Outler, and Dick Heitzenrater rightly draw the primary praise for nurturing the field of Wesley Studies into academic maturity and vigor, Ted has played a key role in bringing systematic theologians outside the confines of this field into dialogue with it.

Thereby they have been able to benefit from its findings and influence its continuing agendas.

This role was not one for which Ted was prepared by the simple fact of his theological education, though his timing was auspicious. After earning a B.A. degree at Lawrence University in 1952, Ted pursued his B.D. degree at Drew University, attaining it in 1955. In general this was a time when little attention was given to Wesley's theology in Methodist seminaries outside of passing comments in Methodist history courses. Drew differed a little in this regard, particularly after the arrival of Franz Hildebrandt in 1953. Hildebrandt was a Lutheran Wesley scholar who would be instrumental in getting Methodists to begin considering Wesley's theology again.[2] While Ted had limited opportunity to study with Hildebrandt, the suggestion of Wesley's relevance was planted. Meanwhile the main focus at Drew, like other Methodist seminaries, was on engaging contemporary culture. Drew was a lively setting for such engagement at the time, with Edwin Lewis capping his distinguished career and Carl Michalson entering his prime. Work under Michalson in particular developed Ted's interest in the emerging "theologies of secularity" and sent him off to Göttingen (where he earned his Th.D. degree in 1958) to study the provocative thought of Friedrich Gogarten and Paul Tillich.

When Ted returned from Germany to start teaching at Candler in 1958, his initial focus remained on the task of engaging theologically such contemporary issues as secularization (including the famous "Death of God" debate on the Emory campus) and the charismatic renewal in the churches.[3] This focus naturally led him into dialogue with the emerging political and liberation theologies.[4] It was in this latter context that the earlier suggestion of Wesley's relevance began to take root and grow.

Ted had become involved in the Oxford Institute of Methodist Theological Studies and was recruited to co-chair the sixth Institute scheduled for 1977.[5] The topic chosen for this institute was a comparison of contemporary liberation theologies and the theology of John Wesley. In preparation for the institute Ted not only recruited prominent Methodist representatives of various liberation theologies as presenters, he began himself an intensive study of Wesley. He was surprised by the insights that emerged from allowing Wesley and liberation theology to engage in mutual dialogue. The addresses from this institute, along with Ted's substantial introductory essay, were published as *Sanctification and Liberation* in 1981.[6] This volume has proven to be pivotal in convincing Methodist theologians that it can be fruitful to bring dialogue with Wesley into their engagement with contemporary issues.

In retrospect, an equally significant essay by Ted was one that was never published! In November 1982 he offered a roundtable discussion paper at the annual meeting of the American Academy of Religion titled "System and Method in Wesley's Theology." This format is a way of "fishing" for interest in new research agendas in the Academy. To the surprise of some, the interest was strong. So Ted took the initiative to start the Wesleyan Studies Group of the AAR, a group that continues to this day and has proven to be the major scholarly arena that allows bridging the gaps (some would say *chasms*) both between the various branches of the Wesleyan family and between the academic specializations of historical studies and theological studies.

In a parallel venture Ted set out to encourage Methodist theologians to reflect specifically on what it meant to do "Wesleyan" theology today. The stimulus was The United Methodist Church's planning for celebrations of the bicentennial of American Methodism. Ted was recruited to host a consultation at Emory University on the topic of "Wesleyan Theology in the Next Century." He chose to focus the consultation more on Methodism's theological contribution *today* across the spectrum of the theological disciplines, with specific attention to the sense in which Wesley informed that contribution.[7] The discussions begun at that consultation have continued to encourage Methodist theologians to rethink Wesley's theology for contemporary Methodism.

Such are the programmatic ways that Ted Runyon has played a key role in fostering the renewed engagement with Wesley by Methodist theologians. His other major contribution has been his own engagement with Wesley, which he has shared in a variety of contexts (including mentoring several doctoral students). The recent publication of *The New Creation: John Wesley's Theology Today*, which offers the fruit of these years of engagement, is sure to continue his valued role in fostering the renewed dialogue with Wesley as theologian.[8]

The contributors to this volume have all benefited from Ted's life and work in a variety of ways. Some of us were students under him, most of us have been his colleagues in a number of settings, and all of us have been informed by his scholarly contributions. The essays we offer here are intended to honor his gift to us by giving in kind.

Kenneth Carder sets the tone for the book in his opening essay. He reflects on his own experience of theological education where consideration of Wesley had little place, and then suggests how engagement with Wesley has served to bring theological grounding and focus to his ministry as a pastor and (now) bishop. True to Wesley, Carder argues that this theological grounding is not a matter of abstract commitments but a grounding that calls all Christians to concerned engagement for and with the impoverished and vulnerable. More implicit but clear in Carder's essay is the suggestion that one of the benefits of the dialogue of Methodist theologians with Wesley is that it can help bridge the too-common gap between academic theology/theologians and the life of the church.

Thomas Langford draws upon Wesley to encourage contemporary theologians to bridge gaps in his essay as well. Langford's focus in chapter 2 is theological method; his specific concern is to argue that instead of dismissing Wesley as an amateur theologian we should recognize that his theological engagement with his setting had a holism and balance than has been lacking in much of subsequent Methodist theology. Unlike Wesley, later Methodist theologians have tended either to turn theology into an isolated and self-interested discipline or to allow the present context to dictate theological judgment.

After the first two more methodological essays come a series of essays on specific theological topics. In each case dialogue with Wesley plays a role in the development of the essay. In some cases the author begins with Wesley and works toward consideration of contemporary relevance. In other cases the author begins with a contemporary issue and dialogues with Wesley as part of the process of addressing the issue. In all cases Wesley is consulted as a partner in the dialogue—one to be corrected at points, and allowed to correct us at points. It is in this mutual dialogue that we can draw upon Wesley as mentor and rethink his theology for contemporary Methodism.

In chapter 3 Marjorie Suchocki reflects on several of Wesley's comments on prayer in *Plain Account of Christian Perfection*, drawing from them insights into what the centrality of prayer to Christian life teaches us about the nature of God, how we participate as co-creators in God's actions, the constitutive nature of our relationship with other persons, and so on.

Theodore Jennings continues the focus on the nature of God in chapter 4, seeking to give concrete meaning to Wesley's insight that

God's sovereignty should never be separated from God's justice and mercy since these belong to the very being of God. Jennings weaves reflections on Scripture together with the insights of Barth, Levinas, and Derrida to argue that the very being of God is constituted as a relationship to the violated and humiliated. As such, Wesley's determination to develop Christian community with and among the disinherited of England was the indispensable concomitant to the truth of the gospel.

Douglas Meeks uses Wesley's model of life among and in service to the impoverished and disinherited in chapter 5 to challenge the contemporary understanding of stewardship in most churches. He argues that the church has become captive to the distorted perspective of modern market economics, which reduces everything to privatized commodities. Through Wesley we can have access to the richer traditional and biblical model of stewardship as providing access for all to the conditions of life and life abundant.

In chapter 6 Manfred Marquardt addresses another area where privatized models have often replaced a richer biblical and traditional understanding. For all of their agreements about the nature and importance of salvation, Marquardt notes that many Methodists share with other Christian groups an uneasiness with the biblical language of "conversion" because of its association with certain caricatured models. He devotes his essay to articulating the authentic nature of conversion as God's saving work that connects our lives with Christ, with one another, and with the world.

James Logan picks up where Marquardt ends in chapter 7, asking what we can learn from Wesley that can help in formulating an authentic approach to evangelism (i.e., seeking conversion). Logan too recognizes that some distorted understandings of evangelism have entered the Wesleyan traditions and focuses his chapter on detailing three characteristics of Wesley's model of evangelism that we need to recover—namely, its theological integrity, personal accountability, and social conscience.

Brian Beck moves us into the theological locus of ecclesiology in chapter 8. His focal question is what the Wesleyan/Methodist tradition might have to gain from and to contribute to the broader ecumenical discussion of ecclesiology. To pursue this he spends time teasing the ecclesiological implications out of Wesley's model of "connexion" and relates them to the current favored ecumenical model of "koinonia."

In chapter 9 Mary Elizabeth Mullino Moore focuses in on the specific ecclesiological topic of ministry. She first provides a case-study analysis to demonstrate that there has been a tendency in Methodist traditions to conceive of ministry in a dichotomized and hierarchical manner. While she admits that this tendency has roots in some of Wesley's practice, she argues that his larger theology— particularly his trinitarian and covenantal emphases—provide resources for developing a vision and practice of ministry that moves beyond dualism and hierarchy, toward diversity and unity.

Beginning with chapter 10 we add another dimension to the dialogue with Wesley in rethinking Methodist theology. All of the previous papers have come out of the North Atlantic setting where Methodism had its origins and earliest development. One of the enriching events of recent decades is the entrance of indigenous Methodist voices from other settings into our theological dialogue. Among other things, these voices have helped to make us more sensitive to the inescapable hermeneutical dimension of all theological work. We never deal with "just the truth" but with truth claims as expressed in certain linguistic, cultural, and historical terms. This recognition highlights both the need to assess the relative adequacy of particular expressions and the question of how one appropriately translates from one expression to another. Our four essays coming from outside the North Atlantic context pay particular attention to these issues.

Justo González actually represents in person a bridge between the North Atlantic context and beyond, with his Cuban roots, his professional location in the United States, and his continual travel and work in the broader Spanish-speaking world. Thus, when he asks "Can Wesley be Read in Spanish?" he is asking not just for Latin Americans but for the peoples of Spain and Equatorial Africa, and for Latinos and Latinas in the United States. The most basic answer to this question is obvious—Wesley has been read by Spanish-speaking peoples for some time. But González seeks to build a base for continued true dialogue of *wesleyanos* with Wesley by gathering the evidence of how Wesley's theology and spirituality were affected by his contact with Hispanic culture.

In chapter 11 José Míguez Bonino moves beyond the question of whether Wesley can be read in Spanish to looking at the ways Wesley was "read" in the various waves of immigration of Methodism to Latin America. Míguez Bonino argues that what actually came to

Latin America was an incomplete and distorted Wesley. He then notes that many in Latin America are finding a reconsideration of Wesley himself to be very fruitful in seeking a theology appropriate to the Latin American situation. The majority of his essay is devoted to identifying aspects of Wesley's theology that are particularly promising in this regard.

Peter Grassow comes to his reading of Wesley in chapter 12 by asking if Wesley might have a political theology that can add insight and direction to the struggle for wholeness in South Africa. He notes that Wesley's refusal to support the American Revolution would appear to place him against all revolutionary change, but argues that there are counter themes in Wesley's larger work that provide a framework for developing a contemporary political theology that can empower the poor and marginalized of South African society.

Chapter 13 by Hoo-Jung Lee is devoted to a comparison of Wesley's understanding of the experience of the Holy Spirit with that of the fourth-century Syriac theologian Macarius. In and through this detailed comparison Lee offers again an argument that the most common "reading" of Wesley is inadequate historically and inappropriate to the situation of Asian Methodists. He then suggests how a reading that gives more emphasis to the Eastern Christian elements in Wesley's spirituality has promise not just for Asian Methodism but for global Methodism (indeed, global Christianity).

The final chapter offers a historical analysis of how Wesley has been viewed and used (or neglected) by Methodist theologians through the course of Methodist history. It demonstrates the earlier neglect of consideration of Wesley as a theologian, reflects on the causes of this neglect, and provides the setting for appreciating the current renewed engagement with Wesley.

CHAPTER 1

What Difference Does Knowing Wesley Make?

Kenneth L. Carder

During a bishop's teaching/listening day in Memphis, a lay person raised a question that no one had asked me before. He asked: "What difference does knowing John Wesley make in your ministry, especially as a bishop?" Aware of my interest in Wesley and my frequent references to him in sermons and writings, the sympathetic layman wanted assurance that Wesley was more than a literary reference or source of historical proof-texting. He wanted to know what difference Wesley makes (or should make) to the contemporary "people called Methodists." His question began a process of reflection on the influence of John Wesley in shaping my role as a pastor and bishop, and on the role that Wesley should play in the formation of leadership in a denomination which claims to be his heir.

The fact that I had to ponder this question reveals the minimal attention that Wesley's contemporary theological and ecclesial significance has received through most of this century. During my seminary years in the 1960s, consideration of Wesley was limited to a course on Methodist history. The relevant date and place were May 24, 1738, at Aldersgate. Wesley's formative contribution to Methodism was focused in his "heart-warming experience," which was portrayed as a prototype of religious experience. Little attention was given to his theological emphases, his passion for the poor, his evangelical commitment to God's reign over all creation, or his reliance on the apostolic faith for forming character and community.

Against this backdrop, I have witnessed a dramatic increase of interest in Wesley's religious thought and practice among American Methodists over the last twenty-five years. Quotes from Wesley show up in increasing numbers in sermons and local church newsletters, while Wesley Studies is gaining respect as a legitimate scholarly pursuit. Both of these developments are laudable, but they need to be brought into conversation with one another if we are to reappropriate the Wesleyan tradition in a theologically rootless church. Confining Wesley to the academy as an object of intellectual curiosity would be as much a negation of our Wesleyan heritage as would be making Wesley a champion of contemporary ecclesial ideological battles, or ignoring him altogether. Fortunately, there are those like Ted Runyon who have been working to bridge the gap between academic study of Wesley and reflection on the life and mission of the church.[1] Drawing on these helpful precedents, I would like to highlight three specific contributions in response to that perceptive layman's question: "What difference does knowing Wesley make to your ministry, especially as a bishop?"

The Contribution to Regaining Theological Grounding and Focus

My serious consideration of Wesley as a viable mentor for pastoral ministry and church leadership began after serving several years as a local church pastor. The only reading related to Wesley during those years consisted of an occasional glimpse at secondary sources in preparation for confirmation and new member orientation classes. At best Wesley seemed peripheral to effective ministry. In comparison to the likes of Tillich, Barth, Bonhoeffer, and Moltmann, Wesley was treated as an antiquated theological lightweight. Besides, psychology and sociology were looked to as the primary sources for insights into pastoral care and institutional leadership. Erich Fromm, Carl Rogers, Rollo May, Peter Druecker, and the like were assumed to have more to offer a pastor seeking to care for people and an institution than an eighteenth-century evangelist.

This began to change, however, as the questions people were asking shifted. The tragedies of Vietnam, the Kennedy and King assassinations, Watergate, the nuclear threat, waning confidence in all authority, and increasing world poverty called for more than psychological counseling and institutional management. A growing awareness of the cultural captivity of the American church, and my own participation in this accommodation, pushed me back to the Bible, historic theology, and our Wesleyan heritage. Wesley's remarkable impact upon an earlier church that had accommodated itself to society seemed to offer hope for addressing the enculturated American church.

Wesley's Model of Theological Grounding and Focus

One fact that caught my immediate attention in reading Wesley was his preoccupation with theology—i.e., with knowing God and responding to God's claim upon all life. This ran counter to the popular images of Wesley as a pragmatist who was indifferent to sound doctrine or serious theological inquiry and was dominated by organizational strategies. I found instead a Wesley who was devoted to understanding, teaching, proclaiming, and appropriating the historic faith. Indeed, he thought theologically, spoke and communicated theologically, preached and taught theologically, strategized theologically, administered the Methodist movement theologically, and he even died theologically—affirming "The best of all, God is with us."[2]

Allusions to the Bible came so naturally to Wesley that it is accurate to say that the Bible was his second language.[3] But while the Bible was his primary authority in matters of faith, tradition (especially as expressed by the early church fathers) was also important. He knew the historic doctrines of the Christian faith and they formed the basic framework of his theological work. While he was familiar with the science, politics, literature, and economics of his time, theology grounded in the Bible and historic Christianity remained the basis from which Wesley responded to personal, ecclesial, and societal issues.

Wesley was obsessed with knowing God, living the reign of God, and proclaiming and teaching the truth of God made known in Jesus Christ and through the Holy Spirit. His sermons, whether oral or written, were theological in content, purpose, and passion. His written sermons served as curriculum resources, as did his *Explanatory Notes on the New Testament*. His letters and journal reflect a man who approached all issues from the perspective of faith. Theological reflection was no occasional diversion from pastoral, administrative, or evangelical duties. It was the thread that held together the fabric of his being, and he expected no less of his preachers and class leaders. He held the early Methodist leaders to strict theological accountability, and his meetings of the Methodist preachers focused on theological/doctrinal issues and concerns. Those present at the first such conference spent one entire day discussing justification by faith, and a second day was devoted to sanctification.[4]

At the same time, Wesley's preoccupation with theology served an evangelical and transformative purpose. Theology was a matter of life and death to him, not a subject of nonpassionate academic speculation. Neither did theology and doctrine serve dogmatic juridical purposes; they were valued for their contribution to evangelization, character formation, and societal transformation. Wesley's interest was "practical divinity," which emphasized the relationship between beliefs and behavior, faith and practice, doctrine and discipline.

For example, in a sermon entitled "On Living without God," dated the year before his death, Wesley reflected on the pervasiveness of what he referred to as "practical atheists." He said that he had only met two atheists (in the technical sense of philosophically rejecting the existence of God) in the British Isles during his lifetime, yet he had met many "Christians" who live "without God in the world." He proceeded to emphasize that what matters is not intellectual *thought about God* but the *shaping of life by the reality and presence of God*:

> I believe the merciful God regards the lives and tempers of [persons] more than their ideas. I believe he respects the goodness of the heart rather than the clearness of the head; and that if the heart of a [person] be filled (by the grace of God, and the power of his Spirit) with humble, gentle, patient love of God and [others], God will not cast him [or her] into everlasting fire, prepared for the devil and his angels because [their] ideas are not clear, or because [their] conceptions are confused. Without holiness, I own no [one] shall see the Lord; but I dare not add, or clear ideas.[5]

In other words, Wesley maintained a healthy and creative tension between doctrine as normative thinking and doctrine as lived reality. Although an avid interpreter and staunch defender of historic faith grounded in Scripture, maintained by tradition, and borne witness in experience and reason, the true goal for Wesley was holiness of heart and life, which was defined by love for God and neighbor:

> . . . see that you begin where God himself begins: "Thou shalt have no other God before me." Is not this the first, our Lord himself being the judge, as well as the great commandment? First therefore see that ye love God; next your neighbor, every child of [humanity].

24

From this fountain let every temper, every affection, every passion flow. So shall that "mind be in you which was also in Christ Jesus." Let all your thoughts, words, and actions spring from this. So shall you "inherit the kingdom prepared for you from the beginning of the world."[6]

Central to Wesley's theological focus was evangelization, the proclamation in word and deed of God's prevenient, justifying, sanctifying, and perfecting grace. This grew out of his conviction that grace transforms persons and societies. As Ted Runyon reminds us, "The essence and purpose of 'real religion,' according to Wesley, is 'a restoration of [humanity] by Him that bruises the serpent's head to all that the old serpent deprived him of; a restoration not only to the favour but likewise to the image of God. . . . Nothing short of this is the Christian religion'."[7]

Evangelization for Wesley was far more than a strategy for institutional church growth. It was a sharing in the transformation of life in response to the coming reign of God over all creation. To cite Runyon again, "The decisive event of conversion and the process of sanctification cannot be properly understood in a purely individualistic context. They must be seen in their organic relation to creation and kingdom. Conversion is decisive to Wesley because it is a participation in God's own renewing of the cosmos."[8] Runyon notes further that for Wesley "conversion does not just change one's *status* before God; it changes the person and the community," and sanctification is about our "becoming an agent of the age to come, joining in the struggle against the forces of sin and corruption, claiming the promise of the new age and living in the hope that the victory over sin is indeed possible."[9]

Maintaining theological focus required intentional discipline for Wesley. In spite of a rigorous travel schedule and multiple demands for administrative attention to a growing movement, Wesley remained theologically centered. He knew the difference between what is foundational and what is instrumental, what is central and what is peripheral, what is permanent and what is faddish. He was ready to adapt and to "plunder the Egyptians" in order to share more faithfully and effectively in God's redeeming and transforming work of grace; but he remained explicitly anchored in theological language, images, and world view. Although he made use of the new tools of the Enlightenment, he never seemed to assume that any tool or method was value-free or theologically neutral. Theological scrutiny was an integral and dynamic component of the Wesleyan revival!

The Potential for Contemporary United Methodism

Perhaps the most valuable lesson Wesley's ecclesial descendants can learn from him is the priority of theology—knowing God and being shaped by the coming of God's reign over all creation. Evidence abounds that United Methodism in North America suffers from theological amnesia and missional anemia. Critical theological reflection and serious appropriation of historic doctrine have become secondary (and often optional) resources for shaping the life and ministry of the church. The market logic of consumerism has supplanted the gift logic of grace as the undergirding framework of the church; and pragmatism devoted to institutional survival, organizational efficiency, and programmatic effectiveness has subtly become the operating philosophy for ministry.[10] The survival, cultural prominence, and statistical success of the institutional church receives more attention from church leaders than the meaning and implications of God's reign over all creation, God's redemption of the world in Jesus Christ, and the forming of a new community through the power of the Holy Spirit.

Anthropologically centered strategies for the bolstering of a sociologically defined church dominate the agendas of many local church and denominational gatherings. The prophetic role of the whole church to be a sign and herald of God's redeemed community of justice, generosity, and joy shaped by Jesus Christ has been replaced with pronouncements on politically "hot" issues by caucuses or specialized agencies. Seldom are the critical issues confronting the world such as racism, economic disparity and injustice, violence and war, the plight of children and the vulnerable, or environmental preservation confronted with a theological seriousness at least equal to that of social, political, and economic analyses.

An anthropologically grounded church is fundamentally different from a theologically formed and focused church. When the consumerist motivation becomes pervasive everything is reduced to a utilitarian market commodity. Worship is reduced to a marketing tool to attract the masses and is shaped by personal preferences and individual tastes. Evangelism is seen more as joining the church than a radical reorientation of life in response to prevenient, justifying, sanctifying, and perfecting grace. Ministry becomes a commodity to be dispensed by the professionals and received by the laity. Institutional participation is equated with discipleship and mission is treated as an optional object of occasional financial support. The church is viewed as another of the many institutions competing for the loyalty and support of people, who shop for the institution that best fulfills their self-identified needs.

The loss of the centrality of theology moves God to the periphery of the church's life or makes God a utilitarian commodity. Thus, some have charged The United Methodist Church in the United States with "atheism."[11] Contemporary Methodists tend to trust planning processes, organizational strategies, institutional structures, and the insights gleaned from the social sciences more than the power of the gospel proclaimed and lived. Without firm theological grounding and critique, as Wesley practiced in the eighteenth century, the methods employed by the church promote a practical atheism under the guise of the Christian faith. The church loses its memory and relies on the surrounding culture to give it identity and purpose.

Recovery of theological focus and doctrinal grounding are necessary in order for United Methodists to be faithful to the gospel as expressed in the Wesleyan movement. Serious theological reflection rooted in the historic faith merits priority attention at every level of the church's life and work. It is particularly important that the role of the pastor as "resident theologian" be nurtured. And the theological work carried out at these levels should, in the words of Wesley, "begin where God begins: 'Thou shalt have no other God before me'."[12] The most critical question confronting the contemporary church and world is, Who is God? We are to be "imitators of God" (Eph. 5:1-2), but not just any god.[13] Whatever shapes, molds, and motivates us is our God; therefore, discerning the nature, purpose, and presence of the Triune God is the church's persistent priority.

There is growing recognition of the importance of theological reflection and formation in The United Methodist Church. Laity are stressing their desire to know who God is, what God is doing in the world, and what they are to do in response. For example, during teaching/listening days in the Nashville Episcopal Area over the last five years, laity have been given opportunity to write questions for response from the bishop. Eighty percent of the questions submitted have focused on theology, beliefs, and doctrines; very few questions have been raised about structures, bureaucracies, apportionments, or even the pastoral appointment process. Likewise, profiles of pastors submitted by Pastor Parish Relations Committees indicate a desire for pastors who are "spiritual leaders" as expressed in preaching, teaching, and pastoral care. The popularity of resources such as Disciple Bible Study and participation in Covenant Discipleship, Emmaus, and other groups devoted to spiritual formation reveal a hunger for depth in Christian education and discipleship formation. Even groups within the denomination calling for doctrinal integrity and theological accountability—while their methods and theological perspectives merit serious critique in the light of the Wesleyan tradition—can be seen as symptomatic of a void created by the church's failure to diligently teach and live out of the historic faith.

Reflecting on this situation of The United Methodist Church, one contribution that knowing John Wesley has made for me and my colleagues in the Council of Bishops has been the incentive to give more attention to the teaching office of the episcopacy. At least one jurisdictional college of bishops has formalized this in a covenant to teach the doctrines and theology of the church and to report at each meeting the ways the covenant is being fulfilled. Such a focus on the primacy of theology for all that the church does helps to reclaim the core of our Wesleyan tradition.

The Contribution to Reclaiming Ministry with the Impoverished and Vulnerable

"What difference does knowing John Wesley make in your ministry, especially as a bishop?" A second contribution has been the recognition of the centrality of ministry with the impoverished and vulnerable to the life and health of the church. Methodism began as a movement of the poor, for the poor, by the poor, and with the poor. Failure to be in friendship and ministry with the poor, the imprisoned, and the vulnerable people of the world is a betrayal of the gospel as communicated through the Wesleyan tradition.

Wesley's Model of Proximity and Ministry with Impoverished and Vulnerable People

Although his modern heirs have been prone to forget it, John Wesley's ministry involved a lifelong commitment to the economically impoverished people of England and his unending devotion to friendship and ministry with marginalized persons.[14] This commitment was motivated and shaped by his understanding of the gospel and the historic faith. It did not emerge from a general humanitarian concern but rather from a conviction that a relationship with the poor is constitutive of the gospel of Jesus Christ—one cannot know and serve Jesus Christ without friendship with the poor. In fact, Wesley considered the poor to be a means of grace, and insisted that "true religion does not go from the strong to the weak, but from the weak to the strong."[15]

Wesley's religious experience and evangelical witness were shaped by his own relationship with the poor. His sense of assurance during the period surrounding Aldersgate in 1738 cannot be separated from his earlier encounters with poverty in his childhood Epworth home, his visitation of the imprisoned and impoverished as a student at Oxford, his failed missionary efforts in Georgia, and the response by the poor to his proclamation of grace. This is why impact on the poor became a principle criterion that Wesley used to determine where, to whom, and what he preached; the design of preaching houses; the composition and content of class meetings; publications written and distributed; and with whom he spent his time. It is also why he considered the establishing of health clinics, lending agencies, sewing cooperatives, or schools as being as integral to the faithful living of the gospel as preaching and praying.

Wesley was convinced that ongoing relationships with the poor and regular visitation with them was as essential to discipleship and spiritual health as was participation in the sacraments. This led him to build expectations of such relationships into his Methodist movement. Tragically, in some "Thoughts Upon Methodism" written near the end of his life, Wesley expressed his fear that the movement was degenerating into "a dead sect with the form of religion but without its power." Two factors, according to Wesley, were leading to such a fate: loss of "the doctrine, spirit, and discipline" with which the movement began and the emerging affluence of Methodists, with the resulting separation from the poor.[16]

Will Contemporary United Methodism Turn Again Toward the Poor?

The current malaise in North American Methodism would suggest that Wesley's fear was not unfounded! The United Methodist

Church, in particular, is permeated by a middle-class ethos. Its organizational structures, management procedures, programmatic activities, curriculum resources, facilities, remuneration of clergy, appointment and budgetary processes, and denominational agencies and gatherings are shaped by middle-class values and methodologies. The poor are absent from most local churches and denominational structures; and whenever they are visible, the poor tend to be treated as objects of charity more than as special friends of Jesus Christ and persons with whom God closely identifies.

As a denomination, we have made great strides in accessing the insights and gifts of technology, the social sciences, and political and administrative procedures. Unlike Wesley, however, our members in the United States presently make little or no access to the insights and gifts of the impoverished people who comprise the largest portion of the world's population and who often live in hidden ghettos near our local churches.

The plight of the impoverished of the world and their absence from our local congregations and connectional structures represents a profound theological and ecclesial crisis for United Methodism. If the poor are constitutive to the gospel of Jesus Christ as practiced and preached by Wesley, separation from the poor is separation from the Triune God and from our theological and missional tradition. Renewed relationships with the impoverished may be the means of evangelizing the affluent and breaking the idolatrous grip of the consumerist market logic to which middle-class North American Methodism has fallen captive.

Some hopeful signs of such renewal are appearing, although prospects for systemic institutional change remain uncertain. The growth and vitality of Methodism among people of the two-thirds world is one source of hope. Globalization of the church provides voices from Africa, Latin America, and Asia to confront the North American church with models for renewal. Although the market logic pervades the world and individualism increases, their grip on the church in Africa and Latin America currently seems less dominant than in the United States. Openness to the experiences and expressions of the gospel among indigenous peoples holds great promise for recovering relationships with the impoverished as a means of grace.

Another hopeful sign is the increasing participation in short-term mission efforts by youth and adults here in North America. This indicates a willingness to be in proximity (at least temporarily) with the impoverished. Informal discussions with youth in the Memphis and Tennessee Conferences indicate that involvement in "hands on" ministry with the marginalized ranks at the top of the preferred activities. Likewise, a growing number of local congregations across the denomination are intentionally turning toward their neighborhoods and seeking to be hospitable to all God's children. However, these churches remain the minority and they often are themselves marginalized in the appointment process and connectional structures of support. United Methodists cannot be content with middle-class homogeneous congregations that merely send financial support to homogeneous congregations composed of the poor. Ongoing relationships with the poor in hospitable communities shaped by the Crucified and Risen Christ must be the norm if we are to be true to the gospel that gave rise to Methodism.

This highlights the potential significance of the Initiative on Children and Poverty recently launched by the Council of Bishops.[17] Implementing this initiative will require systemic changes in the church, including the role and priorities of bishops. The temptations to treat the initiative as an added program or temporary and optional missional emphasis instead of a means to theological and ecclesial transformation are built into all levels of the current structures, perceptions, goals, and procedures of our connectional church. It remains to be determined if the bishops can sustain the focus long enough for the necessary systemic changes to take place.

What is clear is that any turn toward the poor and the marginalized as recipients and agents of God's coming reign must remain rooted in and shaped by theology. The proper undergirding is what Wesley declared to be the essence of true religion, "the love of God and neighbor," and a vision of the kingdom of God brought near in Jesus Christ. Without such a theological grounding, our efforts will lack sustaining power. More important, they will be likely to produce a sentimentalizing of poverty accompanied by paternalistic response, and to solidify the middle-class captivity of The United Methodist Church.

The Contribution to Reclaiming the Ministry of the Laity

"What difference does knowing John Wesley make in your ministry, especially as a bishop?" This inquiry was motivated in part by the lay questioner's appreciation of the Wesleyan heritage of prominent roles for lay involvement. My final response to the question is that my study of Wesley has served to deepen my conviction that pastoral and evangelical power belong to the laity, and that ministry is a shared participation in the presence and work of the Triune God.

Wesley's Model of Reclaiming Lay Ministry

One of Wesley's gifts to the church of his day (although it was not always appreciated!) was reclaiming the understanding that all baptized Christians share in God's ministry to the world. This began with his realization that he could not rely upon ordained clergy in achieving his goal of "spreading scriptural holiness across the land." His empowerment of lay preachers, stewards, and class leaders to aid in this mission is well known and contributed to the strategic success of early Methodism. Part of Wesley's genius was his motivation and formation of leadership of the "plain" people. Following the many examples in the Bible, Wesley often sought out the least noticeable, including the poor, and helped to form them into influential leaders of classes and societies. His persistence in holding the lay leadership to spiritual discipline and theological accountability is a valuable lesson for Methodists of all eras and cultural contexts.[18]

The Loss and (Beginning) Recovery of Ministry of the Laity in United Methodism

The ministry of the laity that Wesley initiated was particularly prominent in the Methodism of the American frontier. The circuit riders, who have been given prominent attention by Methodist historians, played a less significant ongoing role in discipleship formation than the lay persons who provided pastoral care, evangelical witness, religious instruction, and missional engagement during the long intervals between visits by the circuit riders or ordained clergy. However, this prominence of lay ministry did not remain the case.

Some scholars, such as David Lowes Watson, postulate that the current clergy-dominated United Methodist Church had its origin in the transition in the nineteenth century when pastoral power was transferred from the local laity to the "settled" ordained clergy.[19] This transition shifted the role of the laity from primarily a pastoral and evangelical one to that of assisting in maintaining the institutional expressions of religion. Serving on committees, participating in clergy-led activities (including worship), and providing financial support for the institutional church became the standard signs of lay loyalty. The transfer of pastoral leadership from laity to clergy also radically changed the self-image of clergy, who now tended to see themselves as professional leaders charged with enhancing and strengthening the institution. When this self-image was coupled with the pervasiveness of the consumerist market ideology and individualism in North American culture, "ministry" itself was redefined from a sharing in God's transforming mission in the world to a commodity that is dispensed by clergy and received by laity.

Our resulting clergy-dominated church runs contrary to basic Wesleyan theology, which affirms the universality of God's grace available in, to, and for all persons and which invites all to share in God's mission to the world in Jesus Christ. Fortunately, a restlessness and discontent with their passive role in the church's ministry seems to be emerging among United Methodist lay persons. The increase in participation in ministries like lay speaking, Stephen's Ministry, Covenant Disciple Groups, Disciple Bible Study, prayer groups, and Volunteers in Mission represents a willingness on the part of laity to assume pastoral and missional responsibility. The 1996 General Conference affirmation of the ministry of all baptized Christians with the new order of permanent deacon is at least an attempt to support a shift from ministry defined almost exclusively by Orders to ministry as a sharing in God's mission; although the focus remains predominantly directed toward the institutional church rather than the world. Additional intensive theological work is needed to turn the focus to the world where the laity live and work as their primary arena of ministry.

Since The United Methodist Church is made up primarily of small membership churches and the cost of full-time clergy support is escalating, reclaiming lay pastoral leadership takes on particular importance. Fewer churches can afford full-time ordained clergy. An example is a circuit in middle Tennessee made up of five small membership churches. No ordained pastor was available to serve the struggling congregations. Three lay speakers were assigned pastoral responsibility for the churches and two ordained elders were given responsibility for mentoring the lay speakers. The elders and laity meet weekly to discuss pastoral issues, sermon and worship preparation, and other matters of mutual concern. The churches have taken on new vitality and the ordained clergy and lay speakers are growing in their faith and ministries. Such a model is rooted in Wesley's own strategy for ministry and may hold promise for the future. Again, the crucial issue is theological focus and accountability as laity need the tools of theological reflection, Biblical interpretation, and familiarity with and appropriation of the tradition.

Much theological work remains to be done in order to maximize the ministry of the laity. Clergy are trained and conditioned to "run the church" and provide professional expressions of ministry. Sharing proclamation, pastoral care, evangelization, teaching, and worship leadership with laity will require a trained laity and a retrained clergy. Laity will have to revision what it means to be church and see themselves as the church rather than mere participants in a voluntary organization. The shift will demand that pastors be perceptive teachers, grace-filled mentors, and servants of the community of faith more than CEOs of religious institutions. The precedence for such a shift, however, is in our tradition. It is a lesson we can learn from Wesley.

Conclusion

"What difference does knowing John Wesley make in my ministry, especially as a bishop?" Wesley continues to prod me to maintain theological focus in a position now functionally oriented toward institutional management, personnel deployment, and organizational supervision. He constantly reminds me that our theological and missional and evangelical heritage is with the impoverished, the vulnerable, in anticipation of the coming God's reign of justice, generosity, and joy. And Wesley challenges my episcopal preoccupation with clergy concerns, reminding me that all baptized Christians are called to and involved in ministry, and the ordained exist as servants of God's ministry to the world through the church. In these things, of course, Wesley is not unique. His life and ministry, with its limitations and weaknesses, point to the One who is the foundation of all life and ministry—the Triune God!

CHAPTER 2

John Wesley and Theological Method

Thomas A. Langford

My title conjoins two topics that popular caricatures would suggest have little relation to one another. Wesley has frequently been
put forward as a model of methods of evangelization and spiritual
formation. By contrast, positive evaluation of his precedent in theological method has been quite rare. This is true even among his
Methodist descendants; indeed, one senses that a major motivating
force in the development of later Methodist theologies was the desire
to compensate for what were perceived as Wesley's inadequacies.
My goal in this essay is to turn this traditional self-understanding of
the development of Methodist theology on its head. I want to suggest
not only that Wesley had a discernible theological method, but that
this method embodied a holism or balance which later Methodist
theology has struggled—usually unsuccessfully—to maintain.

Wesley's "Experimental and Practical Divinity"

The place to begin discerning Wesley's approach to theology is
with his conception of its purpose. Wesley understood theology to
be intimately related to Christian living and the proclamation of
Christian faith. Theology is actualized in authentic living and true
proclamation. He had little interest in theology for its own sake.
Rather, theology was for the purpose of transforming personal life
and social relations. This was his "practical divinity." For Wesley,
theology was not so much for the purpose of understanding life as
for changing life; theology should help effect the love of God and
neighbor.

What guidelines or corollaries for theological method did Wesley
draw from this conviction about the purpose of theology? Any
answer to this question will need to be indirect. Wesley himself never

discussed his theological methodology and was not explicitly conscious of the issue. His theological mode of operation was developed over time and was organic to his personal experience and his mission. His way of doing theology evolved as his natural way of approaching and dealing with theological issues. Indeed, most of his writings which might appear to be abstract theological constructions, such as *Thoughts Upon Necessity* and *Predestination Calmly Considered*, were actually occasional pieces responding to specific attacks upon his preaching.

One way to do justice to the practical purpose and occasional nature of Wesley's actual theological work is to identify his distinctive theological method as connecting inextricably theological statement with experience or, conversely, experience with theological statement. Robert E. Cushman offered a perceptive account of Wesley's theological method along this line in *John Wesley's Experimental Divinity*. His major points are captured in the following summary:

> The nature of "true living faith" which Wesley has in mind, and which he found expressed in the Homilies of the Church of England, when viewed comprehensively with its full range of implications, embraces the whole of Wesley's "experimental religion" and the substance of his "experimental divinity." The latter is the articulate explication of the former. Viewed in another perspective, the experimental divinity can be seen as a doctrine of salvation, as the "Scripture way of salvation." It amounts to a system of Christian doctrine which issues, quite inevitably, from what he calls "experimental religion," that is, "true, living faith; or the faith that justifies. In his little essay *The Character of a Methodist*, first published in 1742 [1739], Wesley provided an example of his understanding of the relationship between doctrine and the life of Christian experience. In the essay, doctrine and life are viewed as inseparable; the one demands the other. Wesley is saying that the character of a Methodist is (or should be) exhibitive of the individual's Christian doctrine; and, conversely, that essential doctrine is (or should be) constitutive of the Christian life.[1]

I am in full agreement with Cushman's point about the inextricable connection of doctrine and experience in Wesley's theology. However, I would like to focus this connection a little more specifically, in a way that does justice to the primacy of preaching in Wesley's theological work. In making this shift we remain true to Wesley, for he was concerned with theology as an articulation of a transforming experience and as an articulation that transforms experience.

It is of primary significance, as Gordon Rupp has commented, that Wesley did not produce so much a creed as a *kerygma*. Sermons were his chief theological deposit. As such, they represent his theological method more clearly than his scattered theological treatises. Of course, as enacted practical divinity we can expect from sermons more an exemplification of Wesley's method than a definition of it. I would suggest that what we see exemplified in Wesley's sermons is the dynamic interaction between speaking the message and life-changing reception of the message.

The polar dynamic between preacher and hearer, between essential message and existential environment, between what should be said and what can be heard, between the gospel which transforms life and life which can vitalize the gospel is impossible to separate into clearly demarcated units. Preached and received word are so tightly intertwined that they cannot be pulled apart without damage to both.

Preaching intends to evoke response; the gospel is proclaimed in order to transform life, actual life—in its social, intellectual, psychological, and economic location. Wesley's theology is aware of this totality. The message to be proclaimed is basic but the context in which and the people to whom the message is proclaimed must be understood with due sensitivity and adroit interpretation.

It is important to emphasize that Wesley's practical theology was not reducible to applicability, accommodation, or sheer pragmatism. Rather, it had to do with substantial theology being related to concrete life. This theological style refused to draw sharp divisions between theory and practice; each influenced the other—practice shaped theory as much as theory shaped practice. Gospel and Christian life were both necessary (as Wesley's faith and works dynamic affirmed); each helped form the other.

Wesley's practical theology made him especially sensitive to implications of doctrines for Christian life and specific contexts; or, from the other side, his sensitivity to particular situations helped shape his theology so as to make it practical. "Practical theology" was simply a name for bringing the gospel and life together, for making the message clear in expressing God's grace and for structuring gracious Christian living. For this reason Wesley had little time for abstract or self-contained systematic theological exploration. He was not interested in theological self-reflection for its own sake or in refinement simply for the sake of systematic integrity. He was interested in proclaiming the life-changing message.

In his understanding and positive presentation, Wesley held a strong tension between the gospel to be preached and the persons to whom and the situation in which preaching occurred. On the one hand, Wesley faithfully held to the substance of received orthodox teaching about God, Jesus Christ, the Holy Spirit, the Trinity, the created and fallen nature of human beings, justification by grace through faith, and the means of grace. In fact, he assumed this doctrinal inheritance rather than debating its truth or developing its possibilities. On the other hand, Wesley was remarkably sensitive to the situation of those to whom he preached. He spoke in clear, plain English and built upon shared assumptions about inherited doctrines. He attempted rectification of disordered moral lives and he organized bands, classes, and chapel groups to nurture Christian living expressed in holiness of heart and life.

Wesley's central questions were: what must people hear? and how are they able to hear (the gospel)? In answering the first question, he returned to the traditional theology by which he was formed. In answering the second question, he developed an awareness of the intellectual, social, and moral ethos in which the people to whom he preached lived. His astonishing success was in large part due to the balance or holism which Wesley achieved in his sensitivity to both dimensions.

Wesley's primary concern throughout his development was with human salvation. Around this hub his thought was extended like spokes. From this center he developed the central emphases of his theology. Beginning with repentance, salvation was established by justification, affirmed by assurance, found its embodiment in holiness, and reached its final goal in eternal life with God. And all of this was built upon the reality of God's preventing, saving, sanctifying, and completing grace. These classical theological doctrines he set firmly in relation to the experience of those to whom he preached. He attempted to speak to their known condition and he attempted to interpret their condition as sinful persons in need of grace.

The theological issues in the early years of the revival were those of free grace and free will. Free grace was central as it had to do with the availability of salvation for all people and with the moral character of God. Wesley deeply opposed interpretations of predestination, foreordination or election, and especially reprobation or damnation, as expressed through God's eternal decrees—operating as omniscience directed through omnipotence. Both the mediatorial role of Jesus and the responsibility of human beings were by-passed, he contended, by such interpretations.

The character of God and God's mode of relating to human beings was also at stake for Wesley in these debates. He insisted that God was not a despot who arbitrarily chose some for life and others for death. God's relation to humans beings was expressed in Jesus Christ who called upon people to repent and respond in faith, for grace is free to all and for all. "Whosoever will, may come" was the repeated theme and it was explored and expressed in extended discussions.

The free grace of God was the primary and commanding emphasis, but connected with that first principle was human freedom. Prevenient grace made persons morally able and responsible for their sin—both rejection of God and evil actions toward their neighbors—and made them responsible for returning the love of God with their gratitude and faith.

Wesley's sensitivity to the context of his hearers was evident in his awareness of the growing ethos of the Enlightenment. The Enlightenment was a general intellectual movement in Europe, particularly represented in Great Britain by Isaac Newton but extending through British intellectual developments from Bacon to Locke, Hume, and Toland; in France it found clear expression in Descartes, Voltaire, and Rousseau; and in Germany there was special culmination in the philosophy of Immanuel Kant. With all of these thinkers, achievements in the physical sciences were applied to the realm of human intelligence and action.

In many ways, the major themes of Enlightenment mentality were negative in focus, questioning received authorities—including the active sovereignty of God. Autonomous, rational human beings were enthroned as the central value and valuers of reality. This meant that Wesley faced a world increasingly infected by denial of Christian values and by active opposition to received theological convictions.

As such, Wesley's insistence upon the sinful condition of human beings was not only a reaffirmation of classical doctrine, it was set in opposition to the positive anthropology of the Enlightenment. The theme of grace was in sharp contrast to the Enlightenment sense of human self-sufficiency. While Christian perfection was a theme more amenable to concerns of the Enlightenment, Wesley made it dependent upon the action of God. He also affirmed that the valued Enlightenment ideal of human freedom was a reality only as a gift from God. Throughout, insistence upon the priority of God's grace made it possible for Wesley to attend to and transform dominant Enlightenment ideas.

Attention to human experience and cultural context reveals Wesley's way of bringing classical Christian theological themes into tight interaction with the concrete situation and condition of his hearers. Whether unconscious or intentional, Wesley was utilizing a theological method that was holistic and interactive.

Representative Divergence in Later Methodist Theology

The holism that Wesley achieved was difficult either to state with firmness or to maintain with integrity. I want now to explore several critical figures and moments in Methodist theological development which demonstrate how difficult the holistic theological awareness of Wesley was to maintain. The tendency was to stress either theology as an isolated and self-interested discipline, or the context in which the gospel was heard. Our excursion is aimed at making evident the ongoing problem of keeping these two dimensions together in order to develop the adequacy of theological presentation which Wesley achieved.

Richard Watson (apologetic theologian)

Almost immediately with Richard Watson—the first major (British) Methodist theologian after Wesley—the weight between the two was rebalanced. Watson fastened primary attention upon the audience who would hear the message. Special attention was given to the intellectual and cultural sensibilities of those who would hear. His intention was to enhance the communication of the gospel; the effect was to give more basic attention to reception of the communication. Explication of the message gave way to greater influence being asserted by the conditions of reception. There is no doubt that Richard Watson was motivated by an evangelistic passion and a missionary zeal. In this he represented a continuation of John

Wesley's primary commitment. But Watson relegated doctrinal concern to a secondary place in his basic order of priority.

Watson's *Theological Institutes* present a system that is greatly different from that of John Wesley.[2] Watson develops a distinctly apologetic theology, one which begins with an extended consideration of what his readers need to be convinced of before they can appropriate the gospel message. Following more general Protestant theological formations, he treats theology as an intellectual enterprise and one that answers intellectual questions. In this understanding, theology serves preaching at a distance; its primary task is to clear the ground so that the gospel can be received and find root.

It is clear that Watson believed himself to be a theological disciple of John Wesley and wanted to continue the Wesleyan mission. And much of what he wrote contained themes from Wesley. But there is a disjuncture, for Watson deduces from a scriptural base the normative doctrines that he propounds. The tension between the message and its context is released in favor of the context, and especially in favor of what Watson takes to be its intellectual context.

The structure of *Theological Institutes* sets the character of his work. He begins (for over 250 pages) by addressing the objections of opponents ranging from unbelievers (the cultural despisers of religion) to believers with different theological points of view. Theology is to answer questions raised by intellectuals and to deal with issues discussed among intellectuals. Theology becomes a more strictly intellectual undertaking, and to this extent has a limited practical applicability. A specific contextual character becomes central, shifting from the full "practical" dimension characteristic of Wesley's theology.

The issues in this change are subtle. Watson, by functioning principally as an apologetic theologian, allows the context to become the dominant partner. He wants to keep the substance of Wesley's theology and (although he quotes him less than five times in the two volumes) intends, finally, to make the same doctrinal emphases as Wesley. But his method of approach changes the priorities set by Wesley and makes it impossible for Watson to affirm the holistic interrelationship which Wesley espoused.

For instance, he begins with two issues he takes to be of primary concern for those who must judge the message. He argues for biblical authority without making basic the inspiration of the Holy Spirit in providing the text and the interpretation of the text. Likewise, he

41

emphasizes free will utilizing general philosophical arguments and neglects its foundation in prevenient grace that was so central to Wesley. These two themes are foundational to Watson's entire construction; and although he intends to return to much of the substance of Wesley's theology, his mode of approach alters the theological construction.

It is a strange claim to make, but Watson, who became the dominant theological spokesman in Methodism for most of the nineteenth century, probably followed Wesley more closely in all other things than he did as a theologian. His change in theological style and spirit from Wesley leads to a more distant engagement of theological interpretation with concrete practice. He develops a more independent theological statement, one which is completed prior to its being related to Christian living. A reweighing has occurred and the interactive dialectic is broken.

William Burt Pope (Coherent Statement of Methodist Arminianism)

In the final decades of the nineteenth century another British Methodist theologian became a major spokesman; a theologian who moved in the opposite direction from Watson. This commanding figure was William Burt Pope, and his major work was his *Compendium of Christian Theology*.[3]

Pope's scholarly credentials were impressive. He was a thorough student of biblical and classical languages, he read widely in British and German literature, he was disciplined in his thought and achieved a remarkable clarity and succinctness in his theological writing. Descriptions of his character reflect the integrity of his life and thought; he exhibited what he expressed.

At the same time, Pope represented the limitations of a self-restricting tradition, one which stays within its own confines and does not seek interaction with other contemporary intellectual movements. Hence, while he was thoroughly trained in biblical languages, he had little interest in the contemporary work of establishing the most authentic text (which was becoming prominent in the work of F. J. A. Hort and B. F. Westcott in England) and he was hostile to critical biblical work that was common in Germany. Pope's own position was that the text of Scripture as it had been transmitted was sufficient, accurate, and authoritative and that work of biblical scholarship was to provide expositions of that received text.

He was indifferent to current philosophy and hostile to the scientific developments of his day. At no point does he engage the philosophical discussions of British Idealism, which had become prominent with Thomas H. Green in the 1860s and grew to dominate university intellectual life by the end of the century. He dismissed Charles Darwin's scientific work and did not participate in the discussions of encroaching secularism or the relation of Christian faith to the social order. Pope was a tower of strength within an enclosed tradition. He gave impressive expression to the themes that had formed Methodist theology and to the influences that other Christian traditions had upon Methodism. But his statement was a restatement; he did not bring theology into engagement with current issues, questions, or challenges.

With justice, it may be claimed that Pope presented the best formulation yet achieved of Methodist Arminianism in coherent, amicable, and well-structured form. He brought nineteenth-century Methodist theology to finely accomplished statement. The past he presented well, but the present was not addressed. Once again, the balance between message and reception was re-weighted; the holistic theology of John Wesley was not maintained.

The Emerging Distinctiveness of North American Methodist Theology

We have looked at two major nineteenth-century British Methodist theologians. Each represents divergent tendencies in relating the gospel message to concrete human situations. There is no need to attempt a general characterization as to which tendency was more dominant in Britain; every theologian would have to be measured independently and carefully assessed.

On the North American scene the nineteenth century witnessed both tendencies, with Thomas O. Summers following Richard Watson and John Miley more in the mode of William B. Pope. But by the end of the century, under the initial inspiration of Henry L. Sheldon, a transition to apologetic theology set a liberal Protestant agenda which would be followed by Boston personalism and process theology. This tradition has continued until the present. But this approach has been challenged by others who have represented a counter movement working under the influence of European neo-orthodox developments and a rediscovery of John Wesley's theology.

Two mid-twentieth-century Methodist theologians reveal continuing contrasting methods and styles of theological endeavor, namely Schubert M. Ogden and Robert E. Cushman. Both of these represent serious and high quality theology, both intend to bring the Christian message and the cultural context into dialogue, and both do so with intellectual and vocational integrity. Yet they stand in sharp contrast both in terms of approach and content.

Schubert M. Ogden (rational, philosophical apologetic)

Bernard Loomer, then of the University of Chicago, once asked why Methodism in the United States had produced so many theologians who were philosophically grounded. At least a partial answer is that Methodist theologians have attempted to speak to current intellectual concerns, and philosophical analysis is one means of uncovering those concerns and their assumptions. Schubert Ogden represents this interest and has sought to speak significantly to the second half of the twentieth century, specifically by producing a rational apologetic to support Christian faith.

Ogden's basic assumption is that modern people accept the validity of scientific method and findings. This acceptance has left most of his contemporaries fundamentally convinced that we live in a secular world, in a world that does not demand any supernatural explanation. In *The Reality of God*,[4] Ogden challenges this conclusion by exploring the sensibilities of secularity and drawing attention to unexamined dimensions of secular experience common to human life that can be read as evidences of God. In particular, he argues that the sheer affirmation of life, the will to live, is an act of faith. It is an act of valuing human life and an act which may be understood as pointing to God. As such, it provides the possibility of arguing for an objective ground of reality for the ultimate worth of human existence.

Ogden holds that the norms which govern all human reasoning, and only these norms, can be utilized by theology. The argument must be generally convincing and appropriate in ordinary argumentation. This leads him to ask what contemporary people are prepared to hear about God. He proposes two qualities: God is a reality who is genuinely related to life where the actions of people make a difference; and God is supremely relative and supremely absolute at the same time. That is, the ground of being human must be shown to be an incorporating process of cosmic and personal dimensions.

The intellectual background for Ogden's analysis is found in A. N. Whitehead and Charles Hartshorne. Stressing the creative becoming of God and persons—that is, of reality as a whole—this processional character of reality expresses the encompassing mystery of God's love. With sustained investigation and argumentation, Ogden makes a case for this position.

Along with these intellectual sensibilities, Ogden adds, in *Faith and Freedom*,[5] that human beings search for justice and truth in life situations. The expectation of a quality of life that affirms human value, human freedom, and the practical possibility for realized personal and social meaning calls for a gospel interpretation which underwrites these hopes. Faith must be understood as existence-in-freedom and existence-for-freedom; that is, from a Christian perspective, this mode of existence can be seen as life in God and life for God. Life is to be lived within the gift of freedom and faithful disciples must serve the freedom of others through emancipating activity.

To meet this human desire to know the truth and live in freedom, the Christian gospel presents God—whose own nature is free and who in freedom acts as both Redeemer (the affirmer of value in life) and emancipator (the enforcer of value for life). God's self-realization ontologically underwrites the fullest possible self-realization of every creature. Jesus is the primary source and authority for authentic understanding of God and understanding of human life. In *The Point of Christology*,[6] Ogden argues that the human search for freedom sets the context in which the credibility of Christology must be judged. This is significant, for present intellectual-social formation shapes the presentation of the Christian message and shapes the doctrines of God and Jesus Christ.

Ogden is robust and insightful in his analysis of the contemporary secular mind and experience, and he responds with a fresh reading of the Christian message shaped by this analysis.

Robert E. Cushman (Faith seeking understanding)

In contrast, Robert E. Cushman has developed a theology which attempts to let the understanding of God shape the nature of human understanding. For Cushman, true theology is faith seeking understanding; faith, as it has been framed by God, sets the conditions and content of understanding.

45

Cushman laid out his position in a thesis statement, "The Shape of the Christian Faith: A Platform."[7] Beginning with the assertion that religious faith responds to God's initiative, he claims that religious experience is not the source of the knowledge of God, rather it is the medium of God's encounter with human beings. A crisis is precipitated when persons are encountered by God. The entire human person is caught up in this crisis as one comes to know herself or himself as alienated from God and from other persons. Primarily there is a moral estrangement; in the presence of God one recognizes one's self to be sinful. This is not a general experience, it cannot be arrived at by analysis of common human experience; on the contrary, it is a recognition of one's condition when one has "seen" God. The prophet Isaiah set the dynamic (6:1, 5), "I saw the Lord . . . and I said, 'Woe is me!'"

This means that apologetic argument is not concerned to establish theism or to make religious interpretation commendable to everyone, not even to all thoughtful people. True apologetics attempts to turn one's attention on one's existential problem, on the moral problematic of human existence. Cushman's first book was a much praised study of Plato, *Therapeia*.[8] In this book he interprets Plato's primary intention as an effort to overcome moral contrariety. This is Cushman's philosophical background.

Cushman's position culminates in the event of Jesus Christ. Jesus reaches from God's side to overcome human estrangement. The mission and role of Jesus set the model for Christian discipleship in serving human need. This is the center of his thought. Once again, the priority of action, the initiative for reconciliation, the primacy of faith, and the resulting knowledge are all the result of God's activity.

God, for Cushman, is not the question; human beings are. The true religious situation is to know one's self as met by God, to sense the crisis precipitated by that encounter, and to realize the overcoming of alienation by the renewing work of Jesus Christ. The task of theology is to uncover the initiating action of God, to make evident its claim upon human beings and the resulting life of faith. Hence theology derives from faith and functions to induce faith. Theology does not seek to understand life, then root it in faith; quite the contrary, theology begins with faith as the true foundation of life and knowledge.

Cushman represents an effort by a contemporary Methodist theologian to begin with the received gospel and to construe the human condition from that perspective. The message shapes the reception of the message.

Both Ogden and Cushman represent the continuing effort of successors of John Wesley to relate the Christian message to a changing context, to enable transformation of life by authentic preaching of the gospel.

The purpose of Wesley's theology [handwritten note]

Conclusion

John Wesley's mode of theology was distinctive. It did not fall neatly into any received categories. It was neither simply dogmatic nor apologetic theology. He neither concentrated exclusively upon received doctrine, with the intention to convey and explore meanings embedded in traditional doctrines, nor did he concentrate primarily upon the capacity of hearers to understand and accept the doctrines conveyed.

In similar fashion, he did not attempt to find an essential message which endures unchanged over time, remaining the same in every situation; nor did he attempt to construct a contextual theology which finds its primary resources in particular conditions of human existence.

Unlike many modern theological endeavors, Wesley also resisted the division between theory and practice. He did not construct a theological theory which was then applied to any (and all) particular situations; nor did he become a practitioner who undertakes application without allowing the utilization to affect its theoretical substructure.

Wesley struggled to hold divergent dimensions in tight relation: emphasizing both, he allowed each to influence the other. This is the "practical" character of Wesley's thought: theology underwrites Christian proclamation and Christian living; Christian experience, as faithful living, helps set emphases in theological construction. Each requires the other, each enriches the other, each flourishes only as it is bound to the other.

Such intertwining, such balance, is difficult to emulate. Successors have tended to emphasize one pole or the other; bifocality was often lost. Nevertheless, Wesley's effort and achievement have remained a challenge to Methodist theology. He is a theological mentor who demonstrates the value of holistic theological activity and challenges his tradition to attempt this mode of theological effort.

CHAPTER 3

The Perfection of Prayer

Marjorie Suchocki

John Wesley's *A Plain Account of Christian Perfection* is his most succinct statement of his views on sanctification, and as such is a classical resource for Methodist theologians in dealing with this topic. But the book also can serve as a rather astonishing documentation of some of Wesley's views on prayer. This in itself is not too surprising: The life of sanctification is certainly a life of prayer. But the purpose and role accorded to prayer in this small book jolts the imagination, shocking us into new sensitivities about the nature, the effects, and, indeed, the perfection of prayer.[1]

While exhortations to a life of prayer pervade *A Plain Account of Christian Perfection*, it is in the last pages that Wesley's words on prayer soar to amazing heights. Moving through these passages gives rise first to theological reflections on prayer that in turn suggest a Wesleyan theology of prayer.

I

God does nothing but in answer to prayer; and even they who have been converted to God, without praying for it themselves (which is exceeding rare), were not without the prayers of others. Every new victory which a soul gains is the effect of a new prayer.[2]

How can it be that "God does nothing but in answer to prayer"? The words seem mere hyperbole when we consider that God has been creator long before we humans entered the scene. Galaxies swirl into existence, with stars, planets, comets, asteroids, pulsars, and all the phenomena of the universe dancing in patterns that almost infinitely preceded our own entry into the dance. God does much creating long before prayer is possible—at least from our sector of creation. How is prayer involved at all in God's actions?

49

The context may explain the message, for Wesley makes his statement in the midst of a discussion concerning justifying and sanctifying grace. He is speaking not about the creation of the physical world, but about God's continuing creative work in making us spiritually alive within that world. The work of creation is complex and wonderful, involving a dynamic universe in which life in union with the creator is possible. But this form of life is essentially paradoxical: It is life created by God and dependent upon God, but its "aliveness" is wrought not by its automatic responsiveness to God, but by its free responsiveness to God. Its life involves its active openness to and participation in the very grace that calls it into being.

Wesley presupposes here the problematic of existence in the fall of humanity and the necessity of redemption in and through the work of God in Jesus Christ. This is the essential basis upon which the new creation is now possible. But the quality of that new creation requires the acceptance of grace and participation in grace. Prayer is a mode of participation in the creating grace of God; it is an active openness in response to God.

But if prayer is an openness to God, it is also the case that the invitation to pray is God's openness to humankind. It is as if God's will toward our good can take a variety of forms, and prayer invites us to help in the shaping of that form. Through prayer, we are given the opportunity to participate in the shaping of God's love, so that the actual work of love might bear our own imprint as well as God's. But of course if our participation in God's continuing creative work is in and through prayer, and if prayer opens us to conformity with God's love, then that aspect of the work that reflects our own part will be in some respects a finite reflection of God's infinite love.

There is an intentional joining with God in prayer that is also participation in God's love, and therefore participation in God's works of love, which is grace. Prayer is the creation of a circle of activity: God creates out of divine love; Divine love invites us in, not as disinterested observers, but as sharers in that very love. But to share in God's love is to share in God's work. Through prayer, then, we are graciously made participants in God's own works of grace.

In *A Plain Account* Wesley particularly speaks about prayer in relation to God's work of converting and sanctifying grace. One might ordinarily think that conversion and sanctification are totally the work of God, independent of human participation, but this is not so for Wesley. Rather, one might say that for Wesley these activities

50

are totally the work of God in and through God's work with us. God invites us to utilize prayer to become partners with God in the deepest works of divine grace: salvation and sanctification. It is by grace that we are made partners in grace.

How is this possible? Wesley does not spell it out, other than to claim "God does nothing but in answer to prayer." But we can speculate that it is the unitive function of prayer that joins us to God's work—and indeed, that joins us to those for whom we pray. Prayer is the opening of ourselves to God's will. But God's will is boundless love, poured out for creation, inviting creation into itself. This love is not restricted—by definition it is boundless, since its source is the infinite God. Thus when we deign to pray for someone, we can be very sure that the one for whom we pray is loved by God. When we open ourselves to God's will for that person in prayer, we become joined to God's love. Perhaps God takes our own small love and joins it to God's mighty stream of love toward the one for whom we pray. As we are tapped into God's love, our own love for the other grows, and we begin to mirror God's will for his or her well-being. Our actions then become conformed to our prayers, and we become instruments in God's hands to manifest God's love. God pulls us into the divine work, in ways that often go beyond our knowing, in bringing about the results of prayer.

II

Another text expands the message:

> Although all the graces of God depend on [God's] mere bounty, yet is [God] pleased generally to attach them to the prayers, the instructions, and the holiness of those with whom we are.[3]

Here Wesley expands the notion that God works in and through our prayers by stating that God also works in and through our instructions to one another, and in and through our holy living. Earlier in the book Wesley had defined pride as the refusal to learn from another: "If you think you are so taught of God as no longer to need [human] teaching, pride lieth at the door. . . . To imagine none can teach you but those who are themselves saved from sin is a very great and dangerous mistake."[4] In the above passage on prayer, the suggestion is that our openness to God is also an openness to others, and not only toward those others whom we might accord great

51

esteem, but toward all others. The mutual openness of God toward us and us toward God that forms the center of prayer is to be replicated in an openness toward our brothers and sisters as well. This suggestion is foundational for the formation of community insofar as it opens us to the work of God for us in and through one another. For if God works through each of us, then we can look to one another as vehicles of God's grace for us. This takes place through what we say to one another, and in how we live with one another.

This conjunction of prayer, instruction, and holiness of life as together being vehicles of God's grace is not accidental. First, the context of prayer is always communal, whether one prays alone or in company. Second, the community is expected to be faithful in intercessory prayer for each of its members. Third, the life of prayer increases the love of God, and hence affects holiness of life. The individual Christian can expect that he or she is named in prayer by the wider group, even while also exercising faithful prayer in behalf of the group, be it a class band or a congregation. And if prayer is an openness to God, it is also an openness to teachings about holy living. Likewise, opennness to teachings about holy living should result in growth in holy living. Thus God's grace flows through the work of the company of Christians to the strength of each. God works in and through the prayers, teaching, and holy living of the community.

III

Prayer joins us not only to God but to the one for whom we pray. Intercessory prayer weaves the other's needs into who we are. Wesley suggests this with his rather amazing instruction that we should confess the sins of others as our own:

> We ought . . . to bear the defects of others and our own, to confess them to God in secret prayer.[5]

It is as if our intercessions for others join us to them, so that when we feel blockages within them to divine grace we quietly name these before God, not in judgment but in contrition, as if they were our own. And in some cases it may indeed be that we are unwitting participants in the other's sin. Perhaps it is we ourselves who have created the circumstances within which these blockages occur. Attitudes of self-righteousness, or hostility, or condemnation toward the

other—regardless of the "rightness" or "wrongness" of these feelings—can create a spirit of hindrance for the other, and cause the
other to stumble. But regardless of our own direct participation, the
very solidarity that we share in Christ is sufficient for our joining
ourselves to those in whom we perceive "defects," quietly confessing
our perceptions of their sins as well as our own. Wesley suggests that
such prayers are received by God as an opening for converting
and/or sanctifying grace in the ones for whom we so pray.

But what if, having confessed the sins of others as if they were
our own, having confessed these to God in secret prayer, that other
for whom we pray not only seems unrepentant of these sins, but in
fact persists in them—what then? Should we not despair, or fall into
the temptation of feeling better than they, and despise them? Wesley
cautions otherwise: "We are to bear with those we cannot amend,
and to be content with offering them to God."[6] The suggestion is that
our very naming of the sin as we perceive it is at the same time an
offering of that other to God, a releasing of that other to God's mercy,
God's care. For they have their own journey with God, their own
struggles and testings and waverings and victories; and we, though
we confess the sins we perceive, only partially know that situation
about which we pray. We speak to God of a story known best to God
and that other. We intercede in the humility of love, and therefore in
the grace of releasing our prayers and the one for whom we pray to
God. How God uses our prayers is up to God; our work is not to
control what happens as a result of our praying, but to offer the prayer
faithfully for God to use as God can and will. We offer the one for
whom we pray to God, and pray as well for the grace to continue to
relate to that one in Christian love. For as Wesley says, "God is the first
object of our love: its next office is to bear the defects of others. And
we should begin the practice of this amidst our own household."[7]

IV

This next passage is itself a commentary on the Pauline passage
that we should "pray without ceasing." While Wesley repeats this
mandate a number of times in the book, one of his most profound
statements is as follows:

> God's command to pray without ceasing is founded on the neces-
> sity we have of God's grace to preserve the life of God in the soul,
> which can no more subsist one moment without it, than the body

can without air. Whether we think of or speak to God, whether we act or suffer for God, all is prayer, when we have no other object than God's love, and the desire of pleasing God. All that a Christian does, even in eating and sleeping, is prayer, when it is done in simplicity, according to the order of God, without either adding to or diminishing from it by [one's] own choice.[8]

I suggest that the intent of this passage, and indeed, the intent of Wesley's doctrine of sanctification, is that we are to live habitually from and in the sense of the divine presence. There is a holy way of "taking God for granted," of assuming the wonder that the God who is present to all things is therefore also present to you, to me, to us.

So often we in the Christian tradition have been enamoured of what we have called the omnipotence of God that we have allowed it to overshadow the equally traditional, but less valued, understanding of the omnipresence of God. By undervaluing God's presence, we often have the implicit image of our prayers ascending some miles heavenward toward a distant throne, where God deigns to receive our prayers (almost in the caricature of an answering service that assures us our message will be tended to in the order in which it was received). But God's omnipresence puts the lie to that.

When we habituate ourselves to the presence of God it is possible to orient our entire lives to that presence in a prayer without ceasing. There is a great freedom in such habituation, and a great grace. To be habituated to God's presence is to be open continually to God's grace. Such grace does not come to us preceded with some clarion call of trumpet; if it were to do so, we would not be able to hear the quieter call to the work God leads us to in this world, bemused as we would be with the awesomeness of God's felt presence. To the contrary, most often God cloaks that presence with a veil—as with Moses of old—so that we shall not be distracted, but instead shall go about God's work. To be habituated to God's presence is to have at the background of our consciousness the sense that "underneath are the everlasting arms," whatever fortunes or misfortunes take place in the foreground of our lives.

Is it possible to have such a sense; is it possible to "pray without ceasing"? Wesley claimed a triumphant "yes"; it is key to his teaching on Christian perfection. I suggest that this type of prayer is simply the cultivation of the assumption: God is present—here, now. And this God who is present is the God I know through Jesus Christ: This God is for me, willing my good, guiding me even in the worst of times, the worst of fears, the worst of pain. The guidance God gives does not magically eradicate pain—the guidance God gives flows from the loving presence that, as womanist theologians say, "makes a way out of no way," giving the power of endurance, faithfulness, and the form of resurrection that is possible even in the midst of hard times. We are to assume the God of presence.

This assumption does not demand particular forms of piety; clearly, a God of omnipresence is present regardless of how we feel, for God is never absent. God's presence does not depend upon human feeling or human mood; it depends upon God's "godness," God's character, God's very being. Because it is God who makes Godself present, one can simply assume that presence.

Assuming God's presence is not a matter of proof; it *is* a matter of practice. We are to make the assumption of God's presence the groundedness of everything else in our lives, so that God becomes the resting place of our thoughts. Then specific prayers arise naturally from the continuous prayer that is the trusting assumption of God's presence. Wesley indicates that such a trust makes an enormous difference in the way we live our daily lives. Whether we eat or drink or work or rest, we subsist in and through the divine presence. Therefore, we offer every activity to God, and in the process, grow in our love for God. The quality of our lives becomes a reflection of divine presence.

V

But this leads to Wesley's further instructions on prayer:

Beware of thinking, "because I pray always, therefore I need no set time for private prayer."[9]

and:

We ought to be in the church as the saints are in heaven, and in the house as the holiest [ones] are in the church: doing our work in the house as we pray in the church; worshipping God from the ground of the heart.[10]

There is a need for both the assumptive prayer that is the continuous background of our lives, and the specific prayers that arise in specific times as the foreground of our lives. This specific praying should be disciplined into our daily schedules through both individual and corporate worship. Otherwise, it is too easily crowded off the hectic agendas of our days. There will always be something that more insistently demands time than the time of prayer. But Wesley adjures us to reverse this, to let nothing rob us of a daily time of prayer.

The time of prayer is at once personal and corporate. We are called to the specific discipline of daily times of personal prayer, but these are not divorced from the corporate prayers of the full body of Christ. In the deepest sense, all Christian prayer, whether offered in the privacy of one's own home or in public worship, is corporate, for we pray through Christ and in Christ, as members of his one body. When we pray together in public worship, we are joined together not simply with those who are in worship alongside us, but in company with the whole church of God through the ages. Prayer is a unitive thing, sometimes like verses in an unending song, other times like a great chorus of many voices. Prayer, received by the everliving God, is like a participation in God's own everlastingness, and therefore, a participation in the gathered church from all the ages held in God's everlastingness. While we may well pray at times when we are alone, we are nonetheless, in the very act of praying, expressing the unity of the church and participating in that unity through the grace of God. The "prayer without ceasing," that is, living intentionally within the presence of God, issues into specific acts of prayer as the body of Christ. Whether these prayers are offered privately in our daily lives or publicly in congregational worship, they are always corporate. To put it another way, the church offers prayer to God, both in times of public worship and in the daily lives of its members.

Why should we pray specifically? Often it has been said that we do so for the sake of our own souls, but I cannot think prayer should primarily serve so selfish an end. Indeed, Wesley's comments about God's use of prayer to bring things about suggests that a major purpose of intercessory prayer is to open the world—which is so often resistant to grace—to the transformations of grace.

The mission of the church, of every congregation, must entail a proclamation in word and deed, whether it be alleviation of the pains of the poor, or participation in great causes of goodness and justice, or simply ministering to one another in love. But this mission must be bathed in prayer. In carrying out the mission of the church it is God who works through us, and our specific prayers of intercession are our own openness to God's grace so that we shall be channels of God's grace. It is our duty as individuals, as congregations, and as a denomination to engage in intercessory prayer concerning the mission of the church.

For how do we know how God can use our prayer? It is possible that by refusing to pray we are refusing the grace of God and hindering the grace of God in a world so sorely in need of divine grace. Wesley's words, "God does nothing but in answer to prayer," echo Christ's words, "[these things cannot be done] except by prayer and fasting" (Matt. 17:21). The apostle Paul also gives an example, for he begins many of his epistles by recounting his intercessory prayers for the ones to whom he writes. The mission of the church is accomplished only in and through its permeation by intercessory prayer. And prayers of intercession, unlike the continual prayer of "prayer without ceasing," require the work of specific times of prayer, both in the daily lives of Christians and in the corporate worship lives of Christians.

Likewise in this respect, the Lord's Prayer is given to us not as a weekly prayer, or as a "sometime" prayer, but as a daily prayer. Its petitions relate to the hallowing of God's name throughout the earth through the creation of God's reign, which is communities of caring and justice; they relate to the daily need for confession and forgiveness of sins, and for God's strengthening power in adversity. These are specific daily petitions, requiring a specific time of daily prayer. Thus "prayer without ceasing," which is the continuous living in and from God's presence, gives rise to prayers of petitions at set times in our private and corporate lives together.

VI

To continual watchfulness and prayer ought to be added continual employment.[11] . . . Charity cannot be practised right, unless, first, we exercise it the moment God gives the occasion, and second, retire the instant after to offer it to God by humble thanksgiving. . . . [We should] unite ourselves to God, in whom the soul expands itself in prayer, with all the graces we have received, and the good works we have done, to draw from [God] new strength against the bad effects which these very works may produce in us, . . . Good works do not receive their last perfection till they, as it were, lose themselves in God.[12]

Against the misperception that a life of prayer can be separated from a life of works, Wesley deeply connects prayer and works. First, as indicated above, prayer facilitates works, opening us and others to transforming grace. But prayer also prompts us to works of love. For Wesley, love of God is chiefly exercised through love of neighbor: "One of the principal rules of religion is, to lose no occasion of serving God. And since [God] is invisible to our eyes, we are to serve [God] in our neighbor: which [God] receives as if done to [Godself] in person, standing visibly before us."[13] A life of prayer increases our love for God; our love for God yearns for the well-being of the world God loves. Hence, our love for God finds its expression not in prayer alone, but in acts of love for our neighbor; indeed, for all of God's creatures. Prayer impels us to works of love.

But Wesley does not stop there. Prayer precedes work, permeates work, and also follows work. On the one hand, this is to prevent our focusing on the work alone, as if it were totally of our doing, devoid of God's empowering grace, which would be the "bad effect" of which Wesley speaks. But the deeper meaning is that works flowing from the love of God are themselves a kind of prayer. They are at once oriented toward the world and toward God. Thus offering them to God in prayer is a completion of their intent, which is the love of God in and through love for the world.

The final suggestion from the passage is that all works of love, offered to God, are in fact received by God. As such, they enter into God's own everlastingness. Often we think of the praise of God being a vocal thing, a singing that verbalizes the wonder of God. But the works of love that we do in the world, whether individually or corporately, are themselves the praise of God. They become reflections of God's love, mediated through us to the world and back again to God. Insofar as every deed of love is also a deed of righteousness, acting in love is a hallowing of God's name on earth as it is in heaven. Thus all works of love are offered back to God, received by God as God's own echo from the world, to God's everlasting praise. Prayer issues into work, and work issues into prayer.

VII

Our final texts from Wesley concerning prayer speak not only of the gratitude and thanksgiving engendered and expressed by prayer, but of a deep preciousness that haunts the edges of all our praying, and this is union with God. Wesley does not mention prayer in these passages, but he does not have to: the texts themselves bespeak deepest communion, and this indeed is prayer.

> The sea is an excellent figure of the fulness of God, and that of the blessed Spirit. For as the rivers all return into the sea, so the bodies, the souls, and the good works of the righteous return into God, to live there in [God's] eternal repose.[14]

> The love of God is the principle and the end of all our good works. . . . these good works in a spiritual manner die in God, by a deep gratitude, which plunges the soul in God as in an abyss, with all that it is, and all the grace and works for which it is indebted to God; a gratitude whereby the soul seems to empty itself of them, that they may return to their source, as rivers seem willing to empty themselves when they pour themselves with all their waters in to the sea.[15]

These passages go beyond the thoughts suggested by prayers in which we offer our works to God, by suggesting that prayer is a way of offering ourselves to God in anticipation of deepest union. Gratitude, or thanksgiving, is the key. Gratitude is prompted by the gifts of God, but quickly moves from gifts to giver. Indeed, it is the very nature of gratitude to do so. One may be glad concerning a work, or a relationship, or a possession. But gladness is only a prelude to gratitude: gladness focuses upon the condition; gratitude focuses upon the cause of the condition. Gladness can be self-contained; gratitude reaches out to the other in thanksgiving. Thus gratitude is a reaching toward God, a gladness that goes beyond the gifts to glory in the Giver. Gratitude is then a particular form of prayer.

Wesley uses the rather mystical image of gratitude emptying itself into the sea of God. It becomes an apt image for a life of prayer grounded in the God of gracious presence, but it contrasts with images of prayers of intercession. In the latter, an image apt to Wesley's usage is "watchfulness." One prays in intercession, and is watchful for opportunities to act in accordance with one's praying; one prays in confession, and is watchful to avoid repeating those things confessed; one prays for knowledge, and is watchful for occasions to increase in knowledge and wisdom. Thus most prayers orient us to living more faithfully in the world, and call us to attentiveness to the various needs of persons, communities, and the earth itself. Prayer rightly quickens us to loving actions within the world.

But prayers of gratitude have moved beyond the world to focus on God. Our prayers may begin from some facet of God's own acts—creation, redemption, sanctification. But even these terms become confining, for God is greater than all God's works. Hence Wesley's image of the sea connotes that which is deep enough to contain all rivers, broad enough to touch all continents, and yet which remains wholly wondrous in its depth and breadth. Gratitude is a prayer that pours itself into God, beyond all gifts and concerns. Indeed, the prayer of gratitude divests itself of all gifts and concerns, pouring them into God's boundless depths as our gratitude grows from thanksgiving for such gifts to simple rejoicing in God. All gifts are vastly transcended by so great a giver. Prayers of gratitude touch God, empty into God, and in so doing bring intimations of our final destiny, which is everlastingly to participate in the eternal mystery of God, whose depths are love.

VIII

So what are we to conclude, then, about a Wesleyan theology of prayer for today? We have seen passages in which prayer is accorded an awesome place in the providence of God, being used of God as a vehicle of grace in God's work with others. Prayer is a unitive thing, uniting us to one another as well as to God, at so deep a "withness" as to allow us to confess one another's sins to God. Intercessory prayer has a worldward thrust, impelling us toward the very mission for which we pray. Prayer is to be both constant and specific, undergirding our lives. And finally, prayer becomes a vehicle bespeaking the wonder and fullness of God, offering intimations of our eternal destiny.

A Wesleyan theology of prayer suggests an interactive God who draws us into God's own unceasing creativity. This God is no deistic observer of a world finished long ago—to the contrary. Nor does this God appear to exercise unilateral power over the world, as if the world were no more than putty in the shaper's hand. Prayer points to the limitations of these images; they are less than adequate if prayer is to be taken seriously. If God uses prayer to the extent that Wesley indicates, then God works with the world in its ongoing creation. What God does in the world in part depends upon prayer.

One could raise the question, must God work through prayer? Perhaps the question itself is irrelevant. We could find reasons for both a positive and a negative answer. We could argue that God has chosen to create creatures whose gift of freedom enables them to work with or against God's intentions. They (we!) have the possibility of blocking God's creative will for our good. Prayer is an openness to God that is an "unblocking" of our resistance to grace; prayer opens the way for God's work in the world, and for our own participation in that work—first through prayer, which itself opens us to works of love. Our response to God in prayer draws us into degrees of conformity to God's love by the power of God working with our own wills. What those works of love are may not be "foreordained," but may emerge in the creativity of a confluence of instances. There can be joy and spontaneity in the ongoing adventure of participating in God's continuing work of creation. If so, then the answer to whether God must work through prayer is a provisional "yes." Once God decides to create creatures with freedom, then those creatures have the ability to act with or against God's love. Prayer then becomes an essential element in God's positive work in the world.

But perhaps one could also answer reasonably "no, there is no need for God to work through prayer: God can do whatever God wills; God simply chooses to work through prayer." The rationale for such an answer again rests with the freedom with which we have been created. If God chooses to create creatures who are capable of holiness, which is love for God and neighbor, then by definition that love must be voluntary. If it is coerced, it is less than holy. But how is this love to be engendered? The conundrum is that if God simply "plants" it in the creature, then it is not truly love, it is merely an automatic response to a given stimulus. How is the creature to "grow" love? By being loved, of course—we know that from our own experience with children. But how is the creature to "grow" into love of God, except through the experience of God's love? And while God's love can be communicated through the words and deeds of those we know, it is in prayer that we actually touch the love of God for us, and hence grow in our own love for God. And so prayer is a "means of grace" whereby we grow in our knowledge of God and in our experience of love. Perhaps God could have arranged all this in some other way; prayer is not essentially or necessarily the way God works with us. But in the providence of God it is nonetheless a way chosen by and ordained by God.

In either case, what prayer teaches us, particularly as formulated by Wesley, is that God interacts with the world in its own continuing creation, and that prayer is a chief way by which this happens. God is interactive, prompting our prayers and receiving our prayers, and working with them and us according to God's good pleasure.

The caveat in such an understanding of the "why" of prayer is that we can no longer think of prayer as something that is given simply for the benefit of one's own soul. If God is truly interactive, and if God has ordained that prayer shall be an opening for the work of God's grace, then every instance of need or unlove or injustice in the world is an instance demanding the work of prayer. We dare not underestimate what God might do through our prayers. In the nature of the case, of course, we will only see those aspects of "answers" to our prayers in which we ourselves are involved. But God is not limited to what we see. If there is any possibility that our own praying in the world makes a positive difference in what God can do with the world, then we leave off praying to our own and the world's detriment.

Wesley spoke of prayer as a vehicle of grace using the particular instances of conversion and sanctification: Our prayers make a concrete difference in whether or not these events happen. In our own day we are newly aware of injustices within our society against peoples and against the earth itself. Surely the righting of such things is an act of God's love; surely care for such things is an exercise of a Wesleyan understanding of holiness. If Wesley could claim that "God does nothing but in answer to prayer" relative to individual's conversion and growth in love, is it not a reasonable extension to suggest that the same is true in areas of injustice?

The great complicating issue in many forms of injustice, of course, is their deeply rooted societal nature. What can an individual alone do to stop the carnage of genocide or corporate greed or environmental pollution? All of our actions seem so little and ineffective as to turn our zeal to resignation. But prayer means we care and act not in our own strength, but in and through the gracious love of God. To pray in intercession over those matters of injustice that bring such agony to its victims is to offer God an opening in the world toward the good in these situations. Our own small strength is offered to God in prayer, who uses that strength and that opening to accomplish what can be accomplished even in distant places. And the corporate prayers of the church are openings to grace and openness to the moving power of God. The risk, of course, is that God will impel the church toward corporate actions addressing the very things for which it prays. Prayer has the power to transform the church as a society into a transforming agent in society.

A Wesleyan theology of prayer can lead to the conclusion that God works with the world to bring it toward more faithful reflections of God's own love. One might say that God continuously woos us creatures woven of freedom and divine love to become the image of God we were created to be. And prayer is a means whereby grace operates with us and within us to bring such a privilege to perfection.

CHAPTER 4

Transcendence, Justice, and Mercy: Toward a (Wesleyan) Reconceptualization of God

Theodore W. Jennings Jr.

In his "Thoughts upon Divine Sovereignty" John Wesley argues that justice and mercy are not to be disassociated from the divine transcendence, power, and sovereignty but rather are integral to the divinity of God as God.[1] In this way he sought to overcome a bifurcation in the conceptualization of the divine being which seemed to be the consequence, on the one hand, of a deistic conception of God and, on the other, of a Calvinist reflection on the divine sovereignty. In this essay I will argue that a reconceptualization of the understanding of God (drawing on intellectual developments since his time) may help substantiate Wesley's claim.

I hope to demonstrate that the question of the poor, of the violated and humiliated of the earth, is decisive for the doctrine of God.[2] More precisely, I will argue that the being of God is constituted as a relationship to the violated and humiliated; that it is this that distinguishes the God of the Bible from all other gods. By attending to this thesis I hope to give concrete meaning to Wesley's insight that justice and mercy belong to the very being of God, and so are not to be thought of as in some way added to, or in potential conflict with, the absoluteness of the divine being.

I will begin with a hermeneutical reflection on Psalm 82 and the theophany of Exodus 3, highlighting their testimony that the divine being is enacted—and so is real—precisely as a response to the cry of the vulnerable. This testimony will lead me to a theo-philosophical reflection (aided by Barth, Levinas, and Derrida) aimed at demonstrating that the concrete appearance of the divine transcendence is the appearance of the other—every other—who makes an absolute claim upon me. I will then return to hermeneutical reflection, focusing this time on the last parable of Matthew and noting how the gospel radicalizes the insight we have been pursuing by identifying God not only as the hearing and heeding of the cry of the violated but as the cry itself in the dereliction of the cross. This recognition will allow me to conclude that Wesley's determination to develop Christian community with and among the disinherited of England was no mere question of evangelical tactics, it was the indispensable concomitant to the truth of the gospel.

Hermeneutical Reflection

Let us begin with a look at one of the most remarkable passages of the Bible, Psalm 82:

> God sits in the divine council; in the midst of the gods God holds judgment:
> "How long will you judge unjustly and show partiality to the wicked?
> Give justice to the weak and the orphan; maintain the right of the lowly and destitute.
> Rescue the weak and the needy; deliver them from the hand of the wicked."
> They have neither knowledge nor understanding, they walk about in the gloom of night; all the foundations of the earth are shaken.
> I say, "You are gods, children of the most High, all of you; nevertheless, you shall die like mortals, and fall as a single person."
> Rise up, O God, judge the earth; for all the nations belong to you.[3]

It is a most astonishing scene: YHWH seated in a council meeting of all the gods. It is a scene we might imagine on Mount Olympus. The deities of all the nations are present. It is a scene moreover that reminds the Bible reader of the setting of Genesis at the creation, "Let us make humankind in our image" (1:26), or a similar scene in which the divine council takes note of the building of the tower of Babel, "Come, let us go down" (11:7).

In the divine council the gods have acceded to the creation of the earthling in the divine image. In the divine council the gods have acted to prevent the earthling's assault upon heaven. In these scenes all that is divine seems to be of one mind, following the lead of YHWH

Elohim. But in the psalm the God of Israel stands over against all the other gods and calls them to account. The God known to Israel holds judgment over all the other gods and thus steps out from this "divinity in general" of the divine council to be the voice of judgment, the claim of justice. In this way Adonai stands over against the gods (*elohim*).

The one we encounter in this extraordinary scene, then, is not "divinity as such" or "divinity in general" nor some specialized aspect of divinity, but one who stands over against the divine in general or as such and does so precisely as the call for justice for the weak and defenseless, the violated and humiliated. And as this call and claim of justice for those who are vulnerable, this One stands over against all those divine principles that in one way or another, directly or indirectly, through approval or acquiescence, collaborate with the violent of the earth in their rapacious and voracious rule of the earth.

That these gods do not heed this claim makes it clear that they are not true gods after all. Their lack of understanding, their living in bewilderment and gloom is precisely what makes them, in biblical terms, mere idols. They are revealed as idols not because they are made of human hands but because they do not come to the aid of the violated and humiliated. Faced with the claim of justice for the vulnerable these gods stumble into darkness, and thus the foundations of the earth tremble and totter. What Paul would later term the "pillars of the cosmos" become weak and beggarly elemental powers. The principalities and powers stagger under the weight of the claim of justice for the violated and humiliated.

In the psalm they seem to come under the sentence of death: these who seemed to be immortal become mortal, these who seemed to rule over the nations fall "as a single individual." Is this one who falls not the Supreme Being who is the principle of divinity as such, a divine principle that either ignores the plight of history's victims (an unmoved mover, for example) or a supreme being available for appropriation as the legitimation of the existing order (any existing order) of victimage, exploitation, and impoverishment; the divine principle in whose name the violence of patriarchy, of hierarchy, of the "wicked" is sanctified? It is the death of this divine being which is here announced, the death we may say of theism's god, and thus the shaking of the foundations of history and being.

The psalmist glimpses here the becoming God of God, the crumbling of the powerful but false gods of the earth, and calls out to God to do that which the vision has anticipated: become the Lord of all the earth, the Lord of all the nations. And how is it that God may and must do this? Precisely as this claim of justice for the violated and humiliated. In this and in this alone consists the deity of this God whereby ersatz deity is exposed and expelled.

The deity, then, of the God who speaks through the psalmist and is called upon by the psalmist is precisely the deity of this unwavering call and claim: "Give justice to the weak and the orphan; maintain the right of the lowly and destitute. Rescue the weak and the needy; deliver them from the hand of the wicked."

This passage, which is absolutely decisive for understanding biblical monotheism, is too often ignored—and with good reason if theology thinks that in consideration of the deity of God it may take a vacation from the cry of the oppressed and dispossessed. But there is another more familiar passage which makes the same point even if this point is regularly overlooked in traditional theology. I mean the famous theophany of YHWH to Moses at the burning bush (Exod. 3:1-17).

This Exodus passage has not been overlooked in traditional theology, especially in philosophically inclined theology, because the disclosure of the divine name in the theophany is often used to connect God to something like "being itself." That name renders itself as a form of the Hebrew verb "being," often translated as "I Am." But in philosophical theology it is taken more as *ousia* or *essendi*: "the One who is" or "being itself." Whether in the neoplatonism of Augustine or the neo-Aristotelianism of Aquinas the beingness of the divine, and thus the linkage to philosophical reflection upon being, is discerned precisely here.[4]

That this text is central for understanding the nature of the God is clear from the fact that here we have the disclosure of the divine name YHWH, which means not only "I am who I am" but "I will be who I will be," or "I will be the one who is." God's very being, God's innermost essence, is here disclosed in the name which is given to Moses. So near does this approach the very essence of the holy God that Israel adopted the custom of never pronouncing this name, for it was felt to be an encroachment upon the holiness of God: The pure fire at the center of the universe. YHWH—I am who I am; I am who is with you; the very being of God—disclosed to Moses upon the mountain where the flame at the heart of the universe breaks forth into speaking.

Yet what is the meaning of this revelation of the being of the Holy One? We are left in no doubt. It is precisely that this one whose name is disclosed here is the one who has heard the cry of the slaves in Egypt. God is moved to disclose Godself here because God has heard the cry of an afflicted people. "I have *observed* the misery of my people who are in Egypt; I have *heard* their cry on account of their taskmaster. Indeed I *know* their sufferings. . . . The cry of the Israelites has now come to me. I have also *seen* how the Egyptians oppress them" (Exod. 3:7-9, emphasis added). Notice what is disclosed concerning the Holy One. God has *seen* their misery, has *heard* their cry, indeed *knows* their suffering. It is because God has heard the cry of the afflicted and oppressed that God now reveals Godself to Moses, now discloses the essence of the divine being.

That which is not noted in the usage of this passage as a springboard into reflection upon the being of God, upon God as being or being itself, is precisely that the being of God is this hearing and heeding of the afflicted. It is not that God exists in some general sense, and then through anthropomorphic slippage from being and essence to existence and accident, comes to hear and heed the cry of this people. Rather it is in and through both the hearing and the heeding of the cry of the violated and humiliated that this One is, that the being of this One comes to be, that act and being, being as act, irrupts into history.

In this text again the deity of God, the being of God, is precisely this hearing and heeding of the cry of the violated. The being of this God is, so to say, called into being by the cry of affliction, the protest against violation. Now it is simple theological incompetence (or impertinence) when a Christian reflection on the being of God is transposed from this context saturated with the claims of justice for the oppressed and placed instead in the abstract context of the relation of being to beings, or God and the world, or God and human subjectivity, or what have you. For in that case the god of another slaveocracy—that of Athens (and Rome)—has the first and last word over the One who hears and heeds the cry of the impoverished and exploited.

José Porfirio Miranda, in his stunning study of the Bible somewhat misleadingly entitled *Marx and the Bible*, demonstrates that there is a distinctive correlation between the cry of the afflicted and the theophany of God.[5] Already with the murder of Abel the bloodstained earth cries out and God irrupts into Cain's history (Gen. 4:10).

Similarly, in the case of Sodom, the cry of the violated stirs God into action, into being: to destroy the arrogance of those who despoil the poor and violate the vulnerable (Gen. 18:20-21). As Miranda notes, this identification of the deity of God with the claim of justice for the violated is determinative for the whole of the Bible, from Genesis to Revelation. Thus he can rightly maintain that "Yahweh is not among the entities nor the existings nor in univocal being nor in analogous being, but rather in the implacable moral imperative of justice."[6]

To summarize this hermeneutical reflection, the being—and so the deity—of God consists precisely in hearing and heeding the cry of the violated and humiliated, the cry of the poor and marginalized. This is amply demonstrated in the Bible and it is this which distinguishes the god of (many) philosophers (and theologians) from the God of the Bible.

Theo-Philosophical Reflection

We may approach the same insight from a different perspective. Now I turn to the question of the transcendence of God and to the question of the trace of that transcendence which evokes the speaking about God that is something other than idolatry. In order to do this I will briefly recall some of the chief insights of Karl Barth and Emmanuel Levinas.

Karl Barth: God as "Wholly Other"

The adoption by Barth of Kierkegaard's "infinite qualitative distinction between time and eternity" marked his decisive rupture with the liberal theology that had proved itself incapable of a prophetic relation to culture and nation in the debacle of the First World War. The collapse of the easy identification of God with the cultural project of modernity meant that the theism of this synthesis was shown to be properly challenged by the atheism of Feuerbach and subsequently of Marx and even Freud and Nietzsche. For the god of this social order was indeed nothing but the ideological superstructure of the pretensions of Western civilization, the projection of human hopes and fears onto the blank sky.

In contrast Barth proposed that the God of the "strange new world of the Bible" be understood as the "wholly other" who has nothing whatever in common with this system of consciousness and culture, in relation to which God the totality of this system of "man" writ large—of world as culture and society and indeed religion—is brought radically into question so that nothing remains standing. The Other who intersects this world "slantwise from above" brings this world into question, into crisis, into judgment.

Moreover it is in this way and in this way alone that one can speak of transcendence. Otherwise god is but the immanent principle of the world as it is. Thus Barth writes in his commentary on Romans: "We suppose that we know what we are saying when we say God. We assign to Him the highest place in our world: and in so doing we place Him fundamentally on one line with ourselves and with things. . . . And so when we set God on the throne of the world, we mean by God ourselves."[7] But the God of the Bible is one whose otherness is unassimilable to any conception of the human and the world, exceeds the margins and is indeed the frontier by which the wholeness of the world is shattered.

What is critical for our purposes is that the transcendence of God is conceivable as true transcendence by virtue of the otherness of God, the heterogeneity of God with respect to the socially, religiously, and cognitively established totality of the world. Whatever else may need to be said of the "immanence" of God, or indeed of the humanity of God, must pass through the fire of this alterity with its firm and uncompromising "no" to the pretensions of world and humanity to be in some way continuous with the divine.

Emmanuel Levinas: The Other as "Face"

While for Barth the debacle of the First World War occasioned a keen sense of the urgency for a notion of alterity vis-à-vis the cultural and religious synthesis, the gruesome realities of the Second World War precipitated another decisive rupture, this time within the movement of phenomenology. The voice of this rupture is Emmanuel Levinas, for whom as well the theme of the other becomes decisive.

Levinas sees the history of Western philosophy as bound up in a "nostalgia for totality" which pervades the development of epistemology so that "knowledge is in reality an immanence . . . there is no rupture of the isolation of being in knowledge."[8] The history of consciousness aware of itself is a history of the attempt to constitute a totality, a totality which is the indefinite extension of the same and of the self. This is the theme of Western epistemology and of ontology as well.

Opposed to this self/same/totality is the idea of the infinite (Descartes) whose concreteness, according to Levinas, is the appearance of the other as "face." It is this intrusion of the other which renders questionable the egoism of the self at home in a world constituted as the same.

The other with a face is for Levinas the Other that transcends the self and its world, the other who thus invades the realm of the same (constituted as a totality by the comprehension of the self/ego) as a stranger, as alien in the sense of heterogeneous to the self's totalizing operations. It is the intrusion of the other which interrupts totality with an unassimilable "infinity." The other exceeds the world constituted as a totality of the same, of the ego's at-homeness in and enjoyment of the world.

The way in which this other limits and brings into question the self's at-homeness in being is its "face," that in the encounter which—in vulnerability, yet imperially—commands: "thou shalt not kill." In order to express the exteriority of the other to the self, the same, the totality, Levinas speaks of the height, the grandeur, the dignity of the other; the other as the apparition of infinity.

This dignity is precisely the absoluteness of the command not to kill. To be sure it is the very destitution or nudity of the face, its vulnerability, which seems to make murder possible. "The face is exposed, menaced, as if inviting us to an act of violence. At the same time, the face is what forbids us to kill."[9] It is the absolute command present in vulnerability which brings into question the project of self-establishment in the world. For this project of self-establishment (through knowledge, through labor, and so on) is a project which assimilates to the self all that is encountered by the self. Yet here is an other who cannot be so assimilated without violence and violation. It is this "other," the other who invades and evades the net of comprehension, who poses the concrete limit to my self-aggrandizement, to my participation in, or vicarious identification and satisfaction with, a system of self-aggrandizement.

Now of course we cannot doubt that the other with a face is in fact regularly assimilated to the project of self-aggrandizement. But this renders the other both mute and faceless, makes of the other an extension of the self, an expression of the same. And this is, in the last analysis, murder: the annihilation of the alterity of the other. This of course occurs: the erotic other, the beloved, is reduced to an extension of the self, an adornment, an echo; the child in its vulnerability is reduced through violent pedagogy into a perpetuation of the self; the stranger is assimilated or annihilated. To be sure, the otherness of this other may be reduced through co-optation into the system of representation by which the world is constituted as a totality. "The prohibition against murder does not render murder impossible."[10] But it does make murder a crime. It exposes the project of the self as a project of violation and violence. In this sense the appearance of the other as a face renders judgment, brings into question the self, the world, the totality.

As Levinas recognizes, this other is the other signified by "the widow, the orphan, the immigrant." What is it about this trinity of figures that so permeates biblical discourse? It is a cast of characters that stands outside the protective signification of a patriarchal totality of meaning: women without male protectors, children without fathers, travelers without fatherland (*patria*). They are those excluded from the protections of patriarchy. They are formally outside the totality constituted as the household economy of Israel. To be sure this is not an exhaustive enumeration of the ways in which the alterity of the other who calls into question the legitimacy of the totality is represented. There is also the day laborer, the indigent, the beggar, the landless (levite), and so on.

In this list what becomes clear is the vulnerability of the other as that which calls the self and the world into question. In this sense we may discover what is truly at stake in the encounter with any other through the destitution, the nakedness, the vulnerability of the face. For any other as truly other is outside, is a "stranger," is thus vulnerable to the violation which it simultaneously forbids.

Every Other as "Wholly Other"?

Before concluding this reflection we may inquire how these phenomemological reflections on alterity relate to what we earlier noticed with respect to Barth and his rediscovery of the otherness of God as that which brings self and world into question. How are we to relate the other of Barth to the other of Levinas?[11]

Like Barth, Levinas is aware that to speak of the transcendent is to speak of another who cannot be captured in the system of representations by which we constitute the world as the home of consciousness. Rather transcendence points to the coming of an other who intersects, interrupts, and brings into question the totalitarian project of consciousness and culture. Moreover, in both cases the priority of the claim of this other is the contribution of what Barth called the "strange new world of the Bible" to their reflection. We may also note that the consequence of this primacy of the other in the thought of each of these thinkers is the emergence of a certain priority of ethics in their thought. Barth seeks to abolish the division between theology and ethics in his *Church Dogmatics* and discerns in the idea of "command" the category adequate to the alterity of the other as wholly other. Levinas goes even further in that he attempts to demonstrate that ethics is "first philosophy," or that metaphysics (as he terms the reflection upon the encounter with the other) has priority over ontology and epistemology. Ethics becomes the most fundamental "science"; the good, as he says, is more fundamental than the true.

But still we must recognize that Barth understands the other as "God" whereas Levinas understands by the other, the other with a face, the other "person." (We should note that it is precisely the problem that no generic term may unite the self and the other without perpetuating the violence of subsuming the other into the same. Thus if we say 'the other person,' 'the human other,' or what have you, we speak in such a way as to reduce the alterity of the other, making the other simply an alter ego; the very move against which Levinas' ethics seeks to warn us. For in the case of such a common denominator otherness is reduced to an appearance of the same, and to the epistemological strategy which subsumes whatever there is to the categories of the *cogito*.)

Again if Barth restricts the other to the divine, Levinas detects the infinity of the other with a face. But if Barth seems to denude the world of God (and how could it be otherwise if the world is constituted as a totality by the epistemology of the self, the ontology of *dasein*, the conquest of culture) then Levinas finds the other in any other, in the call and claim of this face, this voice. And what then of the name of God?

Levinas anticipates this question when he asserts that "there can be no 'knowledge' of God separated from the relation with men. The other is the very locus of metaphysical truth, and is indispensable for my relation to God."[12] In this sense he can maintain that "In the access to the face there is certainly also an access to the idea of God."[13]

Hence his formula that "*L'absolment Autre, c'est Autrui*" (the absolutely other is the other."[14] This formula is transformed by Jacques

Derrida (whose philosophy is as well a discussion with Levinas) into the even more ambiguous and provocative: "*tout autre est tout autre.*"[15] It may be translated either as "every other is wholly other" or (the) "wholly other is every other." Thus John Caputo remarks concerning Derrida:

> The 'other' is an example of what is named with the name of God; the name of God is an example of what is named by the 'other.' God is the exemplar of every 'other,' the other is the exemplar of God. When John says 'God is love,' 'love' exemplifies what 'God' means, but it is also true that 'God' exemplifies what 'love' means. Is God an example of justice, or justice of God?[16]

However we may seek to decipher this epigram it seems that its biblical provenance is undeniable. Whether in the insistence of the prophets that God demands not worship or prayer or fasting but concrete justice for the violated and humiliated, or in the insistence of Paul that the love of neighbor is the whole command of God, or that of John that the love of the other is the knowledge of God, the Bible is clear that there is and can be no relation to God that is not a relation to the most vulnerable of these. Again Caputo: "When the prophets, for example, use the name of God, they—like Derrida— seem to mean 'justice'; and when they speak of justice, they seem to mean God."[17] Or to return explicitly to the theme of transcendence, I quote Miranda once more: "Transcendence does not mean only an unimaginable and inconceivable God, but a God who is accessible only in the act of justice."[18]

Before taking this analysis forward I want to point to a concrete historical example of what this reflection is suggesting. At the end of the nineteenth century (and thus before either Barth or Levinas) there emerged in Korea a movement of thought and community called Donghak. Initially developed by Ch'oe Che-u and then by his disciple Ch'oe Si-hyong, it sought to develop an "eastern way" to withstand elements of the "western way" associated with formal Christianity, represented at that time by Roman Catholicism. At the same time elements of a kind of "folk Christianity" disseminated through the publication of tracts like the Gospel of Mark by clandestine protestant missionaries were appropriated. The Donghak movement became in time the Donghak rebellion against concrete structures of oppression, especially the corruption whereby the ruling classes (*yangban*) oppressed the underclasses (the *minjung*).

Essential to this movement was the insistence that heaven and earth meet in the concrete presence of the other person. Thus the principle of *in nae ch'on*; man and God are one. The other person was to be seen as the bearer of heaven or god (*si ch'onju*). As such the obeisance rendered to the divine (or by the *minjung* to the *yangban* and especially the emperor) was to be rendered to every person (*sa in yo ch'on* or "treat people as though they were God") and this concretely meant the practice of obeisance to persons of the under-class including women, children, and "slaves." The recognition of the other as the bearer of the divine had revolutionary potential, and in fact issued in revolution, and remains to today as the historical irruption of the *minjung* as the subject of history.[19]

Renewed Hermeneutical Reflection

Can the notion of the divine other as dispersed among or present in the "other" as such be substantiated hermeneutically, or have we now left behind the biblical world with its insistence upon the divine transcendence? In this concluding hermeneutical reflection I wish to suggest that there are important elements of the biblical witness that seem to confirm precisely the direction in which we have been led through a reflection on Barth, Levinas, and Derrida.

The very last parable recorded in the Gospel of Matthew under-lines the whole point of Jesus' mission and ministry. He warns those who hear him that their standing before God is not determined by their belief in Christian doctrine, nor their association with the Christian community, but by whether they have fed the hungry and clothed the naked.

> When the Son of Man comes in his glory, and all the angels with him, then he will sit on the throne of his glory. And all the nations will be gathered before him, and he will separate people one from another as a shepherd separates the sheep from the goats, and he will put the sheep at his right hand and the goats at the left. Then the king will say to those at his right hand, "Come, you that are blessed by my Father, inherit the kingdom prepared for you from the foundation of the world; for I was hungry and you gave me food, I was thirsty and you gave me something to drink, I was a stranger and you welcomed me, I was naked and you gave me clothing, I was sick and you took care of me, I was in prison and you visited me." Then the righteous will answer him, "Lord, when was it that we saw you hungry and gave you food, or thirsty and

gave you something to drink? And when was it that we saw you a stranger and welcomed you, or naked and gave you clothing? And when was it that we saw you sick or in prison and visited you?" And the king will answer them, "Truly I tell you, just as you did it to one of the least of these who are members of my family, you did it to me."

Then he will say to those at his left hand, "You that are accursed, depart from me into the eternal fire prepared for the devil and his angels; for I was hungry and you gave me no food, I was thirsty and you gave me nothing to drink, I was a stranger and you did not welcome me, naked and you did not clothe me, sick and in prison and you did not visit me." Then they also will answer, "Lord, when was it that we saw you hungry or thirsty or a stranger or naked or sick or in prison and did not take care of you?" Then he will answer them, "Truly I tell you, just as you did not do it to one of the least of these, you did not do it to me." And these will go away into eternal punishment, but the righteous into eternal life. (Matt. 25:31-46)

No more rigorous identification of a relation to the divine with a relation to the impoverished and afflicted can be imagined. That God judges the world, every person and nation, on the basis of their response to the poor, the destitute, the humiliated of the earth, is made devastatingly clear. Yet as often as we have heard this passage read from the Gospel of Matthew, can we yet say that it has become our main business to respond to the needs of the most vulnerable members of our society, to the cries of the violated and humiliated of the earth, be they near or far away? And if we have not done this, on what basis shall we persuade ourselves that we have received some special exemption from the clear and manifest command of Christ? When asked by a prosperous person whether it was really good for the poor to help them indiscriminately, Wesley replied that whether it was good for them or not, if we did not do it we should surely go to hell.[20]

But far more is involved here than a reiteration of the familiar prophetic imperative to do justice to the impoverished and vulnerable. For the parable suggests that the divine is present not only in that imperative but also in the very cry or plight of the violated and vulnerable. This suggests a portentous relocation of the divine as precisely the "least of these." Let us see how this works in more detail.

We can begin by noticing a certain slippage in the identification of the "judge."[21] Although the norm of judgment is presented with an almost mathematical rigor, being repeated in virtually the same terms four times, the identity of the judge seems oddly constructed. This judge is first identified as "the human one."[22] Yet this human one is invested with divine appearance. We are referred to his being accompanied by "his angels" and to his being seated on "the throne of his glory." It is precisely as thus identified with attributes of divinity that the human one appears as judge and as "king." Yet there remains a certain distinction between this divine figure and the divine as "father."

What are we to make of the divinization of the human one? Of course so long as this passage is read with the assumptions of post-fourth-century christological formulation in mind the oddity of the passage will not appear. But when we are aware of the problematic features of imposing later doctrinal formulations upon the reading of the text we must find it startling.

Certainly Matthew means us to find it startling, since it is precisely the association of the human one with the divine that leads the high priest to discern blasphemy in the teaching of Jesus: "Jesus said to him, 'You have said so. But I tell you, From now on you will see the Son of Man seated at the right hand of Power and coming on the clouds of heaven.' Then the high priest tore his clothes and said, 'He has blasphemed!'" (Matt. 26:64-5) Nor is this at all the end of the matter. For the author of Acts who retains the scene of the trial also tells the reader that Steven's declaration that he sees the human one "standing at the right hand of God" leads directly to his being stoned for blasphemy (Acts 7:56-8).

What is so startling about this association of the human with the divine is that it seems to encroach upon the divine transcendence and holiness. Yet this association of the human and the divine is not an innovation of Jesus. It already appears, at least suggestively, in the account of Abraham's encounter with the messengers who are on their way to execute divine judgment upon Sodom. There we find a certain slippage between "the Lord" and the three messengers, who are also identified as "men" (Gen. 18:1-2). Something similar appears to happen in Ezekiel's vision of the Glory of God having the appearance of a human being (Ezek. 8:1-4). But it is in Daniel that the divine rule is most closely associated with "the human one" as the coming of a new order or empire that can be described as humane over against previous empires represented as animals of prey (Dan. 7:2-14). Thus the identification of the human with the divine is something not at all unknown to biblical imagery, even if it may appear as horrifying to another sort of (biblical) piety.

Accordingly, in the last parable of Jesus, the (anonymous) human one representing the new humane empire (also known as the reign of heaven or the divine empire) appears as divine. And it is the elevation of the human to stand alongside the divine that is recognizable as blasphemy. This is not a case of incarnation of the divine but the divinization of the human. It is not Jesus as such but "the human one" who is to be invested with divine standing and attribution. It is this divine humanity, this human(e) divinity, then that is represented as "coming," as arriving, in order to pronounce and enact judgment upon history.

The identity of those to be judged has a certain ambiguity as well. For the terminology of the text changes from "nations" to what appear to be persons or people to be divided among the just and the accursed. This ambiguity is not as pronounced as the variation in the identification of the judge. It seems safe to say that what is in view here is no merely individualistic judgment but one that recalls the judgment of nations anticipated in prophetic vision. It is as judge of history, nations, and people, that the human one who is the divine appears.

Now the norm of judgment is, as we have seen, unvarying. It is repeated four times in virtually identical terminology. Nor should the norm as thus reiterated come as a surprise to any familiar with the law and the prophets. What is surprising however is the way in which this norm is grounded. In the prophets and especially the law the response to the vulnerable is grounded in the recollection of the prior status of Israel: "be kind to the alien, for you were aliens in Egypt" (Exod. 22:21; Deut. 10:19; and so on). But here the norm is grounded not in the experience and status of those who are judged but in the location of the one doing the judging. It is because the human to come has already been present as the vulnerable human within history that there can be no appeal of the verdict, "in as much as you did it (or did it not) to them, you did it (or did it not) to me."

The divine to come has already been here as the one who is hungry, naked, imprisoned, and so on. The parable presents this from the perspective of the arrival of the human/divine. But from the standpoint of the hearer of the parable this means that the divine as the human who will come is present now as the hungry, the naked, the imprisoned, and so on. The vulnerable, the humiliated, the violated now is as such the presence of that which comes as the divine judge. The vulnerable other is the transcendent other. Every other is wholly other. The wholly other is every other.

We should note that this last teaching of Jesus (it is his final parable in this gospel) oddly corresponds to the way in which Jesus' first discourse begins. That is, the sermon on the Mount of Olives corresponds with the beginning of the Sermon on the Mount that opens Jesus' public teaching ministry. In that discourse Jesus begins with the beatitudes: "Blessed are the poor in spirit . . . ." That the poor, the grieving, the humiliated, the hungry and thirsty are "happy now . . . for they will be . . ." has an odd correspondence to the reversal of fortunes that appears in Jesus' last parable. But in that last parable the spiritualizing tendencies of Matthew's version of the beatitudes is gone—replaced with literal poverty, hunger, thirst, and so on.

Moreover the parable changes the reversal of fortunes motif in an extraordinary way. For those who are hungry now will be disclosed as the human/divine to come. Now they are the hidden location of the divine (and so are "blessed now"). Then they appear as the divine in order to be the crisis (judgment) of history.

A perhaps even more momentous change takes place between the beatitude and the parable, for now instead of the poor being those who are blessed, they are seen as the site of blessing or cursing for those who will be judged. Those who are not themselves poor (the nations, the peoples) encounter blessing or curse now in the interaction with those who are vulnerable now. The poor who will appear as the humanity of God or the divinity of the human are now the decisive site in which the ultimate felicity or annihilation of historical agents is determined.

The effect of the movement from the beatitudes to the parable is to deepen the identification of the divine with the vulnerable. The one who comes as divine is present now as the needy or vulnerable other. The vulnerable other now is the one who is to come as the divine other. And both the divine other and the vulnerable other are "the human one."

We are then at a point of the radical dissemination or dispersal of the divine among all those who are most vulnerable. It is this vulnerability that is to be recognized as the site now, in history, of the One who comes as the divine. Every other as vulnerable, and especially as humiliated and violated, is the wholly other, the end of history, its judge and goal.

This parable does not stand alone in thus identifying the divine with vulnerable humanity, with the poor, the humiliated and the violated. We have already seen how the parable is a transformation of the beginning of Jesus' teaching of the beatitudes. And we have seen that the image of the human one as divine is connected forward to Jesus' blasphemy and thus to his being repudiated by the Judean authorities. But far more is at stake in this identification in this most Jewish of gospels. For Matthew takes over from Mark the depiction of Jesus' death in which there echoes from his lips the cry of abandoned and violated humanity always and everywhere: "My God, my God, why have you forsaken me?" (Mark 15:34; Matt. 27:46)

Once again: no longer does the voice of the divine sound as the imperative to attend to the cry of the violated but rather it sounds as this cry itself. As the Roman executioner realizes, the cry of destitution, of violation, of abandonment is the cry of the divine itself: "surely this one was divine [a son of God]" (cf. Mark 15:39; Matt. 27:54).

Nor is it right to suppose that this identification is suspended or reversed in the resurrection. For the one who returns is not recognized by his erstwhile companions but rather appears as a nobody, as nobody important; as a vagabond to the disciples on the road to Emmaus (Luke 24:13), as a grave digger to Mary of Magdala (John 20:15), as a kibitzer to the disciples who had gone fishing (John 21:4-6). The dispersion into the nobodies, the nonentities, and so among the vulnerable and the impoverished is not reversed by the resurrection but in a certain way intensified thereby.

Now all of this would require a good deal of interpretive work to make clear, especially since dogmatic presuppositions so overlay the texts as to obscure their radical character and render them virtually harmless. But it is perhaps enough to indicate the textual sites where it is possible to begin the work of demonstrating the significance for theological construction of the radical thesis that the Other is the other.

Conclusion

This may seem to have taken us a long way from Wesley and his attempt to tie the justice and mercy of God more closely to the divine sovereignty, transcendence, and power. I do not intend to claim that Wesley in any way anticipated the more radical claims of Levinas or Derrida. But I do wish to claim that these postmodern conceptualities offer us the opportunity to affirm even more consistently and thoroughly than Wesley could, the identification of the divine (transcendence) as justice and mercy.

We often recall that Wesley directed himself to the poor of England and away from the prosperous and prestigious. We may imagine that this was simply a form of especially idealistic piety or even a misguided and ultimately failed strategy. Whatever else it was, however, it was the rigorous application in the field of proclamation and community formation of the biblical revelation of the being of God. Any other way of seeking to mold, build, or establish the church entails an entire forgetfulness of the God of the Bible. In this sense Wesley's theology was far more systematic (that is, coherent) than that of many of his followers who separate the theme of God from that of the poor and this again from the theme of the church. Before we dismiss Wesley as a folk theologian we would do well to be as clear and as consistent as he is in this respect.

CHAPTER 5

Sanctification and Economy: A Wesleyan Perspective on Stewardship

M. Douglas Meeks

Ted Runyon has opened up a fresh discussion of Wesleyan approaches to the formation of the church and its mission in society.[1] In this essay I will seek to make a contribution to this discussion by treating John Wesley's view of stewardship as the Christian way of being in the world through community as well as the economy through which God works for life against death in the world.

But is such an interest in Wesley somewhat misplaced? How could an eighteenth-century divine who had not mastered the genius of mercantilism, much less capitalism, shed any light on the profound problems of the church's stewardship in a world of globalized capitalism at the turn of the century? What makes Wesley's view of stewardship look either outmoded or revolutionary today is that he so thoroughly inherited the view of God's *oikonomia* in the Torah, the prophets, the teachings and practices of Jesus, the Fathers, and the Catholic and Reformation traditions down to John Locke. Wesley steadfastly held God and economy together. Reappropriating this tradition may seem to some the height of conservatism, but it may be the only way toward a new perspective on Christian stewardship.

To seek to relate God and economy again in this way requires, of course, that we suspend the three-hundred-year concordance according to which theology and economics must be kept as far apart as possible. Pastors and bishops may preach on virtually anything in the market society except economics. Stewardship is thus typically limited to raising the church's budget. The problem, from Wesley's perspective, is that we cannot speak of God biblically without speaking of economy comprehensively.

Stewardship as Economy for Life and Modern Economics

While the science called economics is certainly a relatively recent invention, the word economy (*oikos* + *nomos*) is not; it is an ancient word that means literally the "law or management of the household." "Economy" is found throughout the Septuagint and the New Testament and the phrase *oikonomia tou theou* (the economy of God) is central and decisive for the biblical rendering of God.[2] Economy is about access to the conditions of life and life abundant.[3] Up to the seventeenth century, to pursue economy meant to pursue the question "Will everyone in the household get what it takes to live, will everyone survive (*sur* + *vivre* = "live through") the day and, where possible, flourish?" As the arrangement that makes it possible for the household or community to live, economy was bound to community.[4] In fact, it was clear that economy existed to serve community. Economy in the broadest sense meant the relations of human beings formed for producing the conditions of life against death. Economy was about human *livelihood* and human *flourishing*.

The biblical traditions borrow the language of *oikonomia* to speak of God's most inclusive relationships to creation and understand the church as a peculiar economy in service of what God is doing to redeem creation. In modernity market economics increasingly displaces economy in this sense and offers itself as a pervasive logic by which all spheres of human endeavor can be comprehended and mastered. The logic of the market society has defined the ground of certainty (what can be called true and factual): what can count as the development of human beings and progress of society and the accepted conceptions of order, rule, justice, reason, harmony, and peace. This spirit asserts itself in all spheres of sociality and increasingly proves itself as the one universal order of the world.

The church has not been spared the incursion of this logic. Indeed, the church's widespread malaise is characterized by its idolatrous absorption in this logic. Is it possible that the market logic takes over even in the church, in the way a congregation or a judicatory glues itself together? Productivity, incentive, maximization, and efficiency are the words that are on our lips and that we instinctively understand because we so effortlessly belong to the market society governed by the laws of market economics. Is it not after all often the market logic that in the end governs our clergy appointment system, our view of the effectiveness of ministry, and some of our church growth schemes, some of our evangelism and stewardship programs, and some of our theories of leadership and organizational development? And if the answer is in some sense "yes" to these questions, then must we not ever more urgently teach the logic of the gospel, lest the church in the end have nothing new to say to a public household that excludes many from the conditions of life and life abundant? For in the last analysis the gospel of Jesus Christ is the only new word the church has to say to the world, the only thing the world has not already heard. "Unless the LORD builds the house, those who build it labor in vain" (Ps. 127:1). This is true—even for the church.

Under the assumption of the modern division of life into public and private spheres, the church has been assigned certain social responsibilities in the private sphere. It belongs to the sphere that, according to Hegel, was left free for personal choice. The church loses its public character by submitting to the private roles defined for it by society. But the church can also cease to be public by assuming to itself the logic of the public household. Thus, the church, like all other institutions in this society, has taken over (to be sure most often unwarily and indeed almost as a matter of course) the logic of market exchange as the way of cementing itself together socially and institutionally.[5] The upshot is that the church as *ecclesia* has lost its public manifestation, that is, its ability to appear in the world as an alternative economy serving God's redemption of the world.

This is not the "fault" of the market economy. The church does not have to conform to the logic of the market (any more than it had to conform to slavery, feudal, or mercantilist societies), but so pervasive is the logic of the market as the common sense of human operations that the church will experience freedom for its public mission only as the gift of God's grace. But precisely on the basis of God's grace the church's struggle with the market logic is crucial in our time, for multiple problems of the formation of the church and its mission in our society come to a focus in the question of economy. As one who did not shrink from this grappling with grace and economy, Wesley makes a good partner in our struggle to be faithful.

Modern theology has typically conformed to the spread of the market logic by excluding economy from its central concern. This was not true of Wesley. Economy appears prominently in his theology, not simply as an ethical issue or second thought about Christian practice. Economy is for Wesley at the heart of Christian discipleship and the substance of the way of salvation. This is to say that, for Wesley, *oikonomia* as God's way of redeeming the creation cannot be separated from the life-and-death question of economy, the distribution of what it takes for human beings to survive the day.

Thus, the distinctive contribution of Wesley is the way he connected sanctification to economy in its variegated senses. This is the wisdom of Wesley's view of stewardship. In what follows I will attempt to show how closely Wesley's understanding of stewardship follows the Torah perspectives on God's *oikonomia* as embodied in the grace of Jesus Christ.

Household Rules of the Torah and the Gospel: Sanctification and Stewardship

Sanctification has become mystifying to modern Methodists in large part because they have missed the fact that by sanctification Wesley means simply the righteousness of God given in the Torah and embodied in the grace of Jesus Christ. Holiness is the life lived out of and in accordance with this Torah-gospel gift of life, or, more specifically, it means the return of God's gift of life.

The Torah is God's precious gift, the life-giving rules of the household of life against death.[6] The life question of the people of Israel is how to live in the household of freedom without falling again into slavery. Life in God's household of freedom, then, means living in obedience to God's way of distributing righteousness. Keeping God's Torah economy is life; disregarding God's Torah economy is death. Covenant faithfulness is what the Torah requires in the distribution of what it takes for everyone in the household to live. Torah means guidance for the holy life of righteousness in God's household.

Both liberal and conservative Protestants in the last two centuries have eschewed these household rules, calling them dusty, irrelevant encumbrances of the past, superseded by the gospel. Why would God expect us to keep these outmoded rules?[7] Precisely because the life and death household rules of God's economy are part and parcel of what Jesus teaches! Jesus' gospel of the kingdom makes no sense without the content of God's promises and commands to Israel for God's home-making (stewarding). Whether they are realizable today is precisely the question: whether the church as the economy of God's grace can actually find space and time in which to exist in

86

societies pervaded by the market logic. Jesus does not loosen the household rules; he radicalizes them. As Wesley reminds us, "The imagination that faith *supersedes* holiness is the marrow of anti-nomianism."[9] It is the ruination of stewardship. The "faith that worketh by love" has a context, a shape, an intentionality given by the grace of the Torah epitomized by Jesus.

We turn now to a more detailed consideration of the Torah-gospel household rules to see the origin of Wesley's specific teachings about (1) God and the poor, (2) the necessities of life, (3) dangers of riches, (4) living with the poor, (5) the right use of possessions, and (6) sabbath holiness. The shape of stewardship is to be found in the character of the steward and in the Torah's stewarding commands.

God the Steward and the Poor

The concentration of Wesley's view of stewardship on the poor is not an ideological quirk.[10] It derives from the character of the God of Israel. God has a claim upon all human beings, all things in nature, and all social goods as their Creator. Furthermore, God has a soteriological claim upon the poor, for it is in them that the glory of God's power for life appears. They belong to God! Wesley made clear again and again that the poor belong to the one who has died for them; they may not be treated as if they belonged to another master.

Yahweh's exclusive right to or claim on the household of Israel is based on God's liberation of them from the house of bondage (*oikos douleias*, Exod. 20:2; Deut. 5:6, 7-21). God liberated God's people when they were strangers and oppressed; therefore God's redeemed people should show the same compassion toward the needy in their midst (Exod. 22:21; 23:9). The church states the same logic even more radically: While we were yet enemies of God, Christ died for us. God's grace is made present where it is most contested. Wesley follows the tradition in seeing God's graceful instantiation of salvation in the poor because of the character and will of God.

The peculiar identity of this God has to do with God's identification with slaves. Like all economies, the Household of Israel and the Household of Jesus Christ are created around tables and shaped by what is on the table, the stories that are told around the table, and the relationships of life that result from the table setting. The primary story that makes us who we are is told around the Seder table (Deut. 6). At the Seder table the mother or father does some strange liturgical act that causes the children to ask, "Why are we living in this way?" And that is the signal and the opportunity to tell the precious story that makes us who we are.

This is a primary difficulty with Methodists these days (and Wesley thought the same of Methodists at the end of his life): Our liturgies, our worship, our lives are not strange enough—are not enough out of step with the world around us—for our children to be prompted to ask about the story behind our lives, to ask about the story that makes us who we are. Were we soberly honest, we would have to admit that the first reason we are declining in numbers as a church is that we are losing our own children! And is it not our practice of God's *leitourgeia* by which we serve the children of the poor that will determine whether our own children will listen to the story of the gospel?

The table story that makes us who we are begins one, and only one, way: "Remember that you were a slave (*oiketes*) in the land of Egypt, and the LORD your God brought you out from there with a mighty hand and an outstretched arm" (Deut. 5:15). There is no knowledge of God before, above, or under this story. This is the beginning of our story. We first came to a knowledge of God while we were yet slaves in Pharaoh's economy of slavery. The stench, the chains, the whip, the separation from the ones we loved, the lack of freedom to move and decide our future: These are the things we remember when we ask how we first came to know the God who gave us a home beyond slavery and against slavery. The story that Israel and the Church tell has been credible through the ages to the degree that God's people have accepted the power of God's grace to stand up against slavery—in all its forms (and multiple are its forms even yet in our own societies).

Though the tradition has largely emphasized political metaphors in speaking of God (King, Master, Lord, Judge, Possessor), the primary scriptural narratives speak of God more in economy metaphors. God redeems the world by *creating home* for God's creatures. The story of redemption is the economy of God. Thus the most important name of God is a narrative description of God's economy act: "I am the one who brought you out of Egypt, out of the house of bondage [economy of slavery]" (Exod. 20:1). Though it does not sound "macho" enough to our Western ears, at least in the Moses and Jesus trajectories the Bible speaks of God as a household slave in the sense of a *steward*, that is, the one who is charged with the responsibility of making sure that everyone in the household has what it takes to live. These traditions culminate in the highest christological hymn of the New Testament, the best statement of who God in Jesus Christ is in the redemption of the world:

> Let the same mind be in you that was in Christ Jesus, who, though he was in the form of God, did not regard equality with God as something to be exploited, but emptied himself, *taking the form of a slave* [an economist in the ancient sense], being born in human likeness. And being found in human form, he humbled himself and became obedient to the point of death—even death on a cross. Therefore God also highly exalted him and gave him the name that is above every name. (Phil. 2:5-9)

God redeems the world by becoming a household slave, a steward to the household of the creation. The principal name of God in the New Testament, also a narrative description, is "the One who raised Jesus Christ from the dead." God raises this economist from the dead and creates the Resurrection Household, with new household rules.

The Necessities of Life

The household rules begin with *don't charge interest to the poor.*[11] This seems such an absurd rule in modern economies that run on credit. At least as an American, if you are not in debt, something must be wrong with you. And do we not live in an economy with a highly tuned fiscal apparatus that prevents people from being hurt by debt? No! Debt (personal and national) is still making life miserable for the majority of people around the world.

The reason for this Torah-economy rule is simply that debt leads sooner or later to slavery, and God will not tolerate that the people whom God has freed from the economy of slavery be submitted again to slavery. Debt still causes many kinds of slavery today. Debt robs the poor of what is necessary for life. We who pray "Forgive us our debts as we forgive our debtors," must remember how debt in all its forms closes the household to millions of people.

Even when interest was allowed by the Torah, strict rules prevented the exclusion from access to life: "If you take your neighbor's garment in pawn, you shall restore it before the sun goes down; for it may be your neighbor's only clothing to use as cover; in what else shall that person sleep? And if your neighbor cries out to me, I will

SANCTIFICATION AND ECONOMY

listen, for I am compassionate" (Exod. 22:26-7). The Torah sets limits
on the oppression of the poor by restricting the right of creditors to
seize that property on which the poor depend for life. Nothing that
is necessary for life may be taken as collateral. "For they are my
servants, whom I brought out of the land of Egypt; they shall not be
sold as slaves are sold. You shall not rule over them with harshness,
but shall fear your God. . . . For to me the people of Israel are servants;
they are my servants whom I brought out from the land of Egypt: I
am the LORD your God" (Lev. 25:42-3, 55). It may not sound right to
our Enlightenment-trained sensitivity for freedom, but the biblical
traditions claim that to be a slave of God (or disciple of Jesus) is
freedom.[12] This is where Wesley gets his convictions that freedom is
serving the poor by providing them with the "necessaries" of life.

The Claim of the Poor to Life and the Sin of Riches

A second household rule is *leave gleanings*:

When you reap the harvest of your land, you shall not reap your
field to its very border, neither shall you gather the gleanings after
your harvest. And you shall not strip your vineyard bare, neither
shall you gather the fallen grapes of your vineyard; you shall leave
them for the poor and for the sojourner: I am the LORD your God.
(Lev. 19:9-10, RSV)[13]

There is only one reason for this rule: so that the poor will not have
their faces ground into the dust. The poor are given access to God's
economy of life through the right to share in the harvest.

In the seventh year the vineyards and orchards are to be left
untended not only so that the ground may be rejuvenated but also
so that the poor may benefit (Exod. 21:24; 23:10-11). The Deuteronomic law extends the law of leaving sheaves and fruit beyond the
seventh year to each harvest time (Deut. 24:19-22). It even permits
the poor to enter the field before harvest, although the hungry may
merely satisfy their need and may not take advantage of the owner
of the field (Deut. 23:24-25). Jesus followed this rule by picking grain
for the hungry—on the sabbath! These laws prevent the poor from
begging for their survival and show that God's claim on redeemed
slaves means their right to the means of life. This right supersedes
the right to land and produce.

Isaiah responds to Israel's refusal to recognize these rights in this
way:

90

The LORD rises to argue his case; he stands to judge the peoples. The LORD enters into judgment with the elders and princes of his people: It is you who have devoured the vineyard, the spoil of the poor is in your houses. What do you mean by crushing my people, by grinding the face of the poor? says the Lord GOD of hosts. (Isa. 3:13-15)

For Wesley, the desire to be rich is forbidden by the Lord, and he defined riches as whatever is above the plain necessaries and conveniences of life: "Whoever has sufficient food to eat and raiment to put on, with a place where to lay his head, and something over, is rich."[14] He characterized the sin of hoarding riches in the face of the poor as comparable to adultery or murder, and specified the following contrary guidelines:

> It is allowed, (1), that we are to provide necessaries and conveniences for those of our own household; (2), that men in business are to lay up as much as necessary for the carrying on of that business; (3), that we are to leave our children what will supply them with necessaries and conveniences after we have left the world; and (4), that we are to provide things honest in the sight of all men, so as to 'owe no man anything.' But to lay up more, when this is done . . . is clear proof of our desiring to be rich.[15]

Gleaning rights are not voluntary acts of charity of the rich toward the poor; gleaning rights are the poor's right to livelihood. The commandment "do not steal" means do not take what belongs to the poor because the poor belong to God.[16] This Torah rule is the ground for Wesley's teaching that what one does not need for life (the "necessaries and conveniences") *already belongs to God, and by God's decree—to the poor.*

> [The rich include] all who *possess* more of this world's good than they use according to the will of the Donor—I should rather say of the Proprietor, for he only *lends* them to us; or, to speak more strictly, *entrusts* them to us as stewards, reserving the property of them to himself. And indeed he cannot possibly do otherwise, seeing they are the work of his hands; he is and must be the Possessor of heaven and earth. This is his inalienable right, a right he cannot divest himself of. And together with that portion of his goods which he hath lodged in our hands he has delivered to us a writing, specifying the purposes for which he has entrusted us with them. If therefore we keep more of them in our hands than is necessary for the preceding purposes, we certainly fall under the charge of "desiring to be rich."[17]

It was the failure of Methodists to keep this teaching that most troubled Wesley at the end of his life.[18] This is where we also most severely fail at going on to perfection. Our forgetfulness of this rule of God's economy of life may also be the reason that The United Methodist Church in the United States has remained strangely silent about the dismantling of welfare and the exclusion of children from access to what it takes for life.

Jesus had a lot to say about storehouses and big barns. "Take care! Be on your guard against all kinds of greed; for one's life does not consist in the abundance of possessions" (Luke 12:15). "You fool! This very night your life is being demanded of you. And the things you have prepared, Whose will they be? So it is with those who store up treasures for themselves *but are not rich toward God*" (Luke 12:20-21). Today our storehouses are our insurance and pension funds. They exist of course to secure us, and is this not a good? But what have they done to our freedom to live the gospel?

Whereas artificial scarcity (what Wesley referred to as *pleonesia*, a "desire of having more") is the logical presupposition of the market economy, the abundance (*pleroma*) of God's grace is the ground of the life of the Christian steward. This sense of the "more than enough" of God's grace creates tempers which enable the Christian to use his or her possessions in ways other than assuaging guilt and repressing the fear of death. Life in the *oikonomia tou theou* begins with God's forgiveness of sin and assurance of God's resurrection power against death.

The Use of Possessions

A third household rule is *practice tithing*. Tithing exists for many reasons in the Torah. But the most distinctive reason is for the sake of the poor's access to livelihood (Deut. 14:22-29; Mal. 3:7-12). We often think of the tithe in our context as a means of supporting a religious institution. But the tithe is much more that this. The tithe is a means of building up the household by making certain that no one is excluded from the livelihood of the household. The reason for tithing is the same reason repeated throughout the household codes: "You shall remember you were a slave in Egypt and the LORD your God redeemed you" (Deut. 24:18, 22). Even if the poor are always present, "You shall open wide your hand to your brother, to the needy and to the poor, in the land" (Deut. 15:11, RSV). The tithe is

Torah household redistribution of God's power for life; the tithe is that which belongs to the poor. It is the creation of a commons for the life of God's people.[19]

Wesley's understanding of financial stewardship was profoundly rooted in this Torah household conviction:

> The Lord of all will next inquire, . . . in what manner didst thou employ that comprehensive talent, *money*? Not in gratifying the desire of the flesh, the desire of the eye, or the pride of life? Not in squandering it away in vain expenses, the same as throwing it into the sea? Not in hoarding it up to leave behind thee, the same as burying it in the earth? But first supplying thy own reasonable wants, together with those of thy family; then restoring the remainder to me, through the poor, whom I had appointed to receive it; looking upon thyself as only one of that number of the poor whose wants were to be supplied out of that part of my substance which I had placed in thy hands for this purpose; leaving thee the right of being supplied first, and the blessedness of giving rather then receiving?[20]

He specifically emphasized that the good use of what belongs to God the Proprietor, who is also Steward, precludes wasting what we have been given:

> Perhaps you say you can now *afford* the expense. This is the quintessence of nonsense. Who gave you this addition to your fortune; or (to speak properly) *lent* it to you? To speak more properly still, who lodged it for a time in your hands as his *stewards*? Informing you at the same time, for what purposes he entrusted you with it? And can you *afford* to waste your Lord's goods, for every part of which you are to give an account; or to expend them in any other way than that which he hath expressly appointed? Away with this vile, diabolical cant! Let it never more come out of your lips. This 'affording' to rob God is the very cant of hell. Do not you know that God *entrusted* you with that money (all above what buys necessaries for your families) to feed the hungry, to clothe the naked, to help the stranger, the widow, the fatherless; and, indeed, as far as it will go, to relieve the wants of all [humankind]? How can you, how dare you, defraud your Lord, by applying it to any other purpose? When he entrusted you with a little, did he not entrust you with it that you might lay out all that little in doing good? And when he entrusted you with more, did he not entrust you with that additional money that you might do so much the more good, as you had more ability? Had you any more right to waste a pound, a shilling, or a penny, than you had before? You have, therefore, no

93

more right to gratify the desire of the flesh, or the desire of the eyes, now, than when you was a beggar. O no! do not make so poor a return to your beneficent Lord![21]

Living with the Poor

A fourth rule of God's economy is *practice hospitality*.[22] This means open house for those who are otherwise threatened by death because of their exclusion from home, beginning with orphans, widows, strangers, migrants, and the poor. True worship is living the economy in which God invites into the household all those who are excluded by the denial of God's righteousness. Almost all of the prophets are concerned with the replacement of hospitality in God's household by empty worship and malicious feasts. Isaiah puts together the worship of God and hospitality for the poor and stranger in this way:

> Is not this the fast that I choose: to loose the bonds of wickedness, to undo the thongs of the yoke, to let the oppressed go free, and to break every yoke? Is it not to share your bread with the hungry, and bring the homeless poor into your house; when you see the naked, to cover him, and *not to hide yourself from your own flesh*? Then shall my light break forth like the dawn, and your healing shall spring up speedily; your righteousness shall go before you, the glory of the Lord shall be your rear guard. Then you shall call, and the Lord will answer, you shall cry, and he will say, Here I am.[23]

For Wesley hospitality meant "visiting the poor."[24] He had no doubt that the actual experience of God's economy of grace depended on not hiding from one's own embodiment by turning one's face from the radical other. Grace can be experienced only as we experience God's acceptance of the other who calls into question our definition of ourselves.

Holiness in Time and Space

Finally and perhaps most importantly, God's economy requires *practicing the sabbath*. Though modern theology has stressed God's *rest* as the basis of the sabbath, the sabbath is fundamentally about *God's justice*. The sabbath is the actual presence of God's justice under the conditions of history. In the sabbath those ways in which human beings oppress and exploit one another come to an end; that is, work, property, and consumption cease to be agencies of domination. The household will stay free and will live only so long as the sabbath is kept. Jesus did not do away with the sabbath but rather radicalized it, including the sabbatical (Jubilee) year of Leviticus 25 (Luke 4:18ff).

The Torah works against the disharmony of class and of great discrepancy in wealth through the sabbath year. According to the Torah rules of the sabbath Jubilee Year slaves are to be freed, debts are to be canceled, the land is to lie fallow, and the land (wealth) is to be returned or redistributed to its original holder (Lev. 25:23-24). In God's Torah household the amassing of wealth cannot be justified in the face of the poor who are excluded from what gives them life and future. One can neither take nor withhold from others what they need to contribute to the life of God's economy for God's people.

The Resurrection Household

God's grace creates the resurrection economy. The resurrection household requires that we be gifted by God's grace and that we gift our lives and everything we have in return.[25] But we have forgotten how to be gifted and to gift. So accustomed to the logic of exchange are we that the logic of grace seems foreign. The whole logic of grace at the resurrection table is that God has given God's own Son so that we and the world may have access to what it takes to live. This means, if we think trinitarianly, that God gives God's own life. The answer God expects to God's gift is "much obliged;" yes, we give our lives to what you are doing to redeem the world.[26]

God's economy depends upon the retaught and relearned generosity of God, upon gifts that give in being given and create dignity in being received. Only the gratuitous language of praise can break the suspicion and hatred of gifting and being gifted in our public household. No one in our public household wants to be "much obliged," for it would mean by definition the loss of freedom for exchange. The miracle by which we again understand ourselves and our community as gift to be gifted will have to take place, unless we relent to mean by stewardship only what the market intends.

God's economy begins with a new bread. The people call it *manna* ("what's it") because they do not know what it is. But as its character is uncovered, it proves exactly the opposite of Pharaoh's commodity storehouse bread. It cannot be stored, lest it rot. It cannot be exchanged because it is a gift of God's grace. Because this social good is not a commodity, it must be distributed according to a radically different logic: "they gathered, some more, some less. But when they measured it with an omer, he that gathered much had nothing over, and he that gathered little had no lack; each gathered according to what he could eat" (Exod. 16:17-18, RSV). The economy of God is given shape by this logic of distribution. The history of bread and God culminates for the church when at the eucharist we elevate the bread and give it a new shared communal understanding: "This is my body, broken for you." This bread of life becomes the symbol of all those things which must be distributed if God's children are to live and live abundantly.

Everything in the church should be tested for its appropriateness according to this logic of grace. If we are gifted with the blessing of memory, we know that there is a radical difference between the bread of slavery, bread of tears, bread of death, on the one hand and the bread of freedom, bread of joy, bread of life, on the other hand. Whether the children will eat today depends on which bread determines what we do with our possessions and our work.

The Church and the Market Logic

Does the household of Jesus Christ have a memory that contradicts the notion that all the spheres of distribution of the goods necessary for life should be controlled by the market logic? The church, like all other institutions in our society, is threatened with amnesia and anesthesia. Alcohol, drugs, pain-relievers, unrelieved work, too much television watching, and stoicism in all its popular forms make us forgetful people, unable to experience our own suffering, much less the suffering of others. So it cannot simply be assumed that the church will stand up against the exclusion of human beings from home. The church's "dangerous memories," the ones that would contradict the present arrangements of our public household, must be actively remembered through its scriptures. A church without the Bible and without the memory of God's promises is merely another institution of the market society candidating for inclusion by confirming the market logic.

But if we have a memory, we know that there are certain social goods that should be distributed according to a different logic because these social goods are themselves not commodities. Israel and the church have always known, if memory serves, that healing cannot be distributed according to the logic of exchange. Hospitals were originally the church's way of practicing hospitality (Rom. 12:13) as open house for the stranger, the poor, the sojourner, and the homeless. The church said that they should be given home even if they had nothing to exchange. And, yet, even our church hospitals now are employing a logic which causes them to exclude the very persons for whom hospitals were brought into being.

Israel and the church, if memory is alive, have always known that you cannot distribute learning and the generation of the generations according to the logic of exchange. The church said, we need schools which exemplify two convictions (how quaint they seem in the stupor of our amnesia!): (1) all human knowledge should be related to the truth of the gospel, and(2) no persons gifted for learning should be excluded from home simply because they have nothing to exchange. And yet, even our church colleges and universities (not to speak of our seminaries) are increasingly organized according to the market logic. Decisions about entrance and about learning are increasingly made according to the "bottom line." If the church regains its memory, will we not have to start all over again establishing hospitals, retirement homes, schools and universities, and all sorts of centers that support the humanizing of children's lives according to the logic of the gospel? Else we do not believe that the shalom of the gospel is really meant for this world.

This in no sense means that the church can replace the public institutions for human welfare. But it may mean that as these public institutions are dismantled, the church, as it has done in the past, will apply the imagination of the gospel for modeling new institutions that are governed by life against death for the children of the world.

The market is the greatest mechanism we have ever devised for producing and distributing commodities. But like all of the works of our minds and hands, the market can become an idol. In the market society there is nothing that cannot, in principle, be distributed as a commodity. Everything is for sale. Market economists even suggest that air pollution can be solved as soon as we learn how to make air a commodity. But if something is not a commodity, should it be distributed according to the market logic or is there another logic for the distribution of those things necessary for life and life abundant?[27]

According to the gospel and the depth of human wisdom, *what is necessary for life* cannot be a commodity or exclusively a commodity. Thus social goods such as food, housing, jobs, education and health care should not be exclusively distributed according to the market logic; and social goods such as justice, security, belonging, respect, affection, and grace should not be distributed in any sense according to the logic of exchanging commodities. Otherwise, it is inevitable that those with nothing to exchange will get left out of home.

Modern *economics* has undermined ancient *economy*. In modernity market economics increasingly displaces economy in this sense and offers itself as a pervasive logic by which all spheres of human endeavor can be comprehended and mastered. At one time it was said, "outside the church, there is no salvation" (*extra ecclesiam nulla salus*). Now the poor of the world are faced with a new bitter dogma: *Outside the market, there is no salvation.*

If the church is actually meant to be the living economy of God, then we should go no further without saying that to make a genuine contribution to alternative economy in the world, an economy open to the flourishing of all human beings, the church itself would have to be radically restructured and "recultured" by its own gospel, sacraments, diakonia, and koinonia for its life of stewardship. The great task facing the church toward the next century is how and where to find the actual free space in our market society to become the *oikonomia tou theou*. No other question is so urgent for the church of Jesus Christ. The Methodist contribution to addressing this question will be enriched by taking seriously their Wesleyan origins.

CHAPTER 6

Christian Conversion:
Connecting Our Lives with God

Manfred Marquardt

Salvation—in the Christian understanding of its character and content—is a process of the renewal of human beings as images of God. This "new creation" is presented in scripture as encompassing not only persons as individuals but also their essential relationships with God, other human beings, themselves, and the whole created world. As Ted Runyon has shown, the Wesleyan tradition shares (or *ought* to share) this holistic vision of salvation.[1] Salvation is also understood in scripture and Christian tradition as no less God's work than creation—with one difference: *God, who created us without ourselves, will not save us without ourselves.*[2] This aspect of the *not without ourselves* in God's saving work has been a defining point of consensus in Wesleyan theology and preaching.

But agreement in the Wesleyan tradition begins to break down when attention turns to the use of certain terms for describing salvation. There are a variety of metaphors in scripture and the theological tradition used to illustrate the discernible and yet inseparable constituent aspects of salvation; among these are "justification" as God's pardoning acquittal of our sins, "new birth" as the beginning of the renewal of our whole being by the creative power of the Holy Spirit in the process of sanctification, and "conversion" as a free human response to Christ's invitation of following him, trusting God in faith and obedience. It is the latter term that has occasioned the most debate in Wesleyan circles.

Wesley himself did not use the word "conversion" that often. However, the term is typically taken to carry more connotations of conscious change than the synonym of "new birth," and this emphasis on conscious change had great importance in Wesley's thought.[3]

The debates in Wesleyan circles have usually been sparked when the term "conversion" is restricted to a specific model of how this conscious change takes place. They have often focused on the question of Wesley's own "conversion," but the implications are much broader.

I am not interested in re-entering the debate over the time or style of Wesley's conversion.[4] Rather, I want to invite my fellow Methodists and the broader Christian community to try a fresh consideration about what the disputed and yet essentially biblical term "conversion" may designate, and how and to what extent it may be wise to reintroduce it into theological reflection. I believe that this is an important question to address.

Use of the metaphor of conversion has actually been quite rare in the European context until recently and, when used, it often bears a rather superficial and limited intention: designating the decision of non-Christians to join a Christian church, or the decision of nominal Christians to enter more actively into religious life in their traditional or another church.[5] Largely in reaction to the restrictive use of the complex biblical concept of conversion in the evangelistic crusades of the nineteenth and twentieth centuries, there is an almost complete omission of the term in contemporary theological publications. Meanwhile, in popular society all kinds of changes in personal attitudes, ethical behaviors, or economic programs are called "conversion."

In such a context the salvage of an essential biblical concept deserves new theological investments. My contribution toward this salvage operation will be to contrast popular and traditional caricatures of conversion with its true nature as God's saving work that connects our lives with Christ, with one another, and with the world.

Conversion as Part of God's Saving Work

Many popular accounts present conversion as the human effort to change one's life. Ted Runyon captures well the biblical alternative: "Conversion, strictly speaking, may be seen primarily as the transforming work of God *in* us by the Spirit, literally 'turning [us] around'."[6] As this emphasizes, the human response expressed in conversion is rooted in God's grace, and orients us to a goal far beyond the *status quo* of human existence. The deep desire that precedes and motivates genuine conversion is that of freedom and life in fulfillment; it is the desire of living with the eternal God, who has made himself known as the "fountain of life" (Psalm 36). While it is accompanied by feelings and molded into a personal decision (either instantaneous or at the end of a longer process; one single turn to Christ or a return to God whom one had forsaken), conversion is neither purely emotional nor simply a matter of human decision. It is brought forth by and grounded in God's liberating and empowering work. Otherwise, conversion would become a human work upon which salvation was conditioned—contradicting the central biblical teaching of salvation by grace.[7]

This means that conversion is always in response to God's gracious initiative. God's prevenient and justifying grace, by enabling persons to respond freely to God's love, evokes a process of restitution of their being as images of God, of their partnership and likeness with God as loving and free agents. Conversion is an integral part of salvation, which, in its essence, is the reintegration of human beings into community with God, who—in the triune community of Father, Son, and Holy Spirit—is inclusive, redeeming, and healing love.

Placed in the context of God's saving action, it becomes clear that conversion is not an end in itself. At one pole, it does not mark the *beginning* of salvation. Salvation originates in God's gracious attachment to his human creatures. Conversion is the responsive personal agreement of an individual (though always in community with other persons) to engage in walking with Christ and connecting his or her life with God *Abba*, whose arms are standing wide open. At the other pole, this act of connecting oneself with God may be clear and resolute from the first moment, or it may be rather cautious and only gradually confident, but it will always point to an *end* beyond itself, a future fulfillment. Therefore, the truly converted never assume the status of *beati possidentes*—happy owners of what they pretend to have achieved and now have at their disposal.[8] They rather know—with Paul—that they have nothing which they did not receive (1 Cor. 4:7); and that there is much more which "God has prepared for those who love him," namely "what no eye has seen, nor ear heard, nor the human heart conceived" (1 Cor. 2:9). Conversion takes place in many ways, but always "from grace to grace," from God's initiation to God's completion of the unique community into which God invites us to be members.

And yet, conversion will not take place apart from the personal decision of those who live in connection with God. The freedom they gain by grace may be used—like Adam's and Eve's, according to

101

Genesis 3—*against* living with God in faith and obedience. In his letter to the Galatians, Paul complains:

> Now, however, that you have come to know God, or rather to be known by God, how can you turn back again to the weak and beggarly elemental spirits? How can you want to be enslaved to them again? You are observing special days, and months, and seasons, and years. I am afraid that my work for you may have been wasted. (Gal. 4:9-11)

Those (former) believers were no longer "walking with Christ," they who wanted to be "justified by the law," had cut themselves "off from Christ" and "fallen away from grace" (5:4). Nevertheless the apostle blesses the whole church in Galatia with words that should not be understood as a merely stereotypical formula: "May the grace of our Lord Jesus Christ be with your spirit, brothers and sisters. Amen." Christians may disobey God's will and even "fall from grace," but they do not have the power to defeat the grace of the eternal and loving God, nor does their deserting quench God's love for all humankind.

Throughout the Bible a unique behavior is reported of this sovereign and loving God, who does not forget nor forsake his people: God "visits" his people, whenever and wherever they are gone astray, in order to call or to lead them home. The English word "(to) visit" is a very limited translation for the Hebrew word *pāqad*. The Hebrew word includes meanings like to attend or to punish, but also to look after and to care for. For example, the prophet Isaiah announced in the name of the Lord: "You will be *visited* by the LORD of hosts with thunder and earthquake and great noise, with whirlwind and tempest, and the flame of a devouring fire" (29:6). But there can also be words like these: "For thus says the LORD: Only when Babylon's seventy years are completed will I *visit* you, and I will fulfill to you my promise and bring you back to this place" (Jer. 29:10).

Very often the word *pāqad* is connected with situations of having left God's ways: "I the LORD thy God *am* a jealous God, *visiting* the iniquity of the fathers upon the children unto the third and fourth *generation* of them that hate me" (Exod. 20:5; KJV). After they worshipped the golden calf the Israelites were reminded that God is "merciful and gracious, slow to anger, and abounding in steadfast love and faithfulness, keeping steadfast love for the thousandth generation, forgiving iniquity and transgression and sin, yet by no means clearing the guilty, but *visiting* the iniquity of the parents upon the children and the children's children, to the third and the fourth generation" (Exod. 34:6-7).

When Jesus wept over Jerusalem: "They will crush you to the ground, you and your children within you, and they will not leave within you one stone upon another; because you did not recognize the time of your *visitation* from God" (Luke 19:44), the Greek text uses the word *episkopē* (for "visitation"), which later was used for describing the ministry of a bishop. The intention behind all of these different ways of "visiting" is to bid God's people to turn and come home again.[9] This shows that God's jealousy is an expression of God's love which cannot let his people go into self-destruction, but—by all means—seeks their conversion, their return to living in God's shalom.[10] God's jealousy is simply God's hands of eternal love stretched out for us, making possible conversion to and connection with the living God.

Connecting Our Lives with Christ

While the traditional (or revivalistic) understanding of conversion would agree with the preceding emphasis on God's gracious prevenience, it tends to focus the experience and meaning of conversion in a singular peak event in a Christian's spiritual biography. I do not deny that Christians experience such peak events (though this is not the exclusive, or even the majority, way of "experiencing" conversion), but the biblical meaning of conversion cannot be captured by this narrow focus. I would suggest that this meaning is much better expressed by portraying conversion as essentially "connecting our lives" with God—Father, Son, and Holy Spirit; the three-in-one God whose very being is love.

Consider the New Testament stories about responses to Jesus. All who encountered the man of Nazareth became profoundly aware of their lives and their needs. Those who welcomed Christ, connecting their lives with his life, began experiencing a new community with God. Those who—on whatever grounds—decided not to join Christ excluded themselves from the healing and liberating community with God in Christ. The essential presupposition for any (re-)turn to God—God's gracious and loving turn to them—was offered to all. Those women and men who became disciples of Christ gave a free response to Christ's invitation of following him, trusting God in faith and obedience. This is what conversion simply is.

"Simply," that is, in a non-simplistic sense! The grace of God that enables persons to turn (or return) to the Father of all is not, as many people in our times seem to presume, a kind of magic potion. It is not a mysterious spiritual drug which one can obtain in certain holy places, receive by mystical rites, or imbibe through spiritual exercises. The grace of God, personalized in Christ, is God's loving inclination towards those whom God created in God's image. The encounter with God's grace is personal, taking persons seriously as who they are: creatures who have been enabled to hear, to understand, to discern, to decide, and to respond. Therefore, saving grace can be fully received only by a personal conversion to God in faith. It will never simply be "poured" on humans, rendering their personal decision superfluous. This might seem a more comfortable method of receiving grace, but for at least two reasons it would not achieve "the end of Christ's coming." It would not treat humans as the authentic partners who God created them to be. And it would not lead to the community of life with God which constitutes the essence of salvation. By "comfortable methods" one can only get "cheap grace," which may give good feelings, but in the end is of no worth.

Dietrich Bonhoeffer offered the classic critique of such cheap grace, in a time when Christianity itself was at stake:[11]

> Cheap grace means grace sold on the market like cheapjacks' wares. . . . Grace is represented as the Church's inexhaustible treasury, from which she showers blessings with generous hands, without asking questions. . . . The essence of grace, we suppose, is that the account has been paid in advance; and, because it has been paid, everything can be had for nothing. . . . Instead of following Christ, let the Christian enjoy the consolations of his grace! That is what we mean by cheap grace, the grace which amounts to the justification of sin without the justification of the repentant sinner who departs from sin and from whom sin departs.

Does that mean that those who receive grace have to pay for it, which obviously would destroy the very character of grace? That would be a complete misinterpretation of these lines. No, "cheap grace is not the kind of forgiveness of sin which frees us from the toils of sin. Cheap grace is the grace we bestow on ourselves." Cheap grace is "grace without Jesus Christ, living and incarnate." "Costly grace," instead, is "the call of Jesus Christ at which the disciple leaves his nets and follows him. . . . Such grace is *costly* because it calls us to follow, and it is *grace* because it calls us to follow *Jesus Christ*. . . . [It] confronts us as a gracious call to follow Jesus, it comes as a word of forgiveness to the broken spirit and the contrite heart." True conversion—a willing and honest turning to Christ—is an essential part of the salvation of human beings, by which their entire lives are connected with God's life and thus made whole.

There are times in Christians' lives when they hear their Lord asking them: "Do you also wish to go away?" (John 6:67). The Greek word for "wish" (*thelēte*) expresses a stronger appeal to the Twelve: it asks for a clear and willful decision in a situation when others have left Jesus. There have been several situations in which this decision had to be made anew, situations tempting the disciples to "go away" like others did. This time the Twelve decide not to avert their ways from Jesus, but to stay with him—until the moment when "all of them deserted him and fled." To stay with Christ in moments of danger and temptation implies a decision to keep one's life connected with Christ; and this decision may be harder to make than that of one's initial conversion. And then there is the need of a new conversion for those who had left their Master, betraying or denying him. Christ in his love opens the door again to bid them in, commissioning them (some of whom doubted!) to go and make disciples, entrusting them with the gospel of God's kingdom and with the responsibility for his church: "Tend my sheep" (John 21:16).

One of the biblical metaphors which describes this aspect of the reciprocal relationship between God and God's people is "covenant." I will not rehearse all of the soteriological, ecclesiological, eschatological, and other aspects of covenant. But a few comments may help to understand the presupposition and character of conversion. God's covenants, including the new covenant in Christ Jesus, are the product of his love and faithfulness towards his people. They are the expression of God's abundant grace, as well as God's claim to be the one God of Israel, of the church, of all human beings, and of the whole world. "Then God spoke all these words: I am the LORD your God, who brought you out of the land of Egypt, out of the house of slavery; you shall have no other gods before me" (Exod. 20:1-3). Through the course of revelation history God made himself known as the one and only God. From Isaiah we hear: "O LORD of hosts, God of Israel, who are enthroned above the cherubim, you are God, you *alone*, of all the kingdoms of the earth; you have made heaven and earth" (37:16). And the Christian church is reminded by the apostle: "There is one body and one Spirit, just as you were called to the one hope of your calling, *one Lord*, one faith, one baptism, *one God* and Father of all, who is above all and through all and in all" (Eph. 4:4-6).

The metaphor of covenant has been central to the spirituality of Methodism ever since Wesley recommended that his followers renew their covenant in a yearly service. In this service they reaffirm the decision to connect their lives with Christ, and to be accepted as his disciples who are ready to serve him in the places that he assigns. They hear the invitation "Commit yourselves to Christ as his servants. Give yourselves to him, that you may belong to him," and answer praying: "Let me be your servant, under your command. I will no longer be my own. I will give up myself to your will in all things." They follow Christ, not in order to "earn" their salvation, but because they know and believe: "He is the source of all salvation to those who obey." They anew "put away all idols" and join themselves in a covenant with Christ.[12]

José Míguez Bonino describes conversion ontologically as "the process through which God incorporates the human person, as person, into an active conscious participation in his covenant with humankind, the covenant which he has attested, renewed, and ensured in Jesus Christ."[13] The chance of connecting our lives with Christ is a gift that needs a response, and in most lives more than one. This response sometimes includes dying, giving up our own selves, that we may live in a vivid connection with him. The mystery of Christ's death and resurrection must become a reality in our lives, "for those who want to save their life will lose it, and those who lose their life for my sake will find it" (Matt. 16:25). Connecting our lives with Christ brings life that death cannot destroy.

Connecting Our Lives with God's People

The existence of Christians from the New Testament times until today has been marked by a polar tension between individual and communal, personal and social. The confession of faith is spoken in the singular mode ("I believe"), but it is the faith of the Christian community which is being confessed—whether in the worship service or elsewhere. Likewise in baptism Christians are called by their names, indicating their being unmistakably this individual person, but by the same act of baptism they are incorporated into the body of Christ, the church.

When we understand conversion as a process in which God's Spirit and the believer are involved, and by which the believer's life is being connected with God, it is obvious that the conversion of any individual person is as such an event which connects this person with all other persons who are converted to Christ. As they are connected with Christ, they are necessarily connected with Christ's earthly body, or—to use the metaphor of the letter to the Ephesians—with the church whose head is Christ. John Wesley's statement that there is no religion but social religion, no Christian faith which does not connect the believers with the body of which they are members, has its theological foundation in this essential connectedness of Christ with the church and the members of the church with one another.

To affirm this "social" nature of conversion is to argue against an increasing tendency in our time, the tendency of dissolving "I-belief" from "We-belief," Christian faith from church membership, conversion from connection with the corporate body of Christ. Many people do not realize, or accept, that such separation is a *contradictio in adiecto*. "For," as Paul has made clear, "just as the body is one and has many members, and all the members of the body, though many, are one body, so it is with Christ. For in the one Spirit we were all baptized into one body—Jews or Greeks, slaves or free—and we were all made to drink of one Spirit" (1 Cor. 12:12-13). Our life in Christ and our sanctification are deeply dependent on "the support and backing of a community that provides deep sustenance and spiritual nourishment."[14] As Wesley realized, this abstract theological principle requires very practical implementation. Ironically, Methodists today stand in as much need as anyone of regaining vital small groups in the church to provide communal support and nurture.

Some observers of modern Christianity have charged that a rich spiritual life in the churches has fostered a questionable attitude of spiritual consumerism. This danger can only be avoided if the Christian community understands itself not only as a means of grace but as a means of conversion, leading its members to a self-critical reading of God's commandments and the ethical teaching of the New Testament. Of course, such an approach will be out of step with our societies; it has hardly ever been popular even among Christians.

One thing the church must not do in the face of such criticism is resort to the ever popular search for scapegoats. Instead, as a loving community the church should give scope for repentance and forgiving, for confession of sins and absolution in the name of the triune God, so that people may enter into the healing community of Christ's body (a community of other forgiven sinners). The privilege of inviting repentance is a precious gift that God has entrusted to all who have received God's liberating acceptance, to the church in which the Gospel of Christ is being preached and heard. We may remember what James enjoined upon his readers: "You should know that whoever brings back a sinner from wandering will save the sinner's soul from death and will cover a multitude of sins" (James 5:20).

A no less important task of the church is to lead the young generation growing up in our congregations to a free, joyous, and conscious decision for living with Christ. They grow up in the midst of a congregation, they hear the Christian message in many voices, they experience what it means to be in community with very different people who respect and accept each other, and they quite "normally" become a part of this fellowship. One day they should be able to say "yes, I belong," I want to be a member of this church because I want to be Christian. They ought to be led to confess their faith in Christ, the Father, and the Holy Spirit. There is no single "correct" way to become a confessing member of the church: "The Wesleyan tradition is open to those who are consciously converted to Christianity from a life of egregious sin or from legalism and to those who have been nurtured into the faith in Christian homes."[15] However, it is important that each person, at a time when they are able and willing, choose some way to confirm what they believe and in whom they trust with no limitation. The church should offer them a place and an opportunity—in and beyond the confirmation worship service—for a personal expression of their affiliation. Such a step may be strategic for the whole of their lives.

Connecting Our Lives with God's World

Human beings are prone to the illusion of being the center of the universe. They structure "their world" by relating to everything else as satellites that revolve around the axis of their individual needs and concerns. Even relationships to other humans are often valued, formed, or severed according to the benefits they entail. In the face of this tendency Christian conversion is a very simple, yet revolutionary, change: it is the "Copernican reversal" of removing ourselves from the center of "our world" and instead taking our place alongside all humanity as God's creatures and children, whose lives are truly centered in their creator and parent.

Unfortunately, the understanding of conversion in some Christian traditions has served to foster a contrary attitude—calling into question any commonality with those not among the "converted," and sometimes restricting this designation to only their own little society. They refer to biblical texts like Paul's admonition to the Corinthians:

> Do not be mismatched with unbelievers. For what partnership is there between righteousness and lawlessness? Or what fellowship is there between light and darkness? What agreement does Christ have with Beliar? Or what does a believer share with an unbeliever? What agreement has the temple of God with idols? For we are the temple of the living God; as God said, "I will live in them and walk among them, and I will be their God, and they shall be my people. Therefore come out from them, and be separate from them, says the Lord, and touch nothing unclean; then I will welcome you, and I will be your father, and you shall be my sons and daughters, says the Lord Almighty." (2 Cor. 6:14-18)

How far Paul's words are from urging his fellow Christians to exclude themselves from any community with unbelievers is shown by his own way of life, not to mention the example that Jesus set for his disciples. The meaning of the text may be understood correctly by consulting a similar paragraph:

> I appeal to you therefore, brothers and sisters, by the mercies of God, to present your bodies as a living sacrifice, holy and acceptable to God, which is your spiritual worship. Do not be conformed to this world, but be transformed by the renewing of your minds, so that you may discern what is the will of God—what is good and acceptable and perfect. (Rom. 12:1-2)

To live in this world without making common cause with those who deliberately disobey the will of God, without following the "scheme of this world" (*to schēma tou kosmou toutou*, 1 Cor. 7:31), but as one whose mind (*nous*) is transformed by God's Spirit in order to be able to identify the will of God—that is what conversion is directed to and meant to bring about.

The ability to identify the will of God grows from the new

identity in which believers are "conformed to the image of his Son, in order that he might be the firstborn within a large family" (Rom. 8:29). This fundamental change has consequences for one's attitudes and behavior toward all fellow human beings, who are created in God's image and destined to live in community. As the apostle attests: "You have stripped off the old self with its practices and have clothed yourselves with the new self, which is being renewed in knowledge according to the image of its creator" (Col. 3:9b-10). This "knowledge according to the image of God" (i.e. the image of loving community) knows one rule which is valid in all ways of acting: "You shall love your neighbor as yourself." Christian conversion, as conversion to Christ, is also conversion to our neighbor—who represents Christ according to his own identification: "Truly I tell you, just as you did it to one of the least of these who are members of my family, you did it to me." This behavior is by no means a tactical effort for gaining a top position in heaven, it is the innocent turn to take the other's perspective: "In everything do to others as you would have them do to you!"

Some ethically concerned Christians (following the lead of Blumhardt, Bonhoeffer, and representatives of "religious socialism") have called for a second "conversion to the world" after the first conversion to Christ. In this call they are trying to counter the tendency to merely private piety. In the strictest sense, Christian conversion as conversion to God already necessarily implies a conversion to the world, since it is this world which God's love intends to save.[16] Nevertheless, the Christian individualism so widely spread even among Methodists suggests that it is not superfluous to give this dimension of conversion particular attention.

But how should Christians relate specifically to the non-Christian "world"? The proper relationship will involve both negative and positive dimensions. The negative dimension has been developed into models of Christians living in the world as *Kontrastgesellschaften* (contrast societies) or *Kontrastverhalten* (contrast behavior).[17] These models stress that the community of believers will always be a foreign body in the wider society because of their life-changing relationship with Christ. Accordingly Christians' behavior will necessarily differ from that of their contemporaries in varying degrees from one situation to the next, even to the point of appearing foolish.[18] Such tension with society may be an unavoidable expression of living in faith and obedience to God.

There are also authentic positive dimensions to living as Christians in a non-Christian "world." These dimensions have been gathered under the image of the church living "pro-existence."[19] Those who coined this word were trying to counter the impression that Christians and Christian churches are always "counter-revolutionary" forces in the concern for human (and, now, ecological) rights. But for them, the decision to follow Christ and to let Christ's love be the fountain and rule of their ethical behavior led directly to an identification with the Christ who stood alongside their atheist neighbors defending the rights of the poor, the oppressed, and the excluded.

Within both its negative and positive dimensions, it is important to see that the call of the church to live in the "world" is a call to embrace the whole *kosmos* as the horizon of God's redeeming action.[20] It is in the unmeasurable scope of this *kosmos* that our salvation and conversion must ultimately find their place. The task of discerning specifically how conversion addresses this *kosmos* falls anew to every Christian generation. For our era, on the way into the next century, this discernment has only begun!

CHAPTER 7

Offering Christ:
Wesleyan Evangelism Today

James C. Logan

The rhetoric of evangelism has escalated in the contemporary church. Evangelism ranks high on the agendas of judicatory meetings. Evangelism is a priority issue, in word if not in deed, in local parishes. The cynical quip, "It was *ecumenism* in the 1970s, *renewal* in the 1980s, and now it's *evangelism* in the 1990s,"[1] contains an important element of truth. This change of rhetoric from ecumenism and renewal to evangelism is indicative of a fundamental shift of the placement of the church in Western society.

The Challenge of Evangelism in a Changed Social Situation

Analysts of the church speak of a recent paradigm shift.[2] The church of the Apostolic Age understood itself to be fundamentally a mission people in a time when sharp distinctions existed between the church and the larger society. Shaped by the Jesus story, the early church found within that story an implicit commission to be "in the world but not of the world," to "make disciples." These early Christians understood themselves to be a peculiar people, a culture distinct from the larger culture.[3] They found themselves united by faith in Jesus, gathered around a common meal, sharing their possessions with each other, and venturing into the foreign territory of the marketplace with the story that had formed their own existence. They were an apostolic people, a "sent" people.

With the advent of the Constantinian church a new paradigm emerged. The paradigm known as Christendom was distinctively different from the apostolic paradigm. No longer were the lines drawn sharply between the culture of the Christian community and

Apostolic paradigm

Christendom

113

the society in which Christians found themselves. The church became identified with the larger culture. In a very real sense the church provided legitimization for the society, while depending upon the very economic and political forces which it sought to legitimate.

Christendom was not created in a moment. It evolved over a long historical period. Likewise, the demise of Christendom in the Western world has been a long process. For example, while the founding fathers of the United States (inspired by Enlightenment thought) rejected the notion of an established church, an unofficial establishment or religious coalition of Protestant denominations nevertheless took shape and dominated the religious scene until recent times. From the perspective of most Protestants a variation on Christendom was still assumed. In such a climate it is understandable that the intra-church concerns of *ecumenism* and *church renewal* gained primary focus. Whether the church—local or connectional—is fully aware of it or not, the contemporary rhetoric of *evangelism* is indicative of a societal shift, a shift variously called post-Christendom, post-Enlightenment, or postmodern. As Dorothy said to Toto in *The Wizard of Oz*: "I don't think we're in Kansas any more." When the church in its evangelistic outreach ignores this fact, it succumbs to a culturally defined evangelism that is anachronistic.

Unfortunately much of the hyped rhetoric of evangelism today is more rooted in pragmatic concerns than in a commitment to a contextually appropriate recovery of the evangelical imperative implicit in the Jesus Story. It is driven by the church's institutional concerns of diminishing membership, jaded self-image, and seeming loss of persuasive influence on the dominant society, rarely questioning how these are symptoms of something that goes much deeper.

This pragmatic focus is reflected first in the fact that evangelism did not emerge at the top of the agenda for mainline churches until evidence of a loss of membership surfaced in the 1960s. For example, The United Methodist Church, once the largest denomination of the Protestant establishment, began to report a decline in gross membership in the 1960s. Between the years 1970 and 1984 the denomination lost an average of 1,930 members every week![4] Other denominations were experiencing similar statistical decline.

The decline in membership has been accompanied by a changed self-image of the church. Ecumenical literature in the 1960s called the church from a "come" structure to a "go" structure. By the 1980s the

114

metaphorical self-perception was decidedly a "maintenance structure." This self-image has had a direct influence upon the outreach ministries of the church, especially evangelism. A "maintenance mode" evangelism treats those to whom the church witnesses as means to the end of institutional survival.

The loss of influence and impact upon the public arena goes in tandem with statistical decline and ingrown self-image. The remarks of a suburban couple are instructive: "We know that we should go to church, but, you see, there are so many good causes today." With the increased pluralism of the society, the church has become one option among others in a consumerist "shopping center" of good causes. To the extent that the church accepts this placement in the marketplace exchange by "selling the Jesus story" it legitimates the relativism which undermines the story that defines its existence.[5]

Things were different in Christendom. In a *de facto* Christendom the church could and did function as a sponsor of or chaplain to the public arena. There are plenty of indications that today's society wants neither a sponsor nor a chaplain. If it seeks any legitimations, it wants a pluralism of legitimations. In other words, the church shares a stall among other stalls in the consumerist marketplace.

The Mixed Heritage of Evangelism in the Wesleyan Tradition

I believe that there is reason to hope that John Wesley might be of help in determining the proper means of evangelism in our changed setting. He too stood at a juncture of tremendous cultural, social, and intellectual shift in 1739 when he "submitted to be more vile" and joined George Whitefield in field preaching. His time was hardly the most congenial for Christian belief and practice. Enlightenment skepticism was in vogue among the intellectual elite. Rationalism pervaded the universities and Deism threatened to undercut the claims to Christian revelational authority. While Wesley accepted in modified form the empiricism of Locke and Hume, he refused to accept their conclusions, boldly "offering Christ" as the source of divine grace—prevenient, justifying, and sanctifying. Deistic reductionism was not his diet!

Likewise, in 1739 England was emerging from an agrarian to an industrial society, with all the ferment, social dislocation, and demoralization accompanying such revolutionary shifts. The sharp disparity between wealth and poverty, antinomian immorality, child abuse in the labor market, slum-tenement living conditions, inhumane working conditions in the factories, unjustifiable prison practices, and the abominable African slave trade—all were in full force. Wesley's eye missed little of this social reality, nor did he blink. The religion of the solitary mystics he had left behind in Oxford. The perceived antinomianism of Fetter Lane he had rejected by calling his hearers to avail themselves of the means of grace. Enthusiasm which claimed saving grace but neglected a disciplined life of accountable discipleship he eschewed. He offered Christ in his fullness to the crowds which gathered to hear his words by preaching Christ "in all his offices" as Prophet, Priest, and King.

If these aspects of Wesley's model of evangelism are unfamiliar to many Methodists today it is because the Wesleyan tradition was transmitted to the American church chiefly through the instrumentality of the Second Great Awakening (and its camp meeting revivalism). So powerful was the impact of this phenomenon on American church life that many today assume the conception and practice of evangelism in the Second Great Awakening to be normative Wesleyanism.

But the substance of Wesley's evangelism and that of the nineteenth-century revivalists was no more the same than the structures they utilized. Wesley adopted the Society and the class meeting to nurture his evangelistic movement. The Second Great Awakening pioneered the camp meeting. This latter structure reflected an abbreviated, if not truncated, Wesleyan message. Essentially it was a threefold message: *free grace, free will,* and *conversion*. In the Wesleyan revival, conversion was seen as the *sign* of authentic faith; in the Second Great Awakening, conversion increasingly became the *goal* of faith. Thomas Coke and leaders of British Methodism were repelled by the emotional excesses attendant to the camp meeting, whereas Asbury viewed the camp meeting as "the chief means of grace."[6]

When Albert Outler delivered the Denman Lectures in 1971, he offered a scintillating interpretation of Wesley's theology of evangelism accompanied with a brief critical analysis of the Second Great Awakening. His judgment was:

> The Second Great Awakening represented the effective triumph in the New World of the "radical Protestantism" that had been so sternly suppressed in Europe by the dominant Lutheran, Reformed, and Anglican state-churches. This Protestant tradition was largely

"Montanist" in its ecclesiology (low-church, free-church); anti-sac-
erdotal, anti-sacramental, anti-intellectualist. It made a pejorative
distinction between speculative theology and existential faith. It
was suspicious of a learned clergy. It regarded conversion as more
typically the climax of Christian experience than its initiation.[7]

This is not to deny the positive effect of the Second Great Awakening. The decade and a half following the Revolution were not
auspicious for religion in America. For a time it appeared the proph-
ecy of Voltaire would come true, that a people once having achieved
their political freedom would extend their freedom-project to the
religious sphere as well. The Second Great Awakening turned the
tide! A new birth of religious fervor swept from the frontier to the
eastern coast. The revival gave birth to new denominations, and
strengthened the older ones both spiritually and statistically. The
evangelical revivals shaped much of the religious life of the American
people for almost the entire century.

Admittedly, the theology conveyed in this shaping was often
deficient. Again, Outler's razor-sharp analysis makes the point:

> The typical revivalist preacher knew more about heaven and hell
> than Dante or Milton and took it all much more literally. His
> conception of God was frankly anthropomorphic and his Christol-
> ogy was Eutychian—which is to say, heretical—without his know-
> ing the definition of Eutychianism (i.e., the doctrine that Christ's
> human nature was absorbed into and dominated by the divine
> nature.) For most of them the virgin birth was taken more as a proof
> of Christ's divinity than of his humanity. Substitutionary atone-
> ment was their only theory of the saving work of Jesus Christ. They
> spoke often of the Holy Spirit but usually in terms of *personal*
> charisma rather than the Spirit in the church and the sacraments.
> Their anthropology and psychology were dualistic or trichoto-
> mous; their epistemology pre-critical, pre-scientific, and simplistic.
> In it all, one can recognize the *theologia cordis* of à Kempis, Spener,
> Francke, and Wesley, uprooted from its original church matrix and
> lacking any catholic sense of the church and the sacraments.[8]

No one would ever doubt, however, that they had the evangelical
imperative, and many, many of their converts experienced the saving
grace of Christ.

Remaining largely aloof from the larger cultural and theological
developments of the late nineteenth and early twentieth centuries,
many of the children of the revival continued to nourish an evangelical piety in the churches which generated evangelistic effort and

117

gave rise to the global missionary movement of the late nineteenth century. Their love for Christ and their passion that all persons hear the Christian message sometimes faltered, falling into a self-righteous judgmentalism, but they had managed to tap the evangelistic nerve of the church in a way unmatched since.

Meanwhile, as the mainline Protestant churches moved into the twentieth century they repackaged evangelism as "membership recruitment," relying more and more upon the Sunday school and confirmation education alone to replenish their institutional rolls. Is it any wonder that their congregations presently have a body of members who know just enough about the Christian faith to be immunized from the real thing?

One of the potential results of the mixed heritage just sketched is that we who are Wesley's contemporary descendants may have a difficult time correctly perceiving his approach to evangelism, which was generated in a context quite different from both our own and that of the nineteenth-century revival. A second result is that the implicit dominance of the nineteenth-century model of revivalism may undercut our ability to generate an authentic contemporary evangelism with the power to speak to persons who have been formed by a postmodern world view. These two results overlap to the degree that Wesley's model of evangelism in his setting is considered potentially instructive to our contemporary efforts.

Authentic Wesleyan Evangelism Today

I believe that Wesley can be instructive to us about how to "offer Christ" today. However, we will have to work a little to hear him. We cannot simply listen for familiar vocabulary. He did not share some of the key vocabulary in contemporary discussion of evangelism. For example, Wesley never employed the term "evangelism" itself. This noun was simply not in currency in his day, though he did speak of his itinerant lay preachers as "evangelists," denoting their sole responsibility to preach.

Again, for Wesley it was sufficient simply to "offer Christ," and the motive for such was intrinsically grace itself. He did not appeal, as do contemporary evangelists, to the Great Commission in any of its forms. He was not alone. The reformers, following Augustine, claimed that the text had no binding authority—it had been delivered to the apostles and fulfilled by them. It was one year after

Wesley's death that William Carey rehabilitated the term in his tract entitled *An Enquiry into the Obligation of Christians to Use Means for the Conversion of the Heathen*. For Wesley it was simply the working of the grace of Christ which prompted outreach to others. Grace not shared was grace forfeited!

So Wesley's theological vocabulary may in some instances have to be translated in a new age. His mind fully participated in the thought-world of the eighteenth century. But what is crucial is not the vocabulary; it is the logic of his message. In a similar way, if we are to be instructed by Wesley today, we cannot be content simply to replicate his programmatic efforts. These were designed to fulfill specific purposes for his time and served the cause well. What is crucial is that we recognize the purposes behind Wesley's programmatic efforts (such as providing for personal accountability) and then seek ways to fulfill these same purposes for our time.

In short, the way that Wesley can be instructive to us in our attempt to formulate an authentic approach to evangelism is if we can discern the central trajectories of his approach to evangelism and then focus these for our radically different cultural setting. I want to emphasize three such Wesleyan trajectories that can help us grapple with a faithful ministry of evangelism in our time.

Evangelism with Theological Integrity

Evangelism's heritage from the nineteenth century comes with a minimal theology and a maximal experiential psychology. The advocates of evangelism often have appeared to dispense with serious theological reflection. The discipline of systematic theology in turn tended to ignore evangelism entirely or to subsume it under the rubric of nurture. A double-isolation has occurred: evangelism separated itself from theological reflection, and theological minds in turn chose to consider evangelism as the proverbial "embarrassing cousin."

Such a bifurcation of evangelism and theology was unimaginable to Wesley. Indeed, as Gerald Cragg notes, "The particular emphasis of his theology derived from his preoccupation with evangelism. He included all the traditional elements of the Christian system of belief, but he so arranged them as to bring into the sharpest relief the doctrine of salvation."[9] Wesley's theology was an attempt to describe the true, scriptural, experimental religion.

119

Wesley specifically worried that there be an integrity to the theology that undergirded evangelism. The word "integrity" denotes "wholeness" or "completeness" of truth. A classic indication of Wesley's intention to embody this theological wholeness is seen in his boast of Methodism:

> It is, then, a great blessing given to this people, that as they do not think or speak of justification so as to supersede sanctification, so neither do they think nor speak of sanctification so as to supersede justification. They take care to keep each in its own place, laying equal stress on one and the other. They know God has joined these together, and it is not for man to put them asunder. Therefore, they maintain, with equal zeal and diligence, the doctrine of free, full, present justification, on the one hand, and of entire sanctification both of heart and life, on the other; being as tenacious of inward holiness as any mystic, and of outward (holiness) as any Pharisee.[10]

The Wesleyan message was not striking in its innovation but rather in its intended fidelity to its sources or traditions. Wesley's theology was essentially *descriptive*, not *speculative*. He was not much concerned with theological method nor apologetic program. Convinced that the Christian tradition from the primitive church through the Reformation and Post-Reformation pietism provided the theological logic and categories rendering intelligible and meaningful the human experience of restorative and enabling grace, he announced the accessibility of full salvation—justification and sanctification—to all who would hear. The intent was to tell the Christian Story as witnessed by and received through the traditions of the church as the way of naming or norming Christian experience. Wesley would have had no difficulty in agreeing with a contemporary theologian of doctrine: "To become a Christian involves learning the story of Israel and of Jesus well enough to interpret and experience oneself and one's world in its terms."[11] Wesley's theology was not a "theology of Christian experience" such as that offered later by Schleiermacher; it was an attempt to interpret experience by the delivered scriptural and ecclesial traditions.

To this end, Wesley sought to hold in basic unity the *verbum externum*, the "external word" that molds and interprets oneself and one's world, with the *verbum internum*, the internal action of the Holy Spirit that enables us to hear and receive the healing Word, Jesus Christ. Wesley neglected neither the objective Word of the Gospel nor its subjective appropriation in human experience. He did not

collapse one into the other, making Christ the captive of human subjectivity. Rather, in his typically conjunctive way of thinking, he sought to conjoin the two in an integral wholeness.

The canonical story of Jesus was always the *source* and *norm* of Christian experience. Take note of Wesley's advice to his preachers. "Preach Christ," the Christ of canonical scripture, and preach Christ "in all his offices" as the constant and ready source of saving grace.[12] Christ in his offices as Prophet, Priest, and King was the absolute and sole source of salvation. The Incarnate Proclaimer announces the law of God as judgment to sinners and as "covered promises " for those who are in Christ. As the Incarnate Sacrificial Victim Christ does the divine work of restoring and healing the sinfully broken relationship with God (justification). As the crucified and risen Lord, Christ reigns as the goal of the newly birthed, redirected human will. The single word which encapsulates this canonical story is grace, gift, divine restorative Love, "free in all and free for all."

The offices of Christ

This integral unity or wholeness of the external and internal Word constitutes the occasion for authentic evangelism. The news of a Savior, and hence salvation, is announced. The hearing is by faith divinely and freely given. The response is the free decision nourished by the prevenient working of grace. The masses sang rightly:

> Come, sinners, to the gospel feast;
>   let every soul be Jesus' guest.
> Ye need not one be left behind,
>   for God hath bid all humankind.
>
> My message as from God receive;
>   ye all may come to Christ and live.
> O let his love your hearts constrain,
>   nor suffer him to die in vain.
>
> . . . .
>
> Come thou, this moment, at his call,
>   and live for him who died for all.[13]

Wesley's concern about the integrity of the theology undergirding evangelism led him to enter (reluctantly) the fray of polemics. His scrap with the Calvinists was an incidental matter. For Wesley it was a struggle for the soul of the revival. That which separated him and the Calvinists was not a conviction about divine sovereignty. Rather, the dividing line was their respective controlling models of God. For the Calvinists God was sovereign power, hence election and predestination. For Wesley, by contrast, God was sovereign love. The controlling model of divine love so permeated his thought that universal grace was the only conclusion to be drawn. Universal grace was the fundamental motive giving urgency to the evangelistic efforts of the revival.

Wesley's contest with the Calvinists was not a fight over a theological abstraction. In his sermon "The Lord Our Righteousness," he perceptively cut to the heart of the issue by insisting that while Christ is the *meritorious cause* of justification and sanctification, the *formal cause* is nevertheless faith. Otherwise, the role of human agency in justification and sanctification is minimized to the point of outright loss.[14] Wesley was not compromising with the Pauline principle of "grace alone." However, he insisted that grace entails response and accountability. Grace enables the response but does not coerce it. Such was the manner of the working of prevenient grace. As with justification, faith is the only required condition for sanctification. Through the working of prevenient and justifying grace, one lives the Christian life as one accountable for his or her obedience. Because the righteousness of Christ is imparted to the believer in the new birth, such righteousness cannot but be manifested in willing obedience of love for God and love for the neighbor.

In his later years Albert Outler was asked in an interview with Martin Marty why, with all of his patristical erudition, he had so singularly focused upon Wesley; he replied, "He got the order of salvation right!"[15] And that he did. In our time of rising cultural pluralism accompanied with a pervasive and uncritical relativism the church should do no less than "get the order of salvation right." When the contemporary church is served a menu replete with all kinds of "pop," instant-result evangelism so reflective of the culture itself, the church needs to recover its theological mind. A "thinking" evangelism is the only evangelism which can "offer Christ" with integrity.

Here the contemporary church can be instructed by Wesley. He was no theologian of apologetics to "culture despisers." In a very real sense he countered the prevailing culture of his time. He did not endeavor to reduce the substance of his message to meet the canons of contemporary sensibility or credibility. The result was not a theological scholasticism, arid and removed from the people. His message was contextualized in that he sought to reach the full or whole range of the human *sensorium*: heart, mind, and will. In a deliberate decision he chose a style of delivery that would do justice to the full range of the human condition, hence, "plain truth for plain people."[16] Contemporary evangelism can attempt in our time to do no less. His theological vocabulary no longer resonates with a biblically illiterate public. Maintaining with integrity the logic of grace which was his message, we have to find new words and ways to tell the same canonical story of grace.

Evangelism with Personal Accountability

Wesley was a tired, old man of eighty-four when he retreated to a village in Oxfordshire after having completed an itinerary of the Societies in England, Ireland, and the Channel Islands. The revival had now extended almost fifty years. He reflected on what he had seen and heard on his trip. His mind and heart were not at ease. The words of Isaiah 5:4 came to mind: "What could have been done more to my vineyard, that I have not done in it? Wherefore, when I looked that it should bring forth grapes, brought it forth wild grapes?" (KJV) Building a sermon on this text, Wesley catalogued four contributions which he had made to "the body of people commonly called Methodists": doctrine, spiritual helps, discipline, and outward protection.[17] All of these are important contributions, but I will focus on "spiritual helps" to probe another of Wesley's trajectories.

As important as preaching was for Wesley's evangelism, it was not enough for a full-orbed ministry of evangelism. Experience convinced him that awakening souls without providing follow-up nurture and discipline (i.e., the class meeting) was playing into the hands of the devil. Thus his standard response to reports from his preachers of initial response to their evangelistic efforts became "Follow the Blow!"[18] From the earliest days of the Wesleyan revival the class meeting was an essential, not an elective, alongside preaching.

When hearers inquired, "How may I find this salvation?" Wesley gathered them into small groups to "work out" their own salvation. Under the leadership of lay persons, the class became a "seekers" group, and no doubt more conversions occurred in the context of the class than in open preaching sessions.

The class meeting was Wesley's way of insuring personal accountability in the pursuit of the "scripture way of salvation." While the small group was not an original notion with Wesley (Puritans, Moravians, Anglicans, and others experimented with such), the

123

eclectic but always critical Wesley adapted it for an essential part of his ministry of evangelism. In December of 1739 Wesley drew up governing questions of this nature for his type of class:

Have you the forgiveness of your sins?

Have you the witness of God's Spirit with your spirit . . . ?

Has no sin, inward or outward, domination over you?

Do you desire to be told of all your faults?

Do you desire that, in doing this, we should come as close as possible, that we should cut to the quick, and search your heart to the bottom?

There were five questions which he required to be asked of everyone at every meeting:

What known sins have you committed since our last meeting?

What temptations have you met with?

How were you delivered?

What have you thought, said, or done, of which you doubt whether it be sin or not?

Have you nothing you desire to keep secret?[19]

Wesley regarded these little exercises in "spiritual helps" or accountability to be the "sinews" of the revival.[20] "Couched in the language of ordinary people" and "grounded in solid theological principles," the spiritual aid of these meetings provided a theological grid on which people could plot out their spiritual journey through prevenient grace to justification and sanctification and on to perfection.[21]

Characteristically the class meeting slowly waned across the nineteenth century in American Methodism. By the end of the century it had passed out of the *Discipline* of the Methodist Episcopal Church (North and South). With the passing of the class meeting this group of Wesley's children lost one of the major legacies that he bequeathed them. The eclipse or loss of the class meeting marked a decided decline in the church's ability to nurture accountability and discipleship. We could no longer "follow the blow." The loss of communal accountability meant that the evangelism of the nineteenth century presented itself in the twentieth century not only as a truncated but also as a distorted evangelism. Without structures of accountability, evangelism was reduced to concern for generating an

124

"altar experience" without a "discipleship road." This is an evangelism which knows the Name but doesn't know the Story!

Sociologist Peter Berger has graphically described a society in which an embracing "sacred canopy" has collapsed.[22] In such a situation the problem confronting the Christian witness is not *credibility* but *plausibility*. The social plausibility structures have collapsed. The resultant effect is that "religions enter the marketplace as objects of subjective choices in much the same way as brands of toothpaste and laundry soap. . . ."[23]

In a similar vein, Robert Jensen reminds us that in the postmodern world we have no common story. "Modernity was defined by the attempt to live in a universal story without a universal storyteller." What then shall we do? "The obvious answer," says Jensen, "is that if the church does not find her hearers antecedently inhabiting a narratable world, then the church must herself be that world. If the church is not herself a real, substantial, living world to which the gospel can be true, faith is quite simply impossible."[24]

In other words, the church is really the only plausibility structure of the Christian faith. It was so with the early church (reread The Acts of the Apostles), and it is so in our post-Christendom world. Through this ecclesial reality the Christian world view is potentially expressed in such a way that it can provide a holistic appeal to modern hearers who will not rely on one mode of reality affirmation. Postmoderns can best understand a holy, loving, just, forgiving, life-giving community founded on the grace of God and made effective through discipleship to Jesus Christ.

If the church is its own plausibility structure then it must take seriously the task of forming itself intentionally as a culture of its own. How is this to happen, if the church does not recover structures of Christian plausibility and accountability? The Wesleyan trajectory of personal accountability provides a suggestive precedent for us in addressing our revolutionary and relativistic postmodern setting.

Evangelism with a Social Conscience

Much of our inheritance in evangelism from the nineteenth century is tinctured with an acute individualism and a reactionary social escapism. To be sure, this is not the whole picture. For example, the initial generation of the Wesleyan holiness movement saw the doctrine of entire sanctification inescapably bound with abolition, the plight of the poor, and enfranchisement of women. There can be no denying, however, that this is not the model of evangelism which the twentieth-century church received from the nineteenth century.

Wesley himself has sometimes been criticized as too individualistic regarding the public arena of society and politics. A more careful reading, however, can be instructive. Wesley did not have the tools of critical social analysis which are ours today. Yet when he discovered the poor in his Oxford days and in a more powerful way in 1739 as he took up field preaching, he did not pass by on the other side.

When he addressed the issues of poverty, prison conditions, or the slave trade to the American colonies, these were not auxiliary issues to the gospel of grace which he preached. To address these issues in word, by pen, or by advocacy action were quite simply acts of "faith working by love." As the reality of sanctification is both inward and outward, so the life-in-process of sanctification cannot retreat into a realm of privacy. Such was the logic of grace. Such was the logic of discipleship. Wesley expressed it graphically in a 1775 letter to Miss March: "Go and see the poor and sick in their own poor little hovels. Take up your cross, woman! Remember the faith! Jesus went before you and will go with you. Put off the gentlewoman; you bear a higher character."[25] Or hear him in the final years of his life:

> O that God would enable me once more, before I go hence and am no more seen, to lift up my voice like a trumpet to those who gain and save all they can, but do not give all they can! . . . Many of your brethren, beloved of God, have not food to eat; they have not raiment to put on; they have not a place where to lay their head. And why are they thus distressed? Because you impiously, unjustly, and cruelly detain from them what your Master and their's lodges in your hand on purpose to supply their wants! See that poor member of Christ, pinched with hunger, shivering with cold, half naked! Meantime you have plenty of this world's goods—of meat, drink and apparel. In the name of God, what are you doing?[26]

Those who claim that Wesley had no understanding of systemic injustice should read his *Thoughts on the Present Scarcity of Provisions*. His attack on the distilling industry was directed primarily at the demand it created for grain which then deprived the starving of flour by making it so expensive. And meanwhile the craving for luxury causes landowners to raise their rents. The farmer, paying a higher rent for his land, must then receive a higher price for his produce. "And," says Wesley, "so the wheel runs round."[27]

Likewise, his sharp theological argument against slavery is illustrative of the fact that theological conviction and justice conviction are not separate matters:

> The main argument of the oppressors is that slavery is authorized by law. But can human law change the justice of God's created order? Can it turn darkness into light, or evil into good? By no means! Right is right, and wrong is still wrong. There is still an essential difference between justice and injustice, cruelty and mercy. And slavery cannot be reconciled with mercy or justice![28]

Rarely do we find such thoroughgoing pessimism about the human condition as we find in Wesley coupled with an equally thoroughgoing optimism of the efficacy of grace. His view of evangelism simply would not allow justification and sanctification, faith and works, conversion and holiness of life to be torn asunder. His evangelical ministry constantly reminds us that the conscience restored by sanctifying grace is a conscience simultaneously personal and social. An evangelical ministry that can embody this balance authentically will be central to any effective address to our postmodern situation.

CHAPTER 8

Connexion and Koinonia: Wesley's Legacy and the Ecumenical Ideal

Brian E. Beck

The spelling of the first word of my title betrays the fact that the writer is from the British tradition, which has consistently preserved the "x" in "connexion" as a marker for a technical term. I am glad to offer this essay as a tribute to a colleague and friend from The United Methodist Church, with whom it has been a pleasure to collaborate in the international Oxford Institute of Methodist Theological Studies.

Probably no one would have been more surprised than John Wesley himself to find his connexion discussed as an ecclesiological concept. For him it was essentially a practical and pastoral arrangement in the service of mission. Something had to be done to provide care for those who had discovered faith in Christ and to nurture them in their growth toward holiness. In the context in which the notion was developed, the religious societies of the eighteenth century, there was no reason to think of it in any other terms. The ecclesiological reality, it seemed, was the established church.

This has remained the case until comparatively recent times. Connexion has been regarded by all sides as a constitutional rather than an ecclesiological issue. Throughout the nineteenth century in Britain there were strenuous defenses of the Wesleyan and other varieties of the connexional system, but when systematic theologies of these groups came to treat the doctrine of the church they were curiously silent on the subject of connexion. Only in 1995 in Britain was an ecclesiological statement set before the Conference which seriously addressed the subject. And a theological account of connexion was inserted in the United Methodist *Book of Discipline* first in 1988.[1]

Yet there have always been ecclesiological implications in the practice, and these became greater when the shift took place on his death from a connexion with John Wesley in person to a connexion with a conference. With that shift, the gradual move from existing as a union of societies to existing as a church was accelerated. Sadly, with that development the institutional aspects of connexion were accentuated, and other elements that in fact hold more ecclesiological value tended to become submerged.

This article attempts to tease out some of those ecclesiological values, and to set them alongside a recent articulation of the ecumenical ideal, *koinonia*, to see whether they have anything to say to one another.

Sketching the Wesleyan Connexion

It must be admitted up front that "connexion" was neither an exclusively Methodist word nor exclusively religious. In the eighteenth century it could be used of commercial and political associations as well as religious ones. Among the religious groups using the term were those associated with George Whitefield and Howell Harris and with the Countess of Huntingdon, whose connexion still exists by that name. Wesley, however, gave the word a distinctive character by the way he stamped his own personality and method upon his branch of the revival movement.

In Wesley's usage there were three primary applications of connexion: to members, to societies, and to preachers. The bond, in each case, was with Wesley himself. He exercised authority in various ways over them all. In 1766 he set out his understanding of this authority:

> It is a power of admitting into and excluding from the Societies under my care; of choosing and removing Stewards; of receiving or not receiving Helpers [i.e., travelling preachers]; of appointing them when, where and how to help me; and of desiring any of them to meet me, when I see good.[2]

The relationship was essentially vertical, or, if you prefer, centripetal, from the dispersed units to Wesley himself. From it however developed a lateral relationship. Through their connexion with Wesley the preachers were connected with one another and formed a single body. As he expressed it in 1769 in a passage that looked forward (prematurely as it turned out) beyond his death:

You act in concert with each other, and by united counsels. And now is the time to consider what can be done to continue this union. Indeed, as long as I live, there will be no great difficulty: I am, under God, a centre of union to all our Travelling as well as Local Preachers . . . were it only out of regard to me, they will continue connected with each other. But by what means may this connexion be preserved when God removes me from you?[3]

The answer given to this question in the 1784 Deed of Declaration was the Conference.

The societies were united with each other in a similar fashion. The origin of the term "The United Societies" is not wholly clear, nor is it certain that its meaning remained unchanged. It seems to have begun with the union of two societies in Bristol, and then spread to other societies where there had not been a merger, and eventually was used to refer to all the societies in their union with each other. The paramount importance of that unity for Wesley is seen in his last letter to the American church, where he urges them to declare clearly that "the Methodists are one people in all the world; and that it is their full determination so to continue."[4]

The bonds of this connexion were developed pragmatically, in response to pastoral need or opportunity. These began with band and class meetings, itinerancy, rules, hymns, sermons, *Notes on the New Testament* and other publications, and conference; in due course were added the Model Deed and Deed of Declaration; and for the new church in America were provided the Twenty-five Articles of Religion (which have survived as a standard) and the *Sunday Service* (which did not). Underlying all these is discipline, exercised for the sake of three convictions out of which the entire movement sprang: Christ died for all (so mission is the primary imperative), all are called to holy living (hence the discipline and the need for oversight), and there is no such thing as solitary religion (hence the societies and all that is designed to sustain them). It was those convictions and pastoral needs that prompted Wesley, in frustration at the unwillingness of the Church of England to act, to embark upon ordinations for America, later for Scotland, Canada, and the West Indies, and eventually for England—thereby, from the point of view of canon law, cutting the main hawser mooring the Methodist ship to the Established Church.

Over the decades after his death the movement developed, in different ways on each side of the Atlantic, yet the organizational structure Wesley bequeathed to it has proved remarkably enduring. Its hallmarks are still conference, rules (in Britain, Standing Orders; in America, the *Discipline*), itinerancy, a common hymnal, and above all the expectation that the local church and the conduct of its life are defined not by itself but by a central body that has authority to make the rules by which it is governed, and that to be a (United) Methodist is to belong not just to a local congregation but—as of right—to the wider communion.

In many other ways however, on both sides of the Atlantic, while the framework has remained, the inner life has changed. Not only do Methodist churches perceive themselves as churches and not simply as religious societies, the spiritual quest and the pastoral mechanisms for pursuing it have changed. Gone are the band meetings, the mutual cross-examination, the love-feasts and watch-nights. Week-by-week life in a local Methodist church is not likely to differ over-much from a Presbyterian or Baptist church of similar social complexion. This has made it even more likely for connexion to be seen in institutional terms: as a benefit if it makes grant-aid possible, a convenience in that it guarantees a supply of accredited ministers, and a constraint or imposition if it is felt to inhibit local initiative, or if the local church has to pay what it regards as an excessive amount for the benefits it receives. This description would have to be modified in various ways if one were to attend to those churches in other parts of the world that have grown out of earlier British and American missionary expansion, but it is largely true of the British and American scene. The very insertion of the 1988 statement about the nature of connexionalism into the United Methodist *Book of Discipline* reflected the sense of a need to reclaim a heritage.

In fact independency, whether consciously defined as such, or in the unreflective pragmatic form in which it is encountered among church members in many denominations, has always been the main target for apologists of connexionalism. Nineteenth-century British writers, for example, were willing to regard episcopalian and presbyterian polities as essentially connexional, although less centralized than the Wesleyan connexion. But they viewed congregationalism as another thing altogether. From the eighteenth century on, congregationalism was seen by Methodist writers as posing several serious dangers: the minister's primary function would be to serve the congregation rather than to engage in mission; because appointed by them, ministers would be more likely to be subject to the congregation's influence than the congregation to their leadership; this would make doctrinal heresy and spiritual slackness serious dangers; and if ministers kept their prophetic edge they would be in danger of being sacked, while if they did not they could be there for life and slowly sink along with the church into decline. If one picked on worst case examples (as Methodist apologists did!) there was much in contemporary experience to sustain such fears.

A proper evaluation of connexionalism, however, must begin not from institutional arrangements nor from polemics but from the characteristics of the early period. Both British and American traditions have much to learn and to recover from their earlier heritage, even though (as we shall go on to see) the wider ecumenical debate also poses some questions.

Evaluating Wesleyan Connexionalism

What then are the ecclesiological values that lie behind Wesley's pragmatic and pastoral system? As we have already noted, it was a system for a voluntary society, not for a separate church. Yet it was developed out of assumptions about what the church should be, and for that reason it still has ecclesiological significance. I want to highlight six points that hold value for contemporary ecclesiological reflection.

(1) *The connexion arose out of missionary and pastoral need, not out of a desire to make organization more scriptural.* The nineteenth-century Wesleyan apologists never tired of making the point that, unlike other churches in the Reformed tradition, church organization was not of itself an issue for them. They assumed that the form of the church is dictated by the inner nature of the faith, not juridically by either scripture or tradition. Wesley's convictions on this point cannot be divorced from his Arminianism. He insisted that salvation is to be offered to all, not just to the elect. The structures of the church must therefore serve this goal. Moreover the church's mission has to do ultimately with holiness, in the person and in the wider society. God's design in raising up the Methodist preachers was "not to form any new sect; but to reform the nation, particularly the Church; and to spread scriptural holiness over the land."[5] The structures of the church must therefore serve both to evangelize and to develop spirituality.

To affirm such a principle today is not to deny the significance of tradition (indeed to do so would be to render an examination of the Wesleyan heritage pointless). Still less does it deny the significance of scripture, from which the recognition of the imperatives of evangelization and spiritual formation arise. But in an age when the historical relativity of both scripture and tradition is increasingly acknowledged, and the cultural conditioning of all our inherited structures is recognized, it is important to try to identify core values by which structures are to be assessed and retained or replaced. The mission of the church is one of them.

(2) *The connexion was essentially interpersonal.* Members, societies and preachers were in union with Mr Wesley and thus with one another. The constituent elements in the system—bands, classes, societies, and conferences—were designed to enable people to meet.

> Christianity is essentially a social religion, and to turn it into a solitary religion is indeed to destroy it. . . . I mean not only that it cannot subsist so well, but that it cannot subsist at all, without society, without living and conversing with other [people].[6]

The structures were designed to serve these relationships. Yet ironically, like all other church structures, they have become over time a hindrance to meeting. In our ecumenical age they will need to be overcome, modified, or ignored to make wider meeting possible.

(3) *Relationships were understood to be more than local.* Potentially they were universal. We noted above Wesley's insistence that "the Methodists are one people in all the world; and . . . it is their full determination so to continue." His hopes of keeping the British and the Americans in a single connexion after the War of Independence were soon dashed. The Americans showed themselves determined to go their own way in ecclesiastical matters as in political. In the conditions of the time it was too much to expect otherwise. But note that Wesley's words were more than the declaration of an administrator struggling to hold his organization together. They were rooted in the conviction that the call to that holiness without which no one shall see God is a call to perfect love. Unity therefore, unity without borders, is a gospel imperative.

(4) *In all this there was a stress on accountability.* The purpose of all the tiers of meetings which Wesley organized—bands, classes, society meetings, leaders' meetings, preachers' meetings and conferences—was to "render strict account." The primary concern of the meetings was not "business" in the modern sense, but spiritual and

theological oversight; they met to hold one another to the path in faith, prayer, obedience, faithful pastoring, doctrinal fidelity, and continuing witness and mission. The agenda of the first Conference in 1744 reads, "What to teach; How to teach; and What to do, i.e., how to regulate our doctrine, discipline, and practice."[7] No one should think of himself or herself as autonomous. All answer to one another. (The only exception of course was John Wesley himself. He certainly did not think of himself as answering to the fellowship, although some of the preachers did and his brother, at least, was not afraid to take him on.[8])

(5) *Oversight,* **episcopē,** *was thus in practice a matter of central importance.* John Wesley can rightly be compared with the Ignatian bishop. When he ordained for America, it was not just Whatcoat and Vasey as preachers and pastors, but Coke as superintendent; and to this day in the United Methodist tradition the general superintendency of the whole church is laid upon the collective shoulders of the bishops.

(6) *Finally, Wesley's model of connexion carried some suggestion of the believer's relationship of covenantal obedience to God.* Unfortunately, this suggestion has typically been obscured by the reality that his connexion originated as a voluntary association. In his own time and in the following century this voluntary status was often emphasized as a counter to charges that the connexion was too authoritarian. It was contended that if people did not like the regime, they were free to take themselves off. Actually, it was not always so simple in practice. More important, this emphasis tended to undercut the ecclesiological dimension of covenantal obedience to God.

This danger remains in some modern Methodist accounts of connexion. Consider, for example, the way the 1988 statement in the United Methodist *Book of Discipline* employs the idea of covenant:

> Methodists everywhere have embraced the idea that as a people of faith we journey together in connection and in covenant with one another. Expressing the high degree of cohesiveness and centralized organization among Methodists, the connectional principle became the distinguishing mark which set them apart from the normal patterns of Anglican ecclesiastical organization as well as the more loosely organized Protestant bodies of the day. The acceptance of strong covenantal bonds among the Methodists was no accident. Here were deep theological roots, including the concept and experience of covenant and the resulting emphasis on

135

faith journeying in covenant with God and one another. The connectional idea is a style of relationship rather than simply an organizational or structural framework. . . . It is in essence a network of interdependent relationships among persons and groups throughout the life of the denomination.[9]

Such an account of connexion will not quite do. It may be appropriate to a religious society, but is inadequate as a statement of relationships in the church. It treats connexion as a covenant analogous to our covenant with God, but it does not delineate the relationship between the two. To see the problem, compare the comments on covenant in the report "Costly Unity" published in 1993 after a World Council of Churches consultation on "Koinonia and Justice, Peace, and the Integrity of Creation":

A covenant between human beings carries the biblical sense only if it is made before God with the intention of obedience to God's covenantal requirements. To enter into a covenant means we accept the conditions under which God sets us in the midst of creation.[10]

In other words, connexion (at its best) is not a voluntary association but an ecclesiological discipline. It arises out of the nature of the gospel and the church.

Sketching the Notion of Koinonia

When we turn to the concept of koinonia the most succinct statement is the World Council of Churches' Canberra Statement of 1991, "The Unity of the Church as Koinonia: Gift and Calling."[11] This can be readily supplemented by material in the report of the Fifth World Conference on Faith and Order, held in 1993 at Santiago de Compostela. Some of its flavor is given in the following extract:

(2.1) The unity of the Church to which we are called is a koinonia given and expressed in the common confession of the apostolic faith; a common sacramental life entered by the one baptism and celebrated together in one eucharistic fellowship; a common life in which members and ministries are mutually recognized and reconciled; and a common mission witnessing to all people to the gospel of God's grace and serving the whole of creation. . . . This full communion will be expressed on the local and universal levels through conciliar forms of life and action. In such communion churches are bound in all aspects of their life together at all levels in confessing the one faith and engaging in worship and witness, deliberation and action.[12]

Further quotations from the Santiago report illustrate that koinonia is a far more comprehensive and deeply-rooted concept than connexion can hope to be:

> (4) "Koinonia" is above all, a gracious fellowship in Christ expressing the richness of the gift received by creation and humankind from God. It is a many dimensional dynamic in the faith, life, and witness of those who worship the Triune God, confess the apostolic faith, share the Gospel and sacramental living, and seek to be faithful to God in Church and world. . . . (10) The interdependence of unity and diversity which is the essence of the Church's koinonia is rooted in the Triune God revealed in Jesus Christ. The Father, Son, and Holy Spirit is the perfect expression of unity and diversity and the ultimate reality of relational life. . . . (14) The very structure of the Church is relational. . . . No Christian can exist as an isolated individual exercising a privileged and direct communion with God. . . . (15) Both unity and diversity are expressive of koinonia. . . . (17) The koinonia of the Church is also universal.[13]

The manifest strength of this development of the notion of koinonia is its rooting in the doctrine of the Trinity. There is thus given to the ecumenical goal a central theological paradigm and a Godward dimension. The unity to which we are called is not a blending of structures, nor a reconciliation of human communities, but the drawing of human beings—and ultimately of all creation—into the life of God.

That poses a question not only for our contemporary expressions of ecumenical goals, but for the life and structures of all the churches in our separation. Until that Godward dimension becomes central to our reflection on what the church is and our ordering of its life, our vision will remain distorted.

Engaging the Notion of Koinonia

With some sense of the notion of koinonia before us, I want to engage it now from a Wesleyan perspective. I will do so by examining both parallels and contrasts between the ecclesiological emphases of connexion and koinonia. I begin with some interesting parallels between the model of church as koinonia and the connexional vision.

Parallels between Koinonia and Connexion

(1) Koinonia, like connexion, is not a mere option for the church. The parallel in sentiment between Canberra's "No Christian can exist as an isolated individual exercising a privileged and direct communion with God," and Wesley's "Christianity is essentially a social religion," makes the point.

(2) Koinonia, like connexion, is interpersonal. Again we can pick up the Canberra statement, "The very structure of the Church is relational." It is spelled out there in terms of a common confession of faith, shared sacramental life, and mutual recognition of members and ministries. Although the emphasis would be placed somewhat differently, Wesley's connexion was essentially about people meeting. If Wesley failed to offer the Methodist people a satisfactory doctrine of the Church, he certainly gave them an experience of the Church—meeting in small groups together, sustaining one another—in which the eucharist took on a new significance.

(3) Koinonia, like connexion, is mission oriented: "a common mission witnessing to all people to the gospel of God's grace and serving the whole of creation. . . . The koinonia of the Church is . . . universal," to quote Canberra again. So too for Wesley the connexion was potentially universal, embracing all who will.

If there is a difference between koinonia and connexion on these issues, apart from the language, it might be the starting point. Wesley began at the micro-level, with the needs and relationships of individual believers, and worked outward from them via the local church to the wider connexion. Koinonia, because the setting for the discussion is worldwide ecumenical relations, begins at the macro-level and works inward toward the local church. But we should make no mistake about the fact that what it says about relations between separated churches applies equally to particular congregations and to relationships in any local church.

The Challenge of Koinonia to Connexion

When we turn from similarities to differences, perhaps the most important challenge to Methodist thinking in the concept of koinonia, apart from the Trinitarian framework already mentioned, lies in the insistence that koinonia embraces both unity and diversity. This would not have been obvious to Methodists of the eighteenth or nineteenth centuries, nor indeed in the first half of the twentieth.

The most uncompromising statement of an attitude common in that era is perhaps that of J. H. Rigg, and is worth quoting, if only to show how far British Methodism at least has come in the last fifty years.

> Wesleyan Methodism is a connexional system; there subsists in it an absolute intercommunity of interests; a united people . . . a united and circulating pastorate. This renders it absolutely necessary that both ministers and people should have distinctly adopted or accepted one doctrine and one discipline. No minister can be required to teach and enforce, nor any people to receive and submit to, a system of doctrine which he or they cannot in conscience approve. . . . There *must* . . . be an authority and power in the whole united society to enforce the conditions of the union in every circuit and upon every minister.[14]

I suspect that kind of statement only needs to be made when the rot has begun to set in. Now of course, at least on the British scene, it is the chain stores that present a uniform front and uniform contents to the passer-by, not the Methodist churches. In Britain we have largely legalized that diversity, I suspect more so than in the United States or continental Europe. As a result we struggle with the relationship between unity and diversity, with an inheritance strongly unsympathetic to the latter.

The Challenge of Connexion to Koinonia

If a weakness is to be discerned in the exposition of koinonia summarized above, it is perhaps in the realm of accountability. I use that word rather than its obverse, jurisdiction, because the latter can too readily be seen as something extraneously imposed. Moreover it is legal terminology, somewhat removed from the essentially interpersonal stress of koinonia. Koinonia, however, negates autonomy, and poses the central question in the ordering of the church of how individual members, congregations, and wider groupings answer to one another. Documents on koinonia make much of conciliarity but very little of accountability, except as an agenda item still to be addressed: "Koinonia must not be interpreted as meaning acceptance of our present denominational structures so long as they are 'in communion'. That would make koinonia only a synonym for 'reconciled diversity.'"[15]

It has been one of the strengths of the connexional heritage that it offers an answer to the practical question of creating accountability in the form of the conference—the gathering of representatives of the churches to take counsel together in prayer to discern and declare the mind of God, whose conclusions are binding on the churches they represent. That is the setting in which local churches answer to each other and regulate one another in obedience to Christ. (The reality experienced may be very different; politicking enters in, but that is nothing new.)

Interestingly, the British and American traditions diverge in the application of this principle in ways that mirror more ancient divisions in other traditions. Briefly, in the American tradition (although there are some exceptions) daughter churches outside the United States, while governed in many respects by their own conferences, are bound together by common membership in, and under the discipline of, the General Conference and a single Council of Bishops, which are global in character. In the British tradition, daughter churches (of which America was the first, enjoying "that liberty wherewith God has so strangely made them free"[16]) have become autonomous, linked by agreements about mutual support and cross-representation. Thus the American tradition is more centralist and globalist, akin to the Roman approach with its single college of bishops and universal primacy, while the British mirrors the Anglican and Orthodox traditions in recognizing greater regional autonomy (although in the case of the Orthodox we must not forget the binding character of the truly ecumenical councils). Curiously, one can defend the British Methodist/Anglican position by appeal to a characteristically Roman principle—subsidiarity.

Conclusion

It may seem strange that the contribution of John Wesley to ecumenism should be discussed under the very Methodist heading of connexionalism, rather than in connection with the more often-quoted "catholic spirit." In 1749, in Dublin of all places, he published a document which has had renewed attention in this century, his *Letter to a Roman Catholic*. In it he pleads for tolerance, and sets out those convictions which Protestants and Catholics share, in essence the doctrines of the Creed, and pleads:

> If we cannot as yet think alike in all things, at least we may love alike. . . . Let us resolve, first, not to hurt one another . . . secondly, . . . to speak nothing harsh or unkind of each other. . . . thirdly, . . .

to harbour no unkindly thought, no unfriendly temper ... fourthly, endeavour to help each other on in whatever we are agreed leads to the Kingdom. So far as we can, let us always rejoice to strengthen each other's hands in God.[17]

The sentiments were echoed in a sermon of the same date, "The Catholic Spirit."[18] Certainly in those documents Wesley enunciated an important theological principle, now often referred to as the notion of a hierarchy of truths. Central to that scale of values were the spiritual values of faith and love. But in his day that was, as it remains in ours, a program for reaching across the denominational barriers while those barriers remain, and possibly a means by which we one day will come to see that they are unnecessary and can be removed. But connexion, and its larger, theologically more adequate counterpart, koinonia, look forward to the day when there are no barriers and asks: Shall we still live as though there were barriers? And if not, how shall our common life be ordered?

CHAPTER 9

Trinity and Covenantal Ministry: A Study of Wesleyan Traditions

Mary Elizabeth Mullino Moore

A retired elder approached me at church two weeks before I was scheduled to be ordained as a deacon in The United Methodist Church. He said, "Congratulations on your ordination; you will be almost equal to the rest of us when you are ordained." The man intended this comment in a complementary and celebrative way, and I received it in that spirit, having had much experience in receiving such comments. What the comment reveals however, besides the man's genuine interest in me, is an assumption that diverse forms of ministry exist in a hierarchy of importance. The order of deacon, in his mind, would remain a slightly inferior order to elder, but it was better in his mind than the diaconal ministry, which had been the form of my ministry for twenty years.

During the Annual Conference in which I was ordained, a treasured colleague, who had long advocated the importance of laity (as a lay person for many years, then as an elder), approached me with what sounded like anger in her voice. She said, "What about the laity, Mary Elizabeth; you are not going to abandon them, are you?" This comment stunned me more than the first because this woman is an elder who herself values the ministry of the laity in everything that she does. I thought that she, of all people, would know that I would never abandon my deep commitment to lay ministry. In fact, most of my theological reflection, legislative drafting, and public speaking have been devoted to rediscovering the wholeness of all ministry and the central significance of the *laos*.

These two stories reveal a nervousness about diverse forms of ministry. This nervousness stems from a long tradition of conceptualizing ministry in dualistic, hierarchical ways, and from a common theological practice of dichotomizing unity and diversity. My case reflects only the most recent example of a tension that threads throughout the history of the Wesleyan movement, namely the tension that arises from defining ministry according to discrete hierarchically arranged parts. This tension has endured, in part, because Methodist theologians have given less attention to the topic of ministry than to topics like faith, grace, and holiness. In particular, they have not reflected in depth on how the larger theological insights and methods of our tradition shed light on concepts, structures, and practices of ministry.[1] Discourse around ministry has tended to adopt dualistic, hierarchical patterns.

The neglect of comprehensive theological reflection on ministry is not surprising, given the fact that John and Charles Wesley did not intend to begin a new church. Indeed, Charles roundly criticized the act that brought John to the edge of schism from Anglicanism (ordaining ministers for the new church in the United States). Their specific situation allowed the Wesleys to follow the Anglican pattern of ministry except when matters of mission or necessity required them to do otherwise, as in establishing lay preachers to travel preaching circuits and class leaders to lead classes. For this reason, the early Methodists were agile in creating new structures for missional purposes, but not very thorough in developing a theology of ministry.

Slighting theological reflection on ministry continued in the later Wesleyan movement. Topics like the salvific work of God and the shape of the Christian life, which had preoccupied the Wesleys, continued to draw significant attention. Theologians typically considered diverse positions carefully and sought to mediate differences or weave perspectives together. By contrast, ministry issues have come to the foreground primarily when the church was faced with an immediate controversy or new movement, and they were decided with much less attention to diverse perspectives and the relation among them. Surely such a vital issue as the nature of ministry deserves better than this!

I believe that the time is ripe to reflect critically on the larger Wesleyan theological tradition and to draw upon that wisdom to nourish a theology of ministry. The purpose of this essay is to begin such a process by focusing on a very practical question: *How can the church move toward an understanding and practice of ministry that is based on covenantal community rather than on dichotomy and hierarchy, and on a diversity of forms and functions within a unity of mission?*

Even asking such a question appeals to the Wesleyan tradition of doing theology in a never-ending cycle of theory and practice, and drawing from multiple perspectives in the interest of just and right-eous living in the world. No one has been more committed to a praxis approach in Wesleyan theology than Ted Runyon, in whose honor this essay is presented. Runyon characteristically identified an issue that compelled the church's attention, whether it was the charismatic revival in the 1970s or the urgency of political and liberation theologies in the 1980s.[2] He helped gather people together to reflect on the issue, and devoted his efforts to identifying riches in the Wesleyan theological tradition that shed light on the issue. Further, he frequently presented two or more views, weaving them into a more complete whole.[3] The investigation that follows is shaped deeply by this approach to theological reflection.

This means that I must begin by analyzing the actual practice of ministry—in this instance by focusing on case studies of The United Methodist Church (UMC) and its predecessor bodies. This analysis will reveal a tendency to dichotomize that has influenced ministerial theory and practice through the history of the Methodist movement, from the eighteenth century forward. I will then turn to an exposition of John Wesley, looking particularly at how his trinitarian convictions interweave with his affirmation of covenantal living, thus suggesting a vision and practice of ministry that moves beyond dualism and hierarchy, toward diversity and unity. Finally I will return to the present situation in the UMC, noting both signs of hope in recent developments and the continuing challenge in moving toward a truly covenantal perspective on ministry.

Ministry in the United Methodist Heritage

The purpose of this section is to explore the dynamics affecting the nature and practice of ministry in Methodism in the United States by analyzing case studies from the history of the UMC.[4] What is striking is that these cases, though different in many ways, all reveal a tendency to set up issues in terms of dichotomized categories: hierarchy or chaos, clergy or laity, black or white, women or men. One can see in them the propensity of the church to dichotomize diverse forms of ministry, as well as to dichotomize the very concepts of diversity and unity.

Cases of Conflicts Regarding Ministry

At several points in the history of the UMC and its predecessor bodies issues of full participation in ministry became the center of controversy. A prominent example is the clash in all of these groups over the full inclusion of African Americans and women in the ordained ministry. Other examples (differing in intensity in particular churches) include disagreement over the full participation of laity in annual and general conferences, over the participation specifically of laywomen in these conferences, and over support of missionary societies started and directed by laywomen. This section will explore representative cases of such conflict, seeking to discern what theological assumptions about ministry are reflected in them or contributed to them. The exploration is organized to reveal the range of conflictual issues.

Some of the cases emerged in the *conflict between established traditions of ministry and the immediate needs of the church.* For example, the sacramental controversy of 1772–81 was sparked when the North American societies were not content to depend on the Anglican church or other denominations to provide the sacraments. The situation in North America was quite different from that in Britain, and during this time surrounding the Revolution, people were not willing to continue the Wesleyan pattern of depending on the Anglican Church. Thus, some of the preachers ordained one another and began to exercise sacerdotal leadership in baptism and the Lord's Supper.[5] A few years later, the practice of ordaining lay preachers emerged; these preachers could administer the sacraments, even though the charge where they held membership might be committed to an itinerant who was only a deacon or not ordained at all.[6]

Some cases emerged from *anachronisms in defining ministerial identity and functions in the Methodist Episcopal, Evangelical Association, and United Brethren traditions.* For example, in the Methodist Episcopal Church of the late-eighteenth-century conference membership was the key in defining identity, and also the key in defining the role of church leaders in decision making. Neither laity nor local pastors were members of the conference, which excluded them from governing authority.[7] This meant that traveling lay preachers could participate in the decision making of annual conference by virtue of their itinerancy and conference membership, while ordained local preachers could not, even though they were authorized to administer the sacraments. At times, this practice stood in tension with other concurrent practices, particularly the practice of a three-fold ministry of deacons, elders, and bishops. While the relationship between deacons and elders was understood hierarchically, traveling deacons had governing privileges that were denied to located elders.

Other cases reveal the *diverse ways in which ministerial relationships were defined and embodied.* In the eighteenth-century Methodist Episcopal Church relationships were defined to a large extent by distinctions between orders. Note three examples: (1) Francis Asbury's vision that ministry be modeled on the apostolic example, which he described as being ordained first as deacon and then as elder; (2) the Disciplinary provision that elders would share equally with bishops in administering the sacraments while deacons would share partially; and (3) the common ordination practice that bishops alone would ordain deacons and bishops, but would be joined by elders in the ordination of elders (thus making deacons the only order in which members of the order did not lay on hands in ordination.)[8] During this same period the United Brethren, under Philip William Otterbein's leadership, were less concerned with distinctions. All preachers were members of the annual conference, whether traveling or not; and all participated in decisions about who was authorized to preach, baptize, administer the Lord's Supper, and/or marry (functions that were not necessarily connected to ordination).[9] The actual structure of ministry was a modified presbyterian system in which the preacher was elected by male members of the congregation, the elders were appointed for life by the preacher, and the deacons were elected annually by the congregation.[10] The patterns in these two traditions were quite distinct, and each had its own strengths and limitations.

Within these diverse contexts, further cases reveal *conflicts regarding who would be included and who would be excluded from ordination.* One of the earliest and most devastating conflicts centered around Richard Allen, who was licensed as a local preacher and served as a class leader among the growing number of African Americans at St. George's Church in Philadelphia. When Allen, a former slave, was licensed, he was responsible to the white elders of St. George's. Over time however, he and his people built up their body and sought to have a separate church. Bethel Methodist Episcopal Church was dedicated in 1794, and two years later their charter of incorporation provided that the church would be loyal to the denomination, maintain the property under the authority of their own trustees, and accept the authority of St. George's elder to license and assign local preachers and to officiate in the sacraments "for the time being."[11] The issues were not resolved, however, and in 1807 the Bethel Church issued "The African Supplement," which sought to extend the autonomous authority of the Bethel congregation. According to Will Gravely, the supplement "would not have been necessary, of course, had Allen or other black deacons been advanced to elder's orders or become members of the annual conference."[12] Gravely describes the Methodist practice of providing a limited ministerial standing for African Americans as an "anomaly," and notes that ordinations were not even held in regular conference proceedings, but in private.[13] Throughout this period, two big issues of authority— ordination for black deacons and property control by the black trustees—were focal points for most of the emerging black churches. The failure of the Methodist Episcopal Church to resolve these issues led finally to the establishment of separate black denominations.

Other cases reveal similar processes of exclusion from ordination. One in particular deserves mention because, like the ordination of African Americans, the ordination of women was racked with controversy. Both Anna Oliver and Anna Howard Shaw had been approved by their quarterly conferences for ordination in 1880, but the presiding bishop had announced that he would not present their names to the New England Conference because "the law of the Church does not authorize the ordination of women."[14] From this decision, the case went to the General Conference, and then to the Judiciary Committee, both of which rejected petitions to ordain women. The Committee on Itinerancy at the 1880 General Conference explained its decision by saying that women were already "accorded *all the privileges which are necessary to their usefulness.*"[15] In the end, Anna Howard Shaw transferred to the Methodist Protestant Church where she was ordained (1880); Anna Oliver went back to a local Methodist Episcopal church, but left only a few years later in exhaustion.

During this same period there were a series of *controversies about the participation of laymen and laywomen in the governance of the church.* These questions actually led to division in the United Brethren

Church in 1889, and in the Evangelical Association between 1891 and 1894. Gender was also an issue in the controversies regarding lay leadership; in all predecessors of the UMC, the seating of laymen at both Annual and General Conferences preceded the seating of lay-women. In the United Brethren for example, the first laymen to participate in Annual Conferences did so in 1878, the first laywomen in 1883.[16] The first layman was not actually seated in a General Conference in the Evangelical Association until 1907, the first lay-woman in the 1940s.[17] The issues regarding laity were also related in complex ways to issues of ordination. This is particularly visible in relation to women, who were denied ordination in the same 1880 General Conference (Methodist Episcopal) that denied laywomen the right to serve on the church's governing councils, but approved and supported the Woman's Foreign Missionary Society and the Woman's Home Missionary Society.[18]

Related to issues of lay leadership was the *issue of how to respond to the ministry initiatives of laywomen*. Questions arose as denomina-tions faced initiatives from women to establish women's missionary organizations. The late nineteenth century was a time of evangelistic and missionary zeal, and many Christian women were seeking opportunities to be in service to God and the church. Some women, such as the United Brethren Lizzie Hoffman, discerned a calling to organize women in support of missions.[19] The women's movements shared an impulse to organize, educate, and empower women; to support missions; and particularly to support women missionaries to serve women and children around the world.

Despite common missions, the emergence of the women's socie-ties varied from church to church. Donald Gorrell makes a convinc-ing case that the openness and support in the United Brethren in Christ contributed to a much quicker and easier formation of women's organizations than in the Evangelical Association, the for-mer being established in 1872 and the latter in 1883.[20] Further, the United Brethren women organized in Annual Conferences and later developed a denomination-wide structure related directly to the General Conference. The Evangelical Association women were al-lowed to organize initially only at the local church level under the preacher's supervision; when they did become denomination-wide, they were organized in auxiliary relationship with the male-run Board of Missions.[21] Yet again we see tensions between unity and diversity of ministries!

Dichotomizing Diverse Forms of Ministry: Questions of Power and Community

The cases discussed above share a tendency to dichotomize options into either/or categories. Consider a few of the dichotomies: (1) either we maintain the structures and inheritance from the past or we abandon and destroy the heritage; (2) either we have a strong, powerful clergy or we have a strong, powerful laity; (3) the church either preserves the present definitions and principles of ordination or the church ordains anyone that wants to be ordained; and (4) the church either supports racial minority groups or it supports racial majority groups in structures of ministry and, likewise, it supports either women or men.

This list could be expanded but the basic point is clear—dichotomous thinking underlies much of the church's discussion of ministry. Recognition of this reality is hardly irrelevant to theological reflection and church practice. The pattern of dichotomizing has a direct impact on how power is distributed and how community is experienced in the church. Failure to recognize and address this impact undermines the church's ability to expand theological horizons and to negotiate the rough terrain of decisions regarding ministry.

Consider first the issues of power. These can be illuminated by Val Plumwood's striking analysis of dualisms. Plumwood argues that dualistic thinking and acting undergirds much oppression, whether the oppression be occasioned by gender, race, class, or human-nature relationships.[22] Plumwood defines dualisms as the formulation of contrasts in oppositional and dominant-subordinate terms.[23] I would accentuate the idea that the very formulation of difference in terms of either/or options, between which people are expected to choose, invites the judgment that one option is superior to the other. The history of Western philosophy and theology gives plenty of evidence to that effect, whether in judging mind over body, human life over the rest of the natural world, spirit over matter, or male over female. More subtle, but also demonstrable, have been the valuing of literate wisdom over folk wisdom, free landowners over slaves, rich over poor, Northern hemisphere issues over Southern, Western thought over Eastern, and so forth.

What is particularly important to the present analysis is Plumwood's description of the logical structure of dualism. She argues that in a dualism, the values and spheres of a dualised other "are systematically and pervasively constructed and depicted as inferior"; thus, the possibility of equality and mutuality is unthinkable.[24] She identifies five features of dualism: (1) backgrounding (denial)—the dominating party uses, organizes, and relies on the other, but ignores or belittles the significance of the other's contribution; (2) radical exclusion (hyperseparation)—the dominating party denies or minimizes any similarity with the other, thus justifying domination based on difference; (3) incorporation (relational definition)—the qualities of the dominant party are identified as primary social values, and the dominated party is defined in relation to those values rather than by their own unique qualities; (4) instrumentalism (objectification)—the dominated are expected to subsume their interests to those of the master or master project; and (5) homogenization or stereotyping—the dominated class is identified as homogeneous, at least in matters relevant to the interests of the dominant party, thus allowing them to be stereotyped as inferior and ignored in relation to their diverse interests and achievements.[25]

In developing this description of dualisms, Plumwood is not advocating the elimination of differences in creation, people, social roles, functions, or abilities. What she opposes is the use of existing differences to support patterns of domination in which some are masters over others.[26] This analysis does not negate the value of functional and qualitative distinctions. The issue is domination, not difference. Plumwood's alternative to dualism is integration in theory-building, and upholding equity, mutuality, and respect in social relationships.

A brief look at the cases considered above reveals some interesting correspondence with Plumwood's five features of dualisms.

- *Backgrounding* might be seen in the way in which the early Methodist Episcopal Church relied on the located elders and lay preachers to do the daily work of ministry, but did not allow them to be members of a conference.

- *Radical exclusion* is exemplified by many of the ways that Richard Allen, Anna Oliver, and Anna Howard Shaw were dealt with in the ordination process. The continued refusal of the church to ordain Allen and other African Americans as elders, despite their strong work in building up large, spiritually dynamic churches, fits the denial pattern of exclusion.

Likewise, the explanation given in 1880 for not ordaining women (they were already "accorded *all the privileges which are necessary to their usefulness*") typifies the minimizing of similarity or sympathy by the male decision-makers.

- *Incorporation* is seen in the struggles of laity to get full voice and vote in the governing bodies of the church during the last decades of the nineteenth century. They were defined against the clergy, and were seen as wanting because they lacked the education, experience, and responsibilities of the clergy. Their own distinctive education, experience, and responsibilities were largely ignored.

- *Instrumentalism* is evident in several of the cases, but is most vivid in the desire of the Evangelical Association to allow women to organize for mission, but to bind the organization under supervision of dominant parties (the pastor at the local level and the Board of Missions at the denominational level).

- *Homogenization or stereotyping* is quite visible in all of the cases. African Americans were treated as a unique class, for example, with private ordinations as deacon and no ordinations as elder. And women were seen as people who could appropriately take some roles (Sunday school superintendents, class leaders or stewards) but not others, specifically not the roles of an ordained elder.

This analysis reinforces the claim that dichotomizing tendencies in conceptualizing and structuring ministry have been strong in the UMC heritage. The power of dominant groups has often been reinforced by these dichotomous patterns. The church has frequently responded to nondominant forms of ministry and nondominant people in ministry as if they were other, lesser, and in service to the "more important" leaders.

To be sure, this is the very pattern that—under the surface—has been called into question by the formulations of baptism and ministry that emerged from the 1996 General Conference of The United Methodist Church (to which we will return later in this essay). These formulations did not fall from the sky; they were developed over a period of more than fifty years, drawing from Scripture and the history of the church, as well as from emerging realities in the world and theological discourse in an ecumenical and global forum. In short, many hands have kneaded the dough.[27] But the question now is whether the church, so long formed by dichotomous thinking about the church and ministry, is able to meet the new day without imposing a new set of dichotomous categories: whether clergy and laity, elder and deacon, black and white, Asian American and Native American, or women and men.

Just as in issues of power, people tend to dichotomize in issues of community. In this regard the dichotomizing works against true community by setting up an either/or choice in which some are included and others excluded. Theologically, this process is often reinforced by casting diversity and unity themselves in a fundamental dichotomy, suggesting that a community cannot be diverse and unified at the same time.

This dichotomy between diversity and unity in the community is visible in the cases considered above. The very attempt to limit the membership in Annual and General Conferences is an attempt to create a dichotomy between one group of church members and another, whether it be itinerant and located ministers, clergy and laity, or women and men. When such divisions are based on distinctive roles relevant to the respective groups, they may be justified; but in the cases discussed, the church has decided in retrospect that the divisions were not justified. The decisions are now viewed as having been motivated by clerical prejudice, hierarchical prejudices within the clergy, racial prejudice, gender prejudice, and so forth. The same holds true for the cases focused on issues of who should and who should not be ordained.

The challenge, of course, is that people are easily deceived as to the relevance and appropriateness of a particular distinction. For now, it is sufficient to recognize that the dichotomizing of diversity and unity makes it too easy for people to rule out diversity by imposing a particular unity, to enforce unity by admitting only people of one group to ordination or conference membership, to appeal to the traditions or laws of the past to reinforce the unity, or to deplore diversity as chaotic and destructive of the church. With that awareness we move to the next section of this essay, where I will explore Wesley's affirmation of the central Christian conviction of God's tri-unity in relation to a covenantal understanding of the church—an understanding that holds promise for helping us to move beyond dichotomized community.

Trinity and Covenant in Wesley's Theology

The affirmation of God as Three-in-One has been valued through the history of the church, both for how it holds together the fullness of the distinctive persona of God with the unity of God, and for its correlated implication of unity within diversity in Christian community. This affirmation was also important to John Wesley, appearing at a variety of critical junctures in his thought and ministry (though usually more implicitly than explicitly). For example, Wesley described three things as essential to Christian baptism—an episcopal administrator, the application of water, and administration in the name of the Trinity.[28] In the same setting he defined baptism as "the initiatory sacrament which enters us into covenant with God," a means by which people enter into the new covenant, into the church, into a relationship with God as children and heirs of the kingdom of heaven.[29] Here he was making an implicit link between the community that exists within God and the covenantal relationship that should exist between people and God.

Though this link between a trinitarian view of God and a covenantal view of the church was only implicit, it became somewhat more visible when Wesley argued for the value of multiple forms and locations for the church. He drew parallels between the early church after Pentecost, which soon needed more than one meeting place, and the Church of England in his day, which needed more than one kind of meeting place.[30] Yet he also affirmed the oneness of the catholic church, grounded in "one Spirit, one Lord, one faith, one baptism, one God and Father of all." He recognized that, while churches are diverse according to location or nationality, they are all part of the universal Church.[31] They are bound together by the one God, who is identified in three ways: one Spirit, one Lord, and one God and Father of all.

The possibility of unity in diversity is emphasized as well in Wesley's description of a "true Protestant" (in his "Letter to a Roman Catholic"). He described the beliefs of a true Protestant as centered on one God, who is "Father of all things"; Jesus of Nazareth, who is "Savior of the world"; and "the infinite and eternal Spirit of God, equal with the Father and the Son."[32] The significance of this is not only Wesley's summary of basic Protestant beliefs, but his desire to make the connection clear between Protestant and Roman Catholic faith. Wesley was again affirming the oneness and universality of the

Christian Church, while recognizing the diversity.[33] Of particular interest is that he chose to focus so directly on the Trinity, again pairing trinitarian themes with those of unity in the church.

How did Wesley's trinitarian convictions relate with his beliefs about, structures for, and practices of ministry? To answer this question, one has to move around in early Wesleyan sources and note the interweaving of themes. Certainly John and Charles Wesley, with their colleagues, established a movement structured in a communal way with interlocking societies, classes, and bands, each with distinctive and complementary functions. In seeking to support inward and outward holiness, these groups were focused on the covenantal relationship with God and one another. People in classes, for example, pledged to meet weekly and to follow certain disciplines with one another in order to support the holiness of each and all. Thus, Wesley's writing about the oneness of the church was embodied in the organization that he and others put into place.

Further, while John Wesley recognized the oneness of God and the universality of the Church, he also emphasized the multiplicity of the means of grace and the importance of participating in them. At times he identified the means of grace as prayer, searching the Scriptures, and receiving the Lord's Supper, these being "ordained of God, as the ordinary channels of conveying His grace to the souls of men."[34] Elsewhere, he included church attendance, communicating, fasting, private prayer, and reading Scripture as means of grace, adding a further note about the importance of doing all the temporal good one can and endeavoring to do spiritual good.[35] In every context Wesley emphasized that these practices do not save of themselves, but have the purpose of renewing people's souls in "righteousness and true holiness."[36] If one considers the early Methodist organizational structures alongside his teachings on the means of grace, it is clear that Wesley was cognizant of the importance of communal church structures and diverse church practices. In both cases, the many are held together as one. The many persons and groups within the church are held together in the one universal church, and the many ways of participating in the means of grace are all commanded and used for good by the one gracious God.

Thus far I have suggested that John Wesley held together unity and diversity, and did not participate in the dichotomizing tendencies that were described in the previous section. This is true in many ways, but not in others. The issues were complex in the early

Wesleyan movement, as they are today. Considering just one complexity in Wesley's case can serve to point to some of the messy realities. In 1755 Wesley presented a statement to the Methodist Conference entitled "Ought We to Separate from the Church of England?" In this statement he explained in painstaking detail why the Methodists should *not* separate, beginning with the affirmation that a Church "is a congregation or company of faithful [i.e., believing] people, in which the pure Word of God is preached and the Sacraments duly administered."[37] From this foundation, Wesley addressed item after item (presumably objections that had been raised by people in his movement) and explained that it would be neither expedient nor lawful to separate from the church on these matters. His stated desire to maintain unity is clear throughout. However, his specific actions were not always compatible with unity, nor were they always consistent with his explanations.

One of the most controversial actions from the perspective of the Church of England was Wesley's appointment of (uncertified) people to preach. Wesley's justification for this practice was to invoke God's preemptive appointment: God already appointed you [lay preachers] in your preaching, so when we discerned *God's* appointment, "we permitted you to act in connexion with us."[38] On the other hand, Wesley declared that these appointments did not include allowance for the preachers to administer the sacraments because the ministry of preachers (prophets) is distinct from the ministry of priests and these should not be conflated or confused.[39] For this reason, Wesley had no intention in 1755 of ever ordaining anyone to the priestly, sacramental ministry. Almost thirty years later however, he did exactly that; he ordained Thomas Coke and two other men for the church in the United States. Although Wesley anguished about this decision, he made it because he believed that the action accorded with God's will. Under this same conviction, he ordained a few others in succeeding years, even ordaining three for the Methodist movement in Britain.[40]

In reflecting on this striking departure from his earlier stance, Frank Baker explains that Wesley generally claimed to follow two principles in relating with the Church of England: "to stay as close as possible to her doctrines and discipline and worship, but to make variations in these whenever and wherever this was demanded by the peculiar work of God to which he was called."[41] Here we see a pattern that characterized so much of Wesley's ministry. He sought to follow the law as far as one could without violating the will of God, to seek God's will in Scripture and in the necessities of the present situation, and to be concerned always for the salvation of souls and the holiness and righteousness of his people.

Whatever his variations on specific issues, Wesley clearly wove the themes of Trinity and covenant throughout his theology and ecclesial practice. Further, the two themes were frequently engaged in interplay, both implicitly and explicitly. This pattern is worthy of further exploration, but the present exploration is best concluded with John Wesley's own dying words: "To the Father, Son, and Holy Ghost, Who sweetly all agree."[42]

Trinity and Covenant in Contemporary United Methodism

If Wesley offers resources for rethinking the dichotomized patterns of ministry characteristic of the earlier history of the UMC, are there any signs of receptivity to these resources?

The denomination is clearly in a good position to hear and appreciate the covenantal emphasis on unity in diversity. The UMC is more active in its global interaction than ever before, and also more aware of the distinctiveness of each part of the connection. The reality of difference is often made painfully clear as parts of the church in different parts of the world or in different racial communities divide on critical issues, or when decisions regarding mission and ministry are difficult to negotiate across the diverse contexts of the church. The UMC faces both internal and external pressures. At the same time, it is stirring with a strong yearning to be engaged in mission—in the work of God.[43] This yearning is so strong that unprecedented moves were made at the 1996 General Conference to create more flexibility in church structures, so that mission can be maximized in each local church and in the whole denomination.[44]

Beyond this general openness, I would highlight three specific elements in the current UMC *Book of Discipline* which echo the trinitarian and covenantal themes of unity-in-diversity that we noted in Wesley. The first echo is in the formal theological statement of the denomination, which begins with these words: "United Methodists profess the historic Christian faith in God, incarnate in Jesus Christ for our salvation and ever at work in human history in the Holy Spirit."[45] This statement proceeds to describe the theological task as both critical and constructive, individual and communal, contextual and incarnational, practical and ecumenical. The sources and criteria for faith are identified as Scripture, tradition, experience, and reason.[46] These Disciplinary statements are necessarily broad, but they reveal the central affirmation of God as triune, and they suggest the possibility of engaging in theology in integrative, nondichotomous ways—such that many perspectives, sources, and contrasts are taken into account in the process of discerning the work of God.

A second echo can be found in the Disciplinary account of baptism. In 1996 the UMC adopted "By Water and the Spirit" as a defining document on baptism. Importantly, two statements in the conclusion of this document highlight the connection with the UMC's corresponding reflections on ministry:

> Through baptism we are incorporated into the ongoing history of Christ's mission. . . . Baptism is an expression of God's love for the world, and the effects of baptism also express God's grace. As baptized people of God, we therefore respond with praise and thanksgiving, praying that God's will be done in our own lives. . . .[47]

In the first statement the accent is on the community's participation in Christ's mission, and the role of baptism in incorporating people into that community. In the second statement the accent is on the love and grace of God available to all, and the role of baptism in embracing and celebrating that love and grace. The unifying theme throughout is that baptism is an expression of *God's* love and grace, a covenantal act through which people enter into a covenantal community, a redemptive act, and an expression of God's love for the whole world.[48] The parallels in these affirmations with what we noted earlier in Wesley are striking.

This leads to the third echo, expressed in the Disciplinary statements on ministry. The Study of Ministry that was presented to the 1996 General Conference by the UMC Council of Bishops had as its central theme: "the ministry of all Christians expressed through God's mission to the world through the church."[49] Those words are echoed in the baptism study and in the ministry legislation that passed General Conference and now forms the sections of the *Book of Discipline* entitled "The Ministry of All Christians" and "The Ministry of the Ordained." For example, the former section begins with a pronouncement of covenant:

> From the beginning, God has dealt with the human family through covenants: with Adam and Eve, Noah, Abraham, Sarah and Hagar. . .

In the new covenant in Christ, yet another community of hope was called out and gathered up. . . . Our spiritual forebears stressed this biblical theme of covenant-making and covenant-keeping as central in Christian experience.[50]

Thus, the ministry of all Christians is grounded in God's covenantal intentions, expressed through the diverse gifts of the people, and expressed uniquely through the connectionalism of the UMC. Those who are called to the ordained ministry of deacon or elder are charged to "exercise their ministry in covenant with all Christians." They are further instructed to "live in covenant of mutual care and accountability with all those who share their ordination, . . . with the ordained who are members of the same annual conference and part of the same Order."[51] In other words, their covenantal relationship is first with the whole Body of Christ, and then specifically with the ordained of their annual conference and with those of their particular Order.

The point I would emphasize is that the new Disciplinary statements on baptism and ministry both carefully avoid dichotomizing laity and clergy. They exude instead a hope for covenantal relationship as people engage in the shared mission of serving God in the world. The covenantal inheritance is a gift of God the Creator, or Father; the shared mission is the mission of Christ, and the power to serve is a work of God's Spirit. Thus, the very grounding for the covenant is the work of the triune God—the God who is both Three and One.

Conclusion

This consideration of recent statements added to the UMC *Book of Discipline* suggests that some movement has been made toward the goal set forth at the outset of this essay—to develop an understanding and practice of ministry that is based on covenantal community rather than on dichotomy and hierarchy, and on a diversity of forms and functions within a unity of mission. This movement has not come easily. Through nearly fifty years of study committees, the UMC and its predecessor bodies have wrestled with diverse perspectives, seeking (in the true Wesleyan spirit) practical solutions under the pressures of ecclesial decision making. Two weaknesses are evident in much of this struggling: a lack of consciousness of the *complementary* relationship between diversity and unity, and a lack of sustained reflection on the nature of God (as Trinity) and the God-human relationship (as covenant) as theological ground for understanding ministry.

Although recent work on ministry in the UMC represents significant movement on both of these counts, three challenges persist. The first challenge is to discern and celebrate more explicitly the lively stream of trinitarian and covenantal theology in the Wesleyan theological tradition. The second challenge is to embody that tradition ever more fully in our theological reflection and ministerial practice. The third challenge is to resist the forces of dichotomous thinking by reflecting critically on our own words and actions, and by praying without ceasing that the covenant God has promised will finally be realized.

CHAPTER 10

Can Wesley Be Read in Spanish?

Justo L. González

For the last few years, I have been serving as General Editor of a Spanish translation of Wesley. At present, six volumes have been published; and when the project is completed it will consist of fourteen volumes of Wesley's writings, most of which have never before been available in Spanish translation. Yet this effort to make Wesley speak in Spanish, as any other project of translation, involves more than a mere transposition of language codes, substituting each word in a language for its equivalent in another. Language, as we all know, is much more than a means of communication. It is also, among other things, a conveyor and a shaper of culture. Language reflects the time and the situation in which it was written or spoken. It carries with it implicit presuppositions, values, and perspectives. Thus, a perfect translation is impossible; as the Italians have appropriately put it, *traduttore, traditore*—every translator is also a traitor.

In the case of Wesley, even apart from the technicalities of how to translate this phrase or that, the very notion of translating his works immediately poses the question of the relevance of Wesley for the Spanish-speaking world of the twenty-first century. How relevant can an eighteenth-century Englishman be for Latinas and Latinos in the twenty-first century?

If nothing else, the relevance of Wesley for the Spanish-speaking world of today is established by the sheer number of those who today are his spiritual heirs in Latin America, in Spain, in Equatorial Africa, and among Latinos and Latinas in the United States. Even without a careful counting, one can venture to say that such heirs of Wesley— *wesleyanos* of all brands and denominations—can now be counted by the tens of millions. Many of them may not even know that they are *wesleyanos*; but the stamp of Wesley can be seen in their theology, in their worship, and most clearly in their piety.

161

Thus, it is undeniable that Wesley's theology and spirituality had a significant impact upon later Hispanic culture. But did this interaction go back in at least some incipient ways to Wesley himself? And was it a two-way interaction—was Wesley's theology and spirituality itself affected by his contacts with Hispanic culture? I wish to address these questions as a way of continuing the dialogue initiated twenty years ago at the Oxford Institute under the direction of Ted Runyon.[1]

I will begin at the level of simple linguistic interaction. Wesley began studying Spanish while he was still in Georgia.[2] In his diary for June 28, 1736, he notes that he began this study in order to be able to speak directly with the native inhabitants of Georgia, some of whom had learned Spanish from missionaries, explorers, and colonizers.[3] Some were also descendants of the Spanish, such as the mestizo of a native mother and a Spanish father whom he taught in a plantation on May 27, 1737. Oddly, in his published *Journal* for April 4, 1737, he tells a slightly different story: "I began learning Spanish in order to converse with my Jewish parishioners, some of whom seem nearer the mind of Christ than many of those who call him Lord."[4] Most likely, he studied Spanish with both purposes in mind, as well as simply because he was always fascinated with languages.

Even though part of Wesley's purpose in studying Spanish may have been to be able to converse with the natives of Georgia, he was never able to devote much time to this, for the colonial authorities expected him to serve more as a chaplain to the settlers than as a missionary to the natives. Thus, most of his contacts with Spanish during this time, besides the books that he read and to which we shall return, was through the fairly large Sephardic Jewish community in Georgia. It was one of these, Dr. Moisés Núñez, who gave him Hebrew lessons, in exchange for Wesley's English lessons to his daughter.

As is commonly known, Wesley's fascination with languages led him to write simple grammars for English, French, Latin, Greek, and Hebrew. Although he never wrote a Spanish grammar, he repeatedly spoke with appreciation for the language. On October 11, 1756, after reading Voltaire's *Henriade*, he showed both his anti-French and anti-Scottish prejudices by writing in his *Journal*: "I read over a curiosity indeed, a French heroic poem—Voltaire's *Henriade*. He is a very lively writer, of a fine imagination, and allowed, I suppose, by all competent judges, to be a perfect master of the French language. And by him I was more than ever convinced that the French is the poorest, meanest language in Europe; that it is no more comparable to the German or Spanish than a bag-pipe is to an organ."[5]

Although Wesley continued reading Spanish throughout his life, he apparently never became fluent in it, and soon lost its oral use. That may be the reason why he never wrote a Spanish grammar. In any case, by 1762 it is clear that he could no longer use the language in conversation. In December of that year, at the request of Mr. Maxfield, Wesley baptized two foreigners, one of them dressed as a Turk, and both claiming to be Turks. After the event, for reasons that he does not record, he began having doubts about the supposed "Turks." Since the Turks knew Spanish, Wesley asked a Sephardic Jew to serve as an interpreter as he interviewed them. As is the case so often in his *Journals*, we are not told the outcome of the conversation. But the incident does show that by this time Wesley did not trust his own Spanish sufficiently to interview the "Turks" directly.[6]

Whatever level of fluency Wesley may have had, the significant point is to note how his reading of Spanish writers may have influenced the development of his own convictions on spirituality and theology. This is easy to trace, because the main use that Wesley made of his Spanish was in his religious readings, especially those of the mystics. It was precisely at the time that he was beginning to study Spanish that he became deeply interested in the teachings of Miguel de Molinos—so interested that, just a few days after he began to study Spanish, he translated a mystical poem attributed to Molinos.

Miguel de Molinos was a mystical Spanish teacher who lived some one hundred years before Wesley. His most famous book was *Guía espiritual que desembaraza el alma y la conduce al interior camino para alcanzar la perfecta contemplación*, published in 1665. In six years, the book had seen twenty editions in various European languages. The English edition appeared in 1688 under the title *The Spiritual Guide Which Disentangles the Soul*, and this was probably what Wesley read almost half a century later in 1736. What Molinos taught was essentially an absolute quietism. The soul can do nothing to approach God. All it can do is remain for hours in "mute prayer," in which there are no words, either spoken or silent, but simply an openness that allows God to write on the soul as on a blank sheet of paper. Not even holiness is to be sought, for such active seeking hinders the soul's passivity before God.

One of the foremost Spanish historians of heterodoxy has summarized Molinos' teachings as follows:

The soul will never attain to inner peace unless God purify it first. Spiritual exercises and punishments of the flesh do not lead to that end. The soul's duty is simply to do nothing *proprio motu*, but rather to subject itself to whatever God wishes to impose on it. The spirit must be as a blank sheet of paper, where God can write whatever God wills. It must spend long hours in mute prayer, in humility and submission, without doing, without knowing, without trying to understand anything.[7]

Eventually, Molinos followed these doctrines to their ultimate conclusion, claiming that the passivity of the soul is such that, if the body sins because the demon leads it astray, the soul remains pure of such sin. Brought to trial, he confessed that he had erred, and that his doctrines had led him to immorality. He then spent the rest of his days in prison, still pursuing his mystical ways, but now renouncing the extreme consequences of his quietism.[8]

It is not clear that Wesley knew all of this. It was common in Britain to blame the strictures of the Spanish Inquisition for the outcome of Molinos' career, and therefore to discount reports of his downfall as mere machinations of the inquisitors. Wesley certainly knew the *Guía espiritual* as well as a few mystical poems either written by Molinos or attributed to him. Still, quite apart from the judgment of the Inquisition, Wesley soon became critical of the quietism of Molinos, as well as of mysticism in general. It was only a few months after he translated the poem by Molinos that he wrote to his brother Samuel:

> I think the rock on which I had the nearest made shipwreck of the faith was the writings of the mystics, under which term I comprehend all, and only those, who slight any of the means of grace.
>
> I have drawn up a short scheme of their doctrines, partly from conversations I have had, and letters, and partly from their most approved writers, such as Tauler, Molinos, and the author of *Theologia Germanica*. I beg your thoughts upon it, as soon as you can conveniently.[9]

Typically, in spite of his very negative attitude towards mysticism in general, when Wesley compiled his fifty-volume *Christian Library*, in which he selected what he considered the best available works in English on "practical divinity," he included part of the *Guía espiritual* of Molinos.[10]

The other Spanish author that made a lasting impression on Wesley was Gregorio López, who lived a century before Molinos (and two centuries before Wesley), for he was born in Madrid in 1542 and died in Mexico in 1596. There is considerable mystery and legend surrounding the person of Gregorio López. Some claim that he was actually Don Carlos, the son of Philip II, who supposedly died in prison after being tried by the Inquisition on charges that are still unclear. (Philip never explained why he had ordered his son arrested, except perhaps to the Pope in a letter that has not been found. He repeatedly declared that as a father he was sorry to have had to do this, but as a king and a Christian he had no other alternative. Rumors abounded: the prince was too fond of his stepmother; he had conspired with the Dutch against his father; he had planned to take over the throne; he had been won by heretical doctrines. At any rate, he was declared to have died in prison, and to have been quietly buried. Soon after these events many doubted that he was indeed dead.) According to a fairly common rumor, Don Carlos saved his life by promising that he would disappear, go to the New World, and take a new identity.

Joining the mysterious rumors about Don Carlos with the equally mysterious origins of Gregorio López, the notion soon began to circulate that the two were one. Several factors can be cited in favor of this theory. López never spoke or wrote of his life before coming to Mexico. The date of birth which he gave, 1542, was also the date of birth of Don Carlos. And López arrived in Mexico shortly after Don Carlos disappeared from sight. Finally, some see common physiognomic traits in portraits of Philip II and Gregory López.

What is clear is that Gregorio López, whatever his origin, served as an amanuensis in Mexico City for two years, and that then he went north, to the land of the Chichimecas, where he spent the rest of his life in devotion and caring for the sick. It is said that the intensity of his devotion was such that for thirty years he lived constantly with an abiding sense of the presence of God—and that is the reason why Wesley found him so fascinating, as living proof of Christian perfection. His books include, besides several mystical writings, a *Libro de remedios contra enfermedades* (book of remedies for illnesses), and this is another curious point of contact with Wesley, who also wrote such a book.[11] At the time of his death, López already enjoyed the fame of a saint, and this fame was spread by his writings. Both during his life and after his death miracles were attributed to his intervention, and some thirty years after his death King Philip IV took the initial steps towards his official beatification by the Church of Rome—a process that for unknown reasons never came to a decision. (Although never officially canonized or beatified, he is included in Butler's *Lives of Saints*.) Eventually, López was all but forgotten, to the point that it is difficult to find even a mention of his name in some of the most recent and most thorough histories of the Church in Mexico.[12]

Wesley's first contacts with the writings of López are not recorded. In his *Journal* for August 31, 1742, he says: "I read once more the life of that good and wise (though much mistaken) man, Gregory Lopez."[13] (Note that in this case, as in that of Molinos, Wesley shows that he was capable of distinguishing between various aspects of a doctrine, and between doctrine and practice, and to accept some elements of doctrine and practice while rejecting others.) Two years later, writing about an experience of another cleric, he says: "His experience was of a very peculiar kind, much resembling that of Gregory Lopez."[14] And elsewhere he commented: "I dined with some serious persons in a large, stately house, standing on the brow of a delightful hill. In this paradise they live in ease, in honour, and in elegant abundance. And this they call retiring from the world! What would Gregory Lopez have called it?"[15]

Gregorio López came to serve as one of Wesley's prime examples of a person who embodied true religion even though he held erroneous Roman Catholic theological opinions or doctrines.[16] Indeed, López became one of Wesley's favorite exhibits for proving that holiness was achievable in this life and for defining the standard of holiness. For example, when Wesley preached on the occasion of the death of John Fletcher, he said that "for many years I despaired of finding any inhabitant of Great Britain who could stand in any degree of comparison with Gregory Lopez or Monsieur de Renty. But let any impartial person judge if Mr. Fletcher was at all inferior to them!"[17] Likewise, in a letter to Lady Maxwell he tells her that "I want you to be all a Christian—such a Christian as the Marquis de Renty or Gregory Lopez was."[18]

López also served Wesley as an example of a sort of holiness that, in contrast with that of Molinos and others, is exercised in service to others. He reminded a young disciple that López was able to live in holiness in the midst of all his activities, and encouraged her to seek "such an open intercourse with God, such a close, uninterrupted communion with [God], as G. Lopez experienced."[19] When another correspondent mentioned she was considering a life of withdrawal from society, Wesley related to her that when someone came to López seeking holiness in solitude, López recommended that he go live "as a hermit in Mexico [City]."[20]

Even after he left mysticism aside, Wesley continued admiring, studying, and recommending Gregorio López. When he compiled his *Christian Library* of essential books in "practical divinity," he included in the last volume an abridged version of Gregory's *Life*.[21] And in 1780 he republished this life of López in serial form in his *Arminian Magazine*.

Many other references could be used to illustrate the interaction between Wesley and Hispanic culture and traditions. These should suffice to show that the relationship was much more complex than is obvious at first sight. It is not just a matter of the profound inroads that Wesley and the movement which he began have made among Latinas and Latinos. It is also a matter of the impact that persons of Hispanic culture, and stories of the work of such persons among the native peoples of the Americas, made on Wesley.

Thus, in offering to the world a translation of Wesley into Spanish, we are not only opening the way for a greater influence of Wesley among Spanish-speaking people; we are also calling for new research on Wesley himself—research that will lead to a better understanding of Wesley, by clarifying his relationships with persons outside the Anglo-Saxon world with whom he related, either in person or through his readings, and who significantly influenced his thought and piety. It is our hope that this call will be heeded, not only by Hispanic scholars but also by others interested in the life and works of Wesley.

This is in part—but only in part—what I mean by the title of this brief essay, "Can Wesley Be Read in Spanish?"[22] Reading Wesley in Spanish does not mean merely reading him in a Spanish translation—although that certainly may help. It means also reading him in a way that takes into account not only the British, German, and French roots of his piety, but also its Spanish roots—for in this we may find ourselves coheirs of Wesley in unexpected ways. That is what this essay proposes.

Yet, this is only the beginning of reading Wesley in Spanish. We need to read him from the perspective of Latino cultures, traditions, and social locations. We need to read him from a perspective that, rather than denying such realities and their value, affirms them. That is already happening among the millions of persons of Hispanic tradition who are part of the Wesleyan tradition. If this essay shows that there are contacts between Wesley and our culture that stretch far into the past, the existence of those millions of *wesleyanos* shows that such contacts will extend far into the future.

CHAPTER 11

Wesley in Latin America:
A Theological and Historical Reflection

José Míguez Bonino

As a theologian shaped by both the Wesleyan tradition and Latin American Liberation Theology my consuming interest has always been in asking how theological resources might help address the practical realities of human life. On this occasion, in keeping with the trajectory of Ted Runyon's own recent work, I want to explore the relevance of the Wesleyan tradition for a theological understanding of contemporary Latin American religious and social conditions.

A question like this cannot be explored in the abstract. In particular, any appeal to the Wesleyan tradition in the current Latin American setting must take into account the history of how this tradition was introduced and has functioned in this setting. Therefore, I will organize my discussion in three sections: (1) a brief account of how the Wesleyan traditions were introduced into Latin America; (2) an analysis of the specific "readings" of Wesleyan theology that were brought along with these immigrating groups; and (3) a reflection on the relevance of Wesley's own theology for the present Latin American situation.

The Introduction of Wesley to Latin America

As far as I am aware, Wesley never walked south of the English-speaking areas of colonial America. Moreover, I have found no references in his writings to the Latin American countries—perhaps the indexes of the Bicentennial Edition of his works, when they appear, will uncover some unexpected word! Wesley had learned Spanish during his stay in Georgia, from a Sephardic Jewish colony that he visited on the border of Georgia and Florida. There are reminiscences of John of the Cross and Teresa of Avila in some of his writings, although the names are not identified. It seems that he came to know them (particularly Teresa) through brother Molinos of Avila, whom he includes in the *Christian Library* that he prepared for his Methodist people. We know also that he sharply criticized other Spanish (and French and German) mystics for what he saw as their "quietism."[1]

Between 1840 and 1920 however, Wesley was introduced into Latin America through the missionary efforts of the churches that evolved out of the original Wesleyan revival. This immigration took place in three waves.[2]

The first wave came from "mainline" British and North American Methodism, beginning at the opening of the nineteenth century. The earliest arrival was with British settlers (businessmen, ranch or plantation owners, and immigration groups) who obtained permission to practice their religion—naturally, only in the English language—in an otherwise closed Catholic territory. In the second decade of the century, the Methodist Episcopal Church (MEC) in the United States began to send missionaries. Their early efforts were somewhat tentative: to Haiti (1823), Dominican Republic (1834), Uruguay and Argentina (1835), Brazil (1836), and Mexico (1844–45). In the last quarter of the century the pace picked up: Cuba (1873), Panama and Chile (1877), Paraguay and Peru (1886), Bolivia and Venezuela (1890), and Puerto Rico and Costa Rica (1900). By the end of the century the MEC or the (now independent) Methodist Episcopal Church South had established missions in practically all of Latin America.

These early arrivals had to struggle for religious liberty, together with Baptists, Presbyterians, and other mainline Protestant churches. In this effort, they found allies in the new intellectual liberal elites—freemasons, free-thinkers, and positivists. Some of the most outstanding missionaries developed a twofold ministry: an evangelistic mission among the poor (workers and marginal urban and rural populations, "the dust on the surface of society") and an educational and intellectual task among the intelligentsia. The Methodist churches pioneered in the educational task, creating both large, modern schools catering to the children of liberal elites and more modest parish schools serving the poor children of the *barrios*. Social work—hospitals, orphanages, and cooperatives—was also part of their regular program. One result of this educational and social involvement was a socioeconomic mobility that often elevated this first wave into modest middle-class churches. By the 1930s they were well organized and definitely part of the religious establishment.

Today, however, such mainline Methodism represents less than a third of the total Wesleyan family in Latin America. A significant portion of the remaining percentage trace their roots to a second distinct wave of immigration. This second wave was connected to the "holiness movement" that troubled North American Methodism in the second half of the nineteenth century. Out of the tensions created by this movement eventually emerged such holiness denominations as the Wesleyan Methodists, Free Methodists, Church of the Nazarene, Pilgrim Holiness, Church of God (Anderson), Salvation Army, Christian and Missionary Alliance, and several other small churches. Many of these holiness churches already had a missionary presence in Latin America by 1914 and participated in the great Missionary Congress in Panama in 1916. Their evangelistic commitment has helped them become a significant presence, and their theological influence permeates to some extent all Protestant Christianity in Latin America.

The third wave of Wesleyan-influenced churches impacting Latin America began in 1909 in the Methodist church of the port city of Valparaíso in Chile, where a Methodist missionary (Willis Hoover) and his wife received the news, through a missionary in India, about the Pentecostal renewal that had begun three years before in Azusa Street, Los Angeles. Pentecostal manifestations soon appeared in their church. Two years later a baffled and "orderly" Methodist Church expelled the "rebellious" missionary and congregation on charges of being unbiblical, irrational, and decidedly un-Methodist! The resulting *Iglesia Metodista Pentecostal* (Pentecostal Methodist Church) and the closely related *Iglesia Evangélica Pentecostal* (Pentecostal Protestant Church) make up 75 percent of the total Protestant population of Chile today. Indeed, Pentecostalism now accounts for the majority of Protestants throughout Latin America. Woven through this Pentecostal presence is a major strand of Wesleyan influence, although mixed with several other strands.

It is not terribly important to assess the numerical force of Wesleyan churches in Latin America. Those that officially recognize their Wesleyan origin would probably represent 10 to 15 percent of the total Protestant population of the continent. But the influence of the Wesleyan awakenings has penetrated Latin American Protestantism much more broadly than this official presence suggests.

Which Wesley Was Introduced to Latin America?

With some sense of *how* Wesley was brought to Latin America, we are in position to ask *which* Wesley was brought to Latin America. That is, what influences beyond Wesley himself colored the theology, spirituality, social praxis, worship, and missionary zeal of these three waves of immigration? And how Wesleyan were the resulting churches that took root in Latin America? To answer these questions with any degree of precision would require a major ethnographic study, which has not yet been undertaken. Even so, a few general characterizations can be ventured.[3]

To begin with, Latin America clearly received *a mediated Wesley*. It inherited much of the early Methodist evangelistic zeal. It reproduced some of the original organizational features (certainly a very positive stabilizing factor). In some churches it showed an active social concern reminiscent of Wesley. It also received elements of Methodism's original theological heritage. But all of this was *filtered through the American* (i.e., North American) *experience*. More precisely, the Methodism introduced into Latin America was that shaped by the North American "second great awakening" and holiness movement. One of the clearest evidences of this is the typical hymnal of Wesleyan churches in Latin America. A cursory check will show that they are dominated by the "gospel hymns" of British and American revivalism, and rarely contain more than five or six Wesley hymns. (Given the formative influence of regular singing, this is an important indicator indeed!)

The tendencies of Anglo-American revivalism that were conveyed with the founding of Wesleyan traditions in Latin America continued to influence their development, even in Methodist churches who officially adhered to the classical confessional documents (the Articles of Religion, the General Rules, and Wesley's standard sermons). The polemical conditions in which these churches grew—struggling for their right to exist and to evangelize—reinforced the anti-sacramental and anti-liturgical tendencies already present in that revivalist heritage. One can also discern a strong influence on the self-understanding of Wesleyan-related churches in Latin America (perhaps with the exception of churches related to the MEC) of the polarization between evangelism and social concern that came to characterize American evangelicalism by the early twentieth century (in what Moberg has called "the great reversal").[4] To be sure, many churches were helping the poor at a local level, and some created and supported schools and orphanages. But this service was not integrated into their evangelistic and theological self-understanding.

The ability of Wesley's precedent to counter such tendencies was hampered by the fact that his story, his writings, and his theology have been largely absent from Latin American Wesleyanism. Only the fifty-two "standard" sermons and a few scattered writings have been translated into Spanish, and books on his life and thought numbered less than a dozen until very recently. In fact, one could say that Wesley has been sequestered—albeit probably unconsciously. This situation was ironically demonstrated at recent workshops that the Latin American Council of Churches (CLAI) organized in Peru, Bolivia, and Chile for ministers of churches of Wesleyan origin—including Methodists, Nazarenes, Pilgrim Holiness, Salvation Army, and Wesleyan Pentecostals. The pastors, many of them from rural and small village congregations, were introduced to a wide variety of Wesley's writings. Their interest in these works was intense. They felt a sense of familiarity with them, but it was a spontaneous response that did not come so much from their prior theological education as from the natural connection they found Wesley making with their own everyday pastoral experience.

As with all generalizations, there are some counter examples to the points that I have made so far. In fact, there is a great diversity in the Latin American Wesleyan family. In some cases the response to specific challenges has resulted in new initiatives that have a certain flavor of early Wesleyan practice (though the persons involved are typically unaware of the similarity). One example would be the Church of the Pilgrims in Peru which, under the crisis of poverty in the 1920s and 1930s and the crisis of violence in the 1970s and 1980s, developed local leadership in small towns and villages that is now widely recognized as the main religious and social reference point for the people of the area. Another example are the Chilean Wesleyan Pentecostal churches, who have strongly engaged their culture—in song, methods of expansion, language, and so on—while retaining the connexional organization, ministerial order, and the sacramental life (including infant baptism) of the Methodist tradition. And one could note how the Methodist churches in Argentina, Brazil, Mexico, and Uruguay have joined efforts in CIEMAL (Latin American Council of Methodist Churches) to develop graduate and postgraduate

Methodist or ecumenical seminaries, to launch publishing houses, to support urban ministry, and to articulate—in different ways and contexts—a theology of participation in public life, which they defend as part of their Wesleyan heritage.

On the whole, despite such scattered counter examples, Wesleyanism (and the broader Protestant community) in Latin America has suffered from the impact of Anglo-American revivalism. This is particularly true in the area of theology. What should be a Christological concentration has become instead a *reductionism* in which God the Father frequently appears only as a deistic starter of the world or as a character in an Anselmian-controlled drama of redemption. Christ the Logos, through whom all things were created, and Christ the Lord, the risen One who has defeated the powers and principalities, is given little role in informing or broadening the understanding of what it means to "be saved." Christology is reduced to an individualistic soteriology, and the Holy Spirit is restricted to the subjective experience of conversion and individual (frequently moralistic) sanctification. To be sure, the life of Protestant Christians and churches is much richer than this picture—their love, service, evangelistic passion, and compassion far exceed the limitations of their theology. But this very fact introduces ambiguities and contradictions which are clearly visible, and which seriously impair their mission and testimony in these lands.

The Potential Contribution of Wesley's Theology to Latin America Today

Given the way that the *mediated* forms of Wesleyanism contributed to creating these ambiguities and contradictions, one might expect little interest in turning to Wesley's theology and ministry for help in now overcoming them. Yet there has been noticeable new interest in Wesley in Latin America, not only by his ecclesial descendants, but in the broader Protestant community, and even among Roman Catholic theologians.[5] Somewhat paradoxically, participation in the ecumenical movement has been a positive factor in this development. We have already noticed that it was the ecumenical Latin American Council of Churches that took the initiative in bringing churches of Wesleyan origin together to look at their roots. Likewise, the process that resulted in the autonomy of Latin American Methodist churches in the 1970s, rather than weakening interest in their roots, has freed this interest from purely organizational and legislative concerns, strengthening the consideration of the theological and social richness of the Wesleyan inheritance.

It is in keeping with this new interest that I turn now to reflect on what contribution Wesley's own theology (as contrasted with the *mediated* form with which we are so familiar) might make for the present Latin American situation. But I need to delineate my focus at the outset. On the one hand, I am not interested here in trying to repristinate some real or imagined Wesleyan heritage, lay claim to some private confessional distinctive, or carve out a space in the annals of Latin American Christianity for Wesleyanism. On the other hand, I am not proposing to shape the agenda for Latin American theology by appeal to an eighteenth-century movement, however significant it may have been. That agenda will properly be forged by the testimony and thinking of Latin American Christians and churches as they wrestle with the questions, sufferings, and hopes of the Latin American peoples. If Latin American Protestants (*evangélicos*, as we are called and call ourselves) are to have a place in this agenda, it will be together with other Christians and with the whole of our people. It is precisely in relation to this common task that we can and *must* look at the shortcomings of our own action and thinking, and ponder whether there are any traits and forces in the history that has shaped our identity that might now enrich or correct our participation in this common mission.

This is the sense in which I am raising the question of the potential contribution of Wesley's theology to the present situation in Latin America. I will only be able to offer a few exploratory suggestions of traits in Wesley's theology that I believe hold promise for enriching or redirecting the self-understanding and ministry of Latin American Christians and churches.[6]

A Trinitarian Understanding of Grace

One of the most common charges that critics have made about Latin American approaches to theology is that they are dangerously one-sided. While advocates of these approaches dispute this charge, they do not dispute that misunderstandings and distortions in faith and practice would result from truly one-sided approaches to theology. Indeed, the resolve to do justice to the full range of praxical, theoretical, and spiritual dimensions of human life is at the heart of

175

the Latin American concern for salvation/liberation. The fact that this resolve has often been blunted or obscured in actual presentations of Latin American Liberation Theology has led to a quest for a theological paradigm that might more adequately convey the balance intended. Interestingly, this quest has led to a concentration on trinitarian reflection.[7]

I would suggest that Wesley offers some help in developing this trinitarian paradigm, and bringing greater coherence and wholeness to Latin American theology, particularly in its Protestant forms. His specific contribution lies in his understanding of grace. In their rich and suggestive book on a Wesleyan approach to theology, Walter Klaiber and Manfred Marquardt have called attention to the fact that Wesley's emphasis on prevenient, justifying, and sanctifying grace follows a trinitarian logic.[8] They recognize that, as a whole, the doctrine of the Trinity has played a subordinate role in Methodism; however they argue that Wesley's understanding of God as active, self-giving love leads almost unavoidably to a trinitarian paradigm. They then note how this trinitarian logic becomes more visible in John Wesley's later sermons, and even more apparent in Charles Wesley's hymns.[9] Impetus for, and some guidance in developing, a notion of the trinitarian fullness of grace is a potential contribution of Wesley to contemporary Latin American theology.

Prevenient Grace as Integral to Redemption

The specific notion of prevenient grace is another area where consideration of Wesley may hold promise. This (originally) Augustinian doctrine has drawn the frequent attention of Latin American theologians like Juan Luis Segundo. For Wesley it serves—ironically—as a rebuttal to any interpretation of "total depravity" which seems to leave human beings deprived of all possibility of human freedom, of any spark of good will and human love. Wesley appears to sense that such a view of depravity neither represents human beings as they actually are, nor leaves them the possibility of even hearing God's self-communication. But, unlike other ways of referring to prevenient grace, Wesley wants to see it in the unity of God's loving self-giving to us. He therefore stresses the sometimes underplayed affirmation of the Council of Orange that prevenient grace is "the same grace of redemption," a universal benefit of Christ's atoning work, rather than some pause in original justice, or a piece of "natural goodness" saved from the Fall. I submit that this is not merely a theological trick but a theological way of underlining the necessary unity of God's triune work (*opera trinitatis*)—in which the love of the Father, the presence of "the Lamb slain from the foundation of the world," and the creative Spirit that hovered over the face of the chaos cannot be divided (*indivisa sunt*).

Wesley gives two interesting examples of his use of this doctrine. One is a somewhat romantic view of "the good savage," which experience forced him to correct. The second is his case against slavery, where a deeper insight appears. The rejection of slavery is presented as not merely an ethical question, it is (we would say today) a *status confessionis*: it touches the very heart of faith because slavery denies the freedom—and therefore the God-given possibility—of a human being to make a decision, to assume responsibility, in short to be a human being. When Gustavo Gutiérrez speaks of people who have been reduced to "non-persons" being the focus of God's liberating word, he is speaking the same language.

Wesley himself does not (to my knowledge) refer much to prevenient grace as serving to empower human beings to do the good, however imperfectly and ambiguously. It was the nineteenth-century British Methodist theologian, William B. Pope, who developed this line more coherently. In a carefully woven trinitarian argument (to be sure informed by a pre-Freudian psychology that we could hardly use today) he affirmed human responsibility, building on three theological bases: (1) while sin has distorted and utterly corrupted human existence, it could not reduce us to nonhuman, ethically irresponsible beings; (2) the Holy Spirit brings the universal free grace flowing from Christ's redeeming work (the Atonement) to every human being, restoring to us a sense of moral obligation and a freedom to crave for the good which enables us to act as moral agents; and (3) this "prevenient," "preventive," "initial" or "preliminary" grace tends forward to the realization of full humanity through the free acceptance of sanctifying grace.[10]

Sanctification as Restoration

Sanctification was undoubtedly at the heart of Wesley's entire theology and ministry. My own impression, however, has been that his theological development of the doctrine suffered from serious limitations.[11] It seemed to me that it did not move beyond the area of individual or ecclesial life and, even there, was mostly concerned with individual behavior in everyday private life, as seen from the General Rules. Besides, the meaning of sanctification seemed so exclusively related to the personal soteriological domain that the wider trinitarian dimensions of sanctification in the historical, social, or cultural realm were left out. I was naturally aware that Wesley was deeply concerned with these areas of human life, as his writings abundantly prove. The question was whether he related these concerns to his whole theology, and particularly to his view of sanctification.

The recent work by Klaiber and Marquardt which I mentioned above and a new book by Ted Runyon seriously challenge my earlier interpretation.[12] Runyon in particular argues that Wesley's view of sanctification takes in the whole of "the great salvation" or "the new creation." That is, Runyon suggests that Wesley understood sanctification to include both the full restoration of humanity in the image of God (which involves the totality of human life—spiritual, moral, political, and more) and the restoration of the whole creation (which had been entrusted to human care and disrupted by human sin). On these terms Runyon is able to relate Wesley's emphasis on sanctification to his concrete concern for issues like human rights, poverty and the rights of the poor, the rights of women, environmental stewardship, and ecumenism. Such a reading would also allow Wesley (or later Wesleyans) to open the notion of sanctification to a trinitarian scope, in which creation and eschatology, or christology and pneumatology, could be seen both in their unity and particularity. Scholars will have to debate whether this interpretation of Wesley can be sustained or not. But from the perspective of our Latin American concerns there is no doubt that it offers a particularly fruitful insight.

Christian Obedience as Concrete Action

If indeed Wesley understood sanctification as restoration it would help explain another aspect of his ministry that provides warrant for rethinking some of the models of spirituality and Christian life that were mediated to Latin America. This aspect is Wesley's growing interest in bringing out into the open and denouncing the specific social, political, and even ideological conditions which were producing the contemporary social and economic problems that distorted and thwarted God's design. His interpretation of the causes and cure of poverty, his analysis of the consequences of the laws of enclosure, his discussion of the nature of the slave trade, his subtle denunciations of the causes of war, and even some curiosities like his interest in health and medicine, while limited or inadequate at many points, suggest *a respect for the autonomy of the different spheres of reality.*

Through his example Wesley shows that Christian love cannot remain at the level of generosity or good will when it faces the specific problems of a society; it has to tackle the underlying structural issues. Even the altruistic activities of the Methodist societies needed to be structured and organized in such a way that they did not merely satisfy immediate needs but opened more permanent possibilities and conditions for the beneficiaries of their charity. Similarly, when Latin American theology demands an organic place for social and human sciences in the theological enterprise, it is not merely using an instrument—an "auxiliary discipline" as they used to be called. It is trying to understand the structure of a reality in which God's creation and human sin have intertwined in mechanisms, causalities, possibilities, and impossibilities through which, in the power of the Spirit, Christians and other people can work to restore the design of the Creator, the final goal of the Redeemer.

Christian Life as Synergistic Love

Wesleyan scholarship on the concepts of holiness and perfection has made quite clear that the core of these doctrines was "God's love . . . poured into our hearts through the Holy Spirit that has been given to us." The full recreation of God's image is, in the last resort, for Wesley, nothing but the total control of human intention, purpose, and action by God's love. It is the work of the Holy Spirit and (whether it happens progressively, or suddenly, or both) it is the culmination and perfection of God's redemptive action. "Perfection" is not so much a measure to be filled as a fullness that has no limits. The insistence on "social holiness" or "social Christianity," rather than a sociological conception, is but a way of underlining the centrality of love.

This centrality of love is also at the heart of Latin American Liberation Theology. The "option for the poor" is simply the concrete sign of the universality and intentionality of love. Juan Luis Segundo has made of it what amounts to a confession of faith in the expression: "no action of love is lost in God's world." It is the center of Gutiérrez' spirituality as expressed in *We Drink From Our Own Wells, The Power of the Poor in History,* or *On Job: God-talk and the Suffering of the Innocent.* Even a "hard" theologian like Hugo Assmann will not hesitate to characterize the central concept of faith as praxis as "the personal need to love and to be loved, the giving of one's life for the brothers [and sisters], seen in the wide context of the historical process," or "the new dimension of love in a socialized world."[13]

If sanctification is to be understood as "love poured out into our hearts through the Holy Spirit," i.e., as the very presence of the Holy Spirit (the same Spirit that is active in all of human life as prevenient grace), then human life and action have a "Spirit dimension." Obviously, we have here the old and debated question of synergism. I see little doubt that an assumption of the "incorporation" of the creature in God's acts of liberation—both in the evangelistic call to repentance and conversion and in the liberating acts of justice for the sake of the poor—which is clearly present in Latin American theology, is also central to the Wesleyan perspective. In his article on "Methodism's Theological Heritage," Albert Outler speaks of Wesley's undeniable synergism, which he characterizes as a "covenantal synergism . . . in which both prevenient *and* saving grace are recognized as coordinate providential activities of the one true God of love who, in his love, makes and keeps covenant with faithful [persons]."[14] In a recent dissertation on Liberation Theology, Guillermo Hansen, a young Lutheran theologian, affirms the same point in a very sharply formulated fashion:

> It is in this manner . . . that we reach our final point, namely, that precisely in the enhypostatic nature of Christian praxis, the event of the divine-human "cooperation" coheres, not as a reality pertaining to two causal agential entities involved in a reciprocal-conditional exchange, but as the relationship existing between the hypostatic termini posited by God's decision to be God not without the creatural—i.e. to be triune.[15]

Certainly, this affirmation of synergism needs to be carefully protected by the eschatological proviso: we are not yet at the point where "God is all in all," but in an intermediate time where the human actor still maintains, as Hansen himself says, "the characteristics and constraints of any human witness and praxis (thus always subject to the judgment of God)."

Reclaiming the Christological Balance in Defining Love

The final area where I would suggest that dialogue with Wesley might be fruitful for Latin American Liberation Theology is on the issue of how appeal to Christ serves to define the nature of love. In this case the potential benefit would come in the form of the balance that can derive from dialogue with a contrasting one-sided position. Analyses of Wesley's Christology have generally concurred that the concrete humanity of Christ—the earthly Jesus, as we would put it today—does not play a significant role. One result is that there is little appeal to the earthly Jesus in Wesley's clarifications of the nature of love.

By contrast, in Latin American theology the earthly ministry of Jesus is the paradigm on which both Christology and praxeology (to use Jon Sobrino's expression) are built. For them, love is defined specifically by appeal to Jesus' proclamation and embodiment of the Reign of God—liberating the poor, the oppressed, prisoners, and wounded. On this christological interpretation of love the struggle for justice for the poor is not something secondary to faith and salvation (as a mere consequence of saving faith) but already has, so to speak, "soteriological density."[16]

But the Latin American approach is prone to the opposite weakness of Wesley's Christology. In the justified effort to avoid a dichotomy between faith and social praxis, sacred history and human history, love of God and love of neighbor, they run the risk of blurring the specificity of the Incarnation, the *ephapax* nature of God's intervention in Jesus Christ.

If we treat love simply as an anthropological category, do we not run the danger of losing sight of how God's love incarnate in Jesus Christ serves to define and measure true love? If the emphasis on one single history is not critically confronted with the uniqueness of the Christ event, do not the story of Jesus, the Cross, and the Resurrection become mere models of service, suffering, and hope to be reproduced, rather than a once-for-all event into which we can enter eschatologically through the power of the Spirit? And turning to eschatology, does not the conflictive character of God's action in history tend to be reduced to the progressive—though conflictive—overcoming of structures of injustice and oppression, obscuring the radical nature of "the mystery of evil" to which the apocalyptic tradition bears witness?

Finally, consider the missionary/evangelizing consequences of this imbalance. The one-sided focus on the earthly Jesus has tended to weaken the radicality of the call to conversion: instead of a "turning" or a "new birth," it becomes a growth, a new awareness, or a greater commitment. The specificity of the "personal encounter with Christ"—to use typically evangelical language—is liable to be totally equated with a commitment to the poor and the struggle for justice, with serious loss both for the life of faith and service of the individual Christian and for the community.

Certainly, this criticism does not evacuate the significance of the fundamental affirmation of Liberation Theology concerning the unity of God's action in the world and the understanding of historical liberation as a necessary dimension of salvation. Nor can we forget Gutiérrez' careful qualitative distinction between human achievement and the transcendence of grace. The very life of the thousands of faith communities throughout the continent witnesses to the depth of this spirituality.

But it is important to seek a theological framework in which this foundational element of liberation theology is freed from misunderstanding and deeply rooted in God's self-revelation. A trinitarian basis like that hinted at in Wesley is, in my view, the best protection in this respect.

CHAPTER 12

John Wesley and Revolution: A South African Perspective

Peter Grassow

Over the past five years, South Africa has wrestled with political and social revolution. We have gained a new constitution, a democratically elected parliament, and a respected president in Nelson Mandela. We now have to deal with the realities of the evil generated by our past history—such as has been exposed by the Truth and Reconciliation Commission chaired by Archbishop Desmond Tutu, and is daily being exposed by the rampant crime and corruption prevalent among our citizens. The path ahead will require all of our resources, including religious resources. As a Methodist, this leads me to ponder what my tradition has to offer. In particular, does John Wesley have a political theology that can add insight and direction to the struggle for wholeness in South Africa?

On first consideration, the prospects do not look promising. Wesley's most explicit political writings were opposed to revolutionary political change. As Ted Runyon has summarized: "Wesley assumed that the system was 'justified'—in its basic lineaments capable of being conformed to the will and purpose of God. What remained was 'sanctification', the practice of conformity to that will. Thus the appropriateness of the gradualist, meliorist approach [to political change]."[1] Given this stance, what value is there, apart from academic interest, in taking time out from the struggle to be a Christian in South Africa to investigate the history and traditions of John Wesley?

There is value for South African Methodists, at least, due to the prominent role of Wesley in our theology and practice. If he has a decisive challenge to involvement in revolutionary social and political change, we should hear it. And if his stance is more ambiguous, we deserve to know that as well, because it opens up room for reflection on the most adequate way to be Methodists in our present context. I want to argue precisely that Wesley's stance on the issue of revolutionary change was ambiguous. While there is much in his writings that reflects a conservative orthodoxy, there are also some counter themes that provide the framework for developing a contemporary political theology that can empower the poor and marginalized of our society.

I will develop this case by specific reference to Wesley's response to the American Revolution (or War of Independence). But I must begin by putting this response in larger context—both the larger political context of Wesley's eighteenth-century setting and the larger theological context of relating his convictions concerning political authority and human liberty to his understanding of the relationship between faith and works. After sketching these contexts I will turn to a more detailed consideration of his political praxis in the events of the War of Independence, and ask how these affected his theology after 1764. Finally I will draw together some strands of Wesley's thought that can be useful in framing a political theology for the South African situation.

Wesley's Social and Political Context

John Wesley wrestled with the issues of political and religious authority at a time when John Locke encapsulated the essence of English political ideology. In addition to Locke's advocacy of empiricism and of the necessity of a rational approach to life, his *Treatises on Government* provided the basis for a school of political thought that profoundly influenced American revolutionary thought. This Enlightenment political philosophy held that a republic is necessarily (although often implicitly) based on a contractual agreement with the governed. If this agreement ceases to be honored the republic will descend into corruption and tyranny, becoming a candidate for legitimate revolutionary action by its citizens. The English establishment had drawn upon this line of reasoning to justify the 1688 English Revolution. Less than a hundred years later many in the American colonies were suggesting that it justified revolt against a British government that was oppressively exploiting its colonies.

Wesley's upbringing in the Epworth rectory did not predispose him to share the perspective of the American colonists. It instilled in him an unquestioning loyalty to the English Establishment: "I am a High Churchman, the son of a High Churchman, bred up from my childhood in the highest notions of passive obedience and non-resistance."[2] His mother's puritan piety, which combined an aggressive religion of the will with a disciplined High Church devotionalism, also influenced him away from the exclusive reliance upon the powers of reason that undergirded Enlightenment thinking. His questioning of revolutionary ideology was accentuated in the late 1730s when Wesley came under the influence of the English Moravians, with their strong criticism of *all* human initiative in salvation (or politics!).

However strong one's formative influences, the experiences of life can lead to changes in perspective and commitments. Is there any evidence of such changes in Wesley prior to the American War of Independence? On the specific issue of political liberty there does not seem to have been much change. The 1688 Revolution in Britain had given birth to an undemocratic political dispensation, with its ruling oligarchy resting on the disenfranchisement of the majority of the population, the practice of the "rotten borough" system, and a refusal to grant representation to new manufacturing towns. While Wesley acknowledged all of this, he was convinced that this limited liberty was preferable to the situation before the 1688 Revolution: "We have certainly enjoyed more complete liberty since the Revolution, than England ever enjoyed before; and the English Government, unequal as the representation is, has been admired by all impartial foreigners."[3] Wesley failed to see that only those who enjoy liberty will believe it to exist. Those who lacked political rights were hardly likely to extol the liberty of the English system. His assumption of the admiration of others for English liberty reflected his captivity to the political perspectives of the Establishment.

Not that Wesley was an official representative of the Establishment; he had turned from such official roles to become a persecuted traveling preacher. But the persecution was a fading memory by the time of the emerging conflict in America. He was now the principle organizer of the Methodist movement, which had been meeting in annual conferences for the past twenty years and was rapidly gaining social recognition along with its burgeoning structural discipline. Wesley drew large crowds wherever he spoke, and open air preaching was no longer a "vile novelty" either to him or to his hearers. This would have given Wesley a sense of social acceptability that he had hitherto not experienced, and was probably a major factor in his decision to comment on the economic and political life of the nation in his later years.

Wesley's contacts with his Methodist people also gave him first-hand exposure to the economic conditions of his day. As Eric Hobsbawm notes, Wesley lived at the beginning of an economic crisis which saw "a transition to the era of modern industrial capitalism, to bourgeois society."[4] Hobsbawm suggests that this was not only the beginning of a crisis in which the ties of earlier social and political orders were broken, it was also the beginning of a period of time-saving inventions and new enclosures which uprooted many cottagers from their lands and drove them into squalid factory towns where they constituted a labor supply for the developing industries. In addition to the resulting loss of social cohesion, this gave rise to a developing industrial serfdom and the exploitation of child labor. The developing industrial capitalism created particularly severe hardships for the emerging working classes, who were prominently represented in the Methodist societies that Wesley visited.

Wesley's exposure to the underside of the emerging economic structure eventually led him to criticize elements of the Establishment. For example, he condemned the "enclosing" of farms by wealthy landlords, which he termed "as mischievous a monopoly as was ever introduced into these kingdoms."[5] He also criticized the luxury and waste of "the great, the nobility and gentry," which he suggested caused the increase in rentals and hunger. Finally he was critical of the national debt, which he believed caused "the enormous taxes, which are laid on almost everything that can be named." Wesley argued that the economic hardships of the poor could be lessened by taxing the wealthy, reducing both the national debt and the civil service, and "especially . . . by restraining luxury, which is the grand and general source of want." While his economic analysis may be open to question, and his optimism about change was a little naive, his commitment to the poor is clear and admirable.

By the time of the American Revolution, then, there was an emerging ambivalence in Wesley's political views. On the one hand, he retained the loyalty to the Establishment and the antipathy to human initiative in the process of salvation that had been instilled in earlier years. On the other hand, he had been sensitized to poverty and hardship, and to the discontent that this aroused both in England and in America, and felt an increasing obligation to participate in its solution. While the latter was the chief motivation for developing his political theology, his Tory predilection would prove to determine its content.

Wesley on the Human Role in Salvation

The preceding summary suggested connections between Wesley's developing political theology and his convictions about the human role in salvation. It would be helpful to consider these connections more closely. In particular, it is enlightening to note how some transitions in Wesley's understanding of the nature of salvation are related to his assumptions concerning human involvement in revolutionary political action.

Robert Tuttle has provided a helpful typology for tracing the changes in Wesley's understanding of salvation. He argues that Wesley's assumptions about the role of human faith in the process of salvation underwent a dialectical development: prior to 1738 Wesley reflected the puritan emphasis of his childhood, which assumed humans can initiate faith by their inward and outward works (*thesis*); with the impact of the English Moravians in 1738, Wesley's preaching shifted dramatically to emphasizing that human faith is initiated solely by God's grace (*antithesis*); then, in the mid-1760s his preaching moved to seek a more balanced emphasis on faith initiated by divine grace and confirmed by human works (*synthesis*).[6] I will argue below that the American War of Independence contributed to moving Wesley from *antithesis* to his final *synthesis*. To make this case it is necessary to sketch his views prior to the war in a little more detail, so that they can be compared to his postwar views.

Thesis (pre-1738): The first period of Wesley's life was characterized by two theological imperatives: a radical obedience to God alone, and a commitment to active Christian holiness. Both of these are grounded in his childhood training and underscored by his reading of Jeremy Taylor's *Rules and Exercises of Holy Living and Holy Dying*, which he described as a moment when he understood every area of life as subordinate to the authority of God.[7] His acknowledgment of the sovereignty of God in every area of life provided the foundation to his theological understanding of political authority. At the same time, Taylor's insistence on the responsibility of individuals to use their God-given gifts with the awareness of being in the presence of God persuaded Wesley of the value of human participation within the plans of God.

Antithesis (1738–1764): Wesley's well-known Aldersgate experience is a useful cameo for marking his turn away from Taylor's understanding of obedient service being a correlate to salvation, toward the English Moravian emphasis on salvation *sola fides*. With this appropriation of a radical emphasis on *sola fides*, Wesley verged on excluding human participation from the process of salvation. The political corollary was that social liberation (as an aspect of salvation) was the work of God alone; humans could do no more than trust in the saving power of the divine. When this assumption is correlated with Wesley's tendency in the early years of the Methodist revival to stress the gradual nature of sanctification, little foundation is allowed for justifying or participating in revolutionary political change.[8] If things were wrong with the individual or the society, they would be gradually changed by God's sanctifying influence. Such a view of salvation held little promise for providing a sympathetic hermeneutic with which to respond to the social unrest of England and the American colonies—or for developing a helpful theology for South Africa today.

What Wesley's current (*antithesis*) view of salvation did provide, however, was a foundation for his political theology at the time of the American Revolution. His theology of authority is unchanged—God was still understood to be sovereign. But there was an emerging emphasis being given to the importance of "liberty." Wesley's understanding of salvation as a gift of grace became the theological basis for his understanding of the grace/gift of political freedom.

Wesley and the American Revolutionary War

We have already noted Wesley's ambivalence between criticism of the economic privilege of the ruling classes and loyalty towards the political order of the Establishment. This ambivalence was clearly evident in his initial response to the American discontent. He readily recognized the social problems in both England and America. Indeed, as Ted Runyon notes, his rejection of the common charge that poverty was due simply to the laziness of those affected led him "to oppose new *laissez-faire* economic policies and to call upon the government to return to mercantilist practices, which would assure a more just distribution (e.g., setting the price of bread at a level the poor could afford)."[9]

Wesley also admitted sympathy for the American situation: "I do not defend the measures which have been taken with regard to America; I doubt whether any man can defend them, either on the foot of law, or prudence."[10] What he could not do, however, was make the connection between economic and political structures. For this reason he did not move beyond speaking on behalf of the oppressed, to enabling the oppressed to liberate themselves. Instead he tried to remain neutral.[11] The point came, however, when Wesley discovered events overtaking him, and he was forced to begin defining his political theology—and in the process, to take political sides.

Wesley's political theology can be understood in terms of two major themes: an emphasis on the sovereignty of God, and a concern for the preservation of human freedom. He argued that God, as the giver of all good things, blesses humanity with the gifts of freedom and authority. He defined the gift of human freedom as the rights of the individual "to religion, life, body, and goods."[12] While the freedom of religious belief (which Wesley considered to be an "unalienable right" given by God at the same time as the gift of human understanding) leads this list, it is not defended to the exclusion of the other rights. He was clear to affirm as well the right to "dispose of our lives, persons, and fortunes, according to our own choices, and the laws of our country."[13]

Wesley's limitation of individual freedom by "the laws of our country" is intentional, for he assumed that these laws have divine sanction. He argued that no authority is a law unto itself, but discovers its legitimacy—initially, continually, and ultimately—in the all-powerful and all-knowing God: "Now I cannot but acknowledge, I believe an old book, commonly called the Bible, to be true. Therefore I believe 'there is no power but from God; the powers that be are ordained of God' (Rom. 13:1). There is no subordinate power in any nation, but what is derived from the supreme power therein."[14]

The first gift, God's gift of freedom, is thus to be preserved by the second, God's gift of authority: "There is no supreme power, no power of the sword, of life and death, but what is derived from God, the Sovereign of all."[15] Furthermore, human authority is to be a reflection of the divine, given by God to humanity to represent God on earth: "As [humanity] has the government of the inferior creatures, [humanity] is as it were God's representative on earth. Yet [our]

189

government of [ourselves] by the *freedom of God's will*, has in it more of God's image, than [our] government of the creatures."[16] The task of human authority is to act on behalf of God in the preservation of human freedom. No authority exists by its own merits, but instead is the result of the grace of God.

This emphasis on governments existing by God's permission, and of God's choosing, in order to preserve the people's liberties could be taken in a direction that justifies revolt against governments that do not preserve liberty. However, Wesley took the opposite tack. He stressed that God gives authority to governments, not the people being governed—which undercut the right to popular revolt; and he argued that *true* human liberty is found in obedience to the authority of God and those appointed by God—which made democratic government incompatible with liberty.

Wesley offered practical warrant for his political theology from his own observations of different systems of government. His examination of democracy led him to conclude that it tended to "unhinge all Government, and to plunge every nation into total anarchy."[17] More important, if one's concern is liberty, Wesley argued that experience shows that "the greater the share the people have in government, the less liberty, either civil or religious, does the nation in general enjoy. Accordingly, there is most liberty of all, civil and religious, under a limited monarchy; there is usually less under an aristocracy, and least of all under a democracy."[18] Thus, democratic principles should be rejected as "incompatible . . . with the universal practice of [humankind], as well as with sound reason."[19]

By contrast, Wesley's experience of (constitutional) monarchy under King George was positive. This led him to encourage his fellow citizens to make support for "King George, whom the wise providence of God has appointed to reign over us" a key criterion in deciding whom to elect to parliament, since George had been "a minister of God unto thee for good."[20] Once again we see that Wesley was incapable of recognizing his ideological captivity (the Marxian "false consciousness"), and so he universalized his ruling class values in support of his argument.

Ironically, then, it was his concern for human liberty that prompted Wesley's opposition to the American Revolution. He believed that the colonies enjoyed liberty to the fullness of their wishes and insisted that "none take away their lives, or freedom, or goods; they enjoy them all quiet and undisturbed."[21] He was unable to grasp the exploitation inherent in the economic relationship between England and its colonies, or to come to terms with the American sense of injustice in being taxed without parliamentary representation.

As Wesley had feared, what began as a cry for "the rights of Englishmen" and the redress of their grievances, became a war for American independence. Thus began a six year struggle, with fighting in every colony between people who had formerly been fellow citizens but were now divided into Loyalists and Patriots, English and American. John Wesley found himself trapped between Methodists who supported King George, and those who supported American independence. Throughout this struggle his political theology remained consistent: God was the ultimate authority, and all freedom was a gift given by God alone.

Wesley's belief that the King was appointed by God to preserve human freedom led him to support England's decision for war. His subsequent campaign of preaching and writing emphasized that the one who supported the revolution not only rebelled against the Crown, but against God: "Let us put away our sins! the real ground of all our calamities; which never will or can be thoroughly removed, till we fear God and honour the King!"[22]

For Wesley the correctness of the decision for war was confirmed by the initial English successes subsequent to the general fast called by King George: "There is all reason to believe that God was well pleased with it. We now openly acknowledged him, and he openly acknowledged us."[23] Here we see the unfortunate hermeneutic found wherever religion is used to justify the activities of the powerful.[24] Victory is taken to be a sign of God's support, and conversely defeat as a sign of God's disapproval. Such a theology is starkly imprinted on our South African memory. The alternative hermeneutic would hold that theological justification of oppression by the powerful over the weak, victorious though it may be, is a heresy. This alternative has the warrant of the Biblical revelation of God who is in solidarity with the poor—or alternatively with those who suffer defeat and oppression.[25]

The longer the war continued, the clearer it became that England was losing. This raised the painful question for Wesley of why England had not sustained its initial triumphs. His theology could not admit to anything other than divine sanction for the war, for he had defined the rebellion as against both King and God. Neither could he suppose that God was too weak to prevent English defeat, for this denied God's sovereignty. By the reverse logic, he could not attribute defeat to the superior ability of the Americans, for they were in rebellion against God—and thus powerless. Wesley took the only other option open to him, which was to blame the people of England. He accused them of being "openly and insolently wicked," warning them that "the time is come . . . [for] the windows of heaven to be opened, to rain down judgments on the earth."[26]

This response kept Wesley's understanding of God's sovereignty intact. While it was right that God initially supported the efforts of the English to restore freedom to the American colonies, it was also God's sovereign right to withdraw support from the English because of their sinfulness. What Wesley was unable to even consider was whether King George was right to engage in war in the first place. While he implied that those in authority lose their legitimacy when they were no longer a reflection of the divine, his social perspective effectively silenced this revolutionary potential within his thinking. Instead he supported the political order of the status quo.

Wesley was hard pushed to maintain theological consistency when American independence was granted. He had formerly balanced the authority of God with the divine grace/gift of liberty by appeal to how the English monarch protected liberty. But now King George had lost authority over America. Wesley found his answer:

> As our American brethren are now totally disentangled both from the State, and from the English hierarchy, we dare not entangle them again. They are now at full liberty simply to follow the Scriptures and the primitive church. And we judge it best that they should stand fast in that liberty wherewith God has so strangely made them free.[27]

Herein Wesley's dilemma of the authority of God is resolved: it was God who had given liberty to the Americans. This assumption allowed him to affirm the authority of God over the actions of both the English and the Americans, providing a practical synthesis in his theological relationship with the Americans.

But the ambiguity within Wesley's political thought did not disappear. While he ascribed the new American order to God, Wesley avoided reconciling the democratic ideals of the new American order with his theological legitimation of the monarchy. Wesley would never be a democrat. Although recognized for pioneering lay preaching in his Methodist societies on the basis of the doctrine of the priesthood of all believers, he never allowed Methodists to choose their own leaders. Indeed, the year before his death he insisted that "the people shall have no share in choosing either stewards or leaders among the Methodists. We have not, and never had, any such custom."[28]

The (Partial) Theological Synthesis of the Mature Wesley

Despite his inability to shift political ground, Wesley's theology of salvation did undergo a profound change subsequent to his excursion into American politics—the shift described above by Tuttle as "synthesis." That Wesley was able to change should come as no surprise. Not only should a changed context affect the theology operative within it, but Wesley's doctrine of Christian Perfection provides a hermeneutic that demands change. Wesley, who described Christian Perfection as "the indispensable necessity of having 'the mind which was in Christ', and of 'walking as Christ also walked',"[29] believed perfection to involve salvation from sin and a subsequent growth in holiness as the one purpose of religion.

While the great Protestant watchwords of *sola fides* and *sola Scriptura* remained central to his doctrine of justification, Outler discovers in the sermons of the "mature" (i.e., the "synthesis") Wesley an interpretation of *solus* as "primarily," rather than as "solely" or "exclusively" (the reading during his "antithesis" period). He notes that for the mature Wesley "faith is the primary reality in Christian experience but not its totality."[30] Wesley urged that faith "is only the handmaid of love," and that the goal of the Christian life is holiness, "the fullness of faith," which means the consecration of the whole self to God and the neighbor in love.[31] His concept of holiness changed from an absorption with the mystical to a striving for the realization of the fruits of holiness within this world.

The Wesley of the "synthesis" period thus restored balance to *sola fides* by recovering some of the ideas of his earlier "thesis" days. Richard Heitzenrater notes that Wesley was willing to admit that perhaps his middle views were wrong and that his Oxford days had merit.[32] Wesleyan biographers agree that in his latter years Wesley taught that "faith not properly nourished by its fruits might well prove to be illusory."[33] However this does not mean that Wesley had come to terms with social salvation.

This "mature" Wesley continued to understand salvation in the individualistic terms of the "antithesis" period described above.

Human participation in salvation remained confined to a striving for personal holiness. While Wesley affirmed that "The Gospel of Christ knows . . . no holiness but social holiness,"[34] Runyon points out that this must not be understood to be a holiness committed to changing the social order.[35] Wesley's holiness was social only insofar as it impacted the personal life and relationships of the individual—first of all with God, and then with fellow Christians, friends, and neighbors.

The move from antithesis to synthesis remained incomplete in Wesley's thought and practice in another way as well. While his theological hermeneutic changed to an affirmation of human participation in personal salvation within this life, he never explored the political potential of this change, choosing instead to retain the model of unilateral divine action for the social, economic, and political dimensions of salvation.[36]

Expanding the Limits for the South African Situation

This brings us back to the question posed at the beginning of this essay: Does John Wesley have a political theology that can add insight and direction to the struggle for wholeness in South Africa? Any positive answer to this question will require expanding Wesley's insights beyond the limits he retained. For Wesley was unable to see the political implications of his theological development, and so ended up as one who like a strong rower, "looked one way and rowed another."

For example, while Wesley was concerned about poverty and social injustice, he and the other early Methodist leaders were ill-equipped to analyze or interpret their political or economic situation.[37] Lacking an understanding of the structural causes of injustice, his Tory ideals easily controlled his perspective. Like Wesley, South African Methodists have a sincere concern for the poor. If we are to avoid Wesley's inadequacies we need to develop a rigorous social analysis. At the same time—drawing some precedent from Wesley!—the church needs to geographically relocate its leadership and administrative functions to the areas of the poor (the informal settlements, the shanty towns, the inner-city tenements, and the backyard dwellings), for it is only here that it can develop a perspective that will be liberating for all our people.

A second example would be Wesley's doctrine of salvation. While his own accounts focused largely on the personal dimension, the revolutionary implications of the doctrine began to show through in his opposition to the economic injustices of English society. The teleological nature of Wesley's doctrine of perfection, taken in conjunction with the concept of social holiness, demands that the status quo constantly be called into question. His is not a doctrine that accepts holiness as a theoretical goal, while settling for what is possible within the limitations of society (like Niebuhr's ethic of the impossible possibility[38]); rather, it rests content with nothing less than the goal, and in the process radically challenges every interim-ethic as being inadequate. This bears an affinity with the Barthian ethic of the "positive possibility," and its understanding of God's grace that brings into question all human thought and action. For Methodists (and all others) in South Africa this means that the struggle for human liberty continues, despite the new democratically elected government.

In particular, we can never relax our vigilance over the issues of authority and human liberty. In this regard the emphasis on the authority of God in Wesley's thought has two helpful implications. First, Wesleyan theology challenges the powers that be to recognize their subordinate nature, for all authority is "derived from God, the Sovereign of all." Second, this subordinate authority is legitimate only insofar as it recognizes God's sovereignty in its willingness to reflect God's image. The task of the Christian church is to remind those in authority of their responsibility to act on behalf of God in the preservation of human freedom.

But, finally, the task of the church in the social/political realm goes beyond trying to preserve freedom to seeking to nurture greater justice and wholeness. This means that we will have to move beyond Wesley's limits in his affirmation that "the Gospel of Christ knows . . . no holiness but social holiness," seeking a holiness committed to the social order. Our task as Methodists must be to bring salvation to every aspect of our society. But in this process we have something to learn from the "mature" Wesley's acceptance of faith in others on the basis of the fruits of holiness shown in their lives. This precedent challenges those Methodists in a context of social reconstruction who, while agreeing with the goals of the new government, refuse to share their programs because of theological or ideological differences. We need to recover the Wesleyan conviction that affirms the service of God as a higher priority than ideological unanimity: "If there were a difference of opinion," says Wesley, "where is our religion, if we cannot think and let think?"[39]

CHAPTER 13

Experiencing the Spirit in Wesley and Macarius

Hoo-Jung Lee

In his sermon "The Scripture Way of Salvation" John Wesley used an excerpt from the *Homilies* of Macarius to illustrate a believer's experience in the spiritual journey:

> How exactly did Macarius, fourteen hundred years ago, describe the present experience of the children of God! "The unskilful (or unexperienced), when grace operates, presently imagine they have no more sin. Whereas they that have discretion cannot deny that even we who have the grace of God may be molested again. . . . For we have often had instances of some among the brethren who have experienced such grace as to affirm that they had no sin in them. And yet after all, when they thought themselves entirely freed from it, the corruption that lurked within was stirred up anew, and they were wellnigh burnt up."[1]

This excerpt suggests how Wesley drew upon the wisdom of this spiritual master for guidance in directing the spiritual growth of his Methodist people. These *Homilies* were originally composed as spiritual guides within early Syriac Christian monasticism, and they impressed Wesley with their depth and experiential realism about the life of grace.

Albert Outler has emphasized how Wesley chose to respond to the growing need for doctrinal and spiritual guidance among his Methodist people with "something analogous to a set of Methodist 'Homilies,'" and suggested that "this decision that a cluster of *sermons* might serve as doctrinal standards for a popular movement is a significant revelation of Wesley's self-understanding of his role as spiritual director of 'the people called Methodists'."[2] While Outler's intended analogy was between Wesley's sermons and the Anglican *Book of Homilies*, I would suggest that the purpose of the Macarian *Homilies* (to offer "experienced" spiritual guidance and wisdom) is also reflected in Wesley's decision to circulate his collected sermons among the Methodist societies. Just as Wesley had drawn wisdom from this spiritual master, he drew from him a model of how to share that wisdom with those under his direction.[3]

I want to probe the specific relationship between Wesley and (the one he knew as) Macarius in their understanding of the experience of the Holy Spirit. While they share a conviction of the importance of experiencing the grace of the Spirit, I will argue that Wesley did not mine the full depths of the Syriac Christian tradition embodied in Macarius' *Homilies*. This makes renewed dialogue with this tradition by Wesley's current theological descendants a very desirable agenda. Such dialogue is particularly desirable in the context of emerging postmodern, "global" Christianity. Christians can no longer simply assume the superiority of their received models of spirituality. They must engage more seriously the profound spirituality and virtuous practices of other religions, particularly the Oriental religions.

The goal and result of such engagement need not be an insipid syncretism. Rather, it can serve to help discern authentic enculturations of Christian faith and life in the various world contexts, in part by encouraging us to be instructed and enriched by the ecumenical breadth of the Christian family. To take our specific case, the traditional scholarly reading of Wesley, which accentuates one-sidedly his similarities with the Western Christian traditions, does not speak uniformly to worldwide Methodism. As an Asian Methodist, I find that his voice is heard in a more positive, welcoming way when Wesley is read in the wider context of ecumenical spiritual traditions.

This is what led me to explore Wesley's connections to Macarius, the Syriac Christian. I will first sketch briefly the historical connections that support seeking a creative synthesis of Wesley and Macarius in developing an authentic Wesleyan spirituality. Then I will examine in some detail the understanding of the experience of the Spirit in both Wesley and Macarius. These expositions will uncover the parallels between the two, but they will also highlight areas where Macarius' insights can enrich the spirituality of the worldwide Wesleyan family.

Wesley and Macarius: Toward a Creative Synthesis

Albert Outler has done the most to remind us of Wesley's theological indebtedness to early Eastern Christian writers. It was from these Eastern writers, he insisted, that Wesley derived the distinctive pneumatology that became foundational to his "most distinctive ideas about prevenient grace and human freedom and, most crucially, of his peculiar doctrine of perfection as *teleiosis* (perfecting perfection) rather than *perfectus* (perfected perfection)."[4] In other words, Wesley's Eastern-derived pneumatology enabled him to see sanctification and perfection not as a static state but as a dynamic, growing process that is rooted in the life of the Spirit and aimed at perfect love. The person and work of the Holy Spirit were construed as "God's personal presence in the believer's heart and will, and in the Spirit-filled community and its sacraments." Therefore, Wesley could "think of the Christian believer as indwelt and led by the Spirit within rather than being possessed by the Spirit as if by some irresistible force."[5]

In accounting for these shared themes, Outler suggested that the specific Eastern Christian theologians who were most influential upon Wesley in framing his pneumatology and his central conviction of divine-human participation were Macarius, Gregory of Nyssa, and Ephrem Syrus.[6] His suggestion became the starting point for my doctoral dissertation, which tried to determine more precisely the patristic roots of Wesley's pneumatology and ascetical spirituality.[7] My conclusion was that the Macarian *Homilies* played the most prominent role (even if often implicitly) in shaping these two aspects of Wesley's theology. This conclusion differed somewhat from Outler, because he had supposed that what we have in the Macarian *Homilies* is actually the "slightly filtered" theology of Gregory of Nyssa. Drawing on more recent patristic scholarship, I argued that the *Homilies* are not a second-hand expression of Gregorian Byzantine spirituality but an authentic expression of distinctively Syriac ascetic spirituality. It is in this Syriac tradition that we should see the "real" patristic source for Wesley's pneumatocentric theology and spirituality.[8]

Supposing this connection is true, what is its significance beyond mere historical interest? I believe that it holds promise for helping contemporary Methodists (and the broader Christian family) in our quest for Spirit-filled, life-giving community and spirituality. Ours is an age that values concrete experience more than abstract theories and systems. In this postmodern context, Wesley's emphasis on experiential Christianity and affective spirituality can have a great appeal. Macarius also shows a deep concern with inner subjectivity, stressing the importance of conscious awareness of the Divine Presence. As Kallistos Ware indicates, his Christianity "consists above all in the awakening of our spiritual senses, so that we attain a direct, palpable awareness of God's Holy Spirit dwelling in our hearts."[9] This shared emphasis suggests that a creative synthesis of Wesley and Macarius could be an important resource for spiritual renewal and reawakening in global, ecumenical Christianity.

Of course, if they were in full agreement there would be no need for a synthesis. For all my appreciation of Wesley's emphasis on affective spirituality, I find that he remained too bound by the dominant focus on logic and reason that pervades Western culture (including the Western Christian tradition). In this postmodern context we need a more inclusive model of Christian life that presents it as highly *religious*. We need a model with richer and deeper symbolism, a model that values mysticism as much as it values virtuous, sanctified living. It is precisely at this point that a creative synthesis of the Syriac mysticism of Macarius with Wesley's spirituality of holiness holds the most potential relevance. It can help address the growing yearnings of ecumenical Christianity for more mutual, universal sharing among spiritualities of various forms and traditions.

Wesley on the Experience of the Spirit

Wesley centered his spirituality and theology in the transforming work of the Holy Spirit.[10] God was not an object of philosophical reasoning for him, but the Life-giving Spirit who encounters us, empowers us, and dwells in us. If Jesus Christ is in us, we are experiencing the presence of his Spirit in us. And this presence of the Spirit of Jesus Christ is what enables us to participate in the Divine nature and life—that is, to become true children of God.

Charles Wesley's sermon "Awake, Thou That Sleepest" provides a representative statement on the experience of the Spirit in Wesleyan terms: "Art thou a 'partaker of the divine nature'? Knowest thou not, that 'Christ is in thee, except thou be reprobate'? Knowest thou, that God 'dwelleth in thee, and thou in God, by his Spirit, which He hath given thee'? Knowest thou not that 'thy body is a temple of the Holy Ghost, which thou hast of God'?"[11]

This parallels John Wesley's insistence that the root of religion "lies in the heart, in the inmost soul," and is aimed toward "the union of the soul with God."[12] Charles described this goal of religion as "a participation of the divine nature, the life of God in the soul of man: Christ formed in the heart."[13] And John clarified such participation in the divine nature as "being renewed in the image of God, and having communion with [God], so as to dwell in God and God in you."[14]

Note how prominent the language of "indwelling," "communion," and "participation" is in these accounts. The Wesleys also frequently termed the revivifying work of the Spirit "inspiration," meaning a breathing of God's very being into our hearts, making our life "a habitation of God." Such indwelling or inspiration of the Spirit of God was affirmed to be "the common privilege of all believers, the blessing of the gospel, the unspeakable gift, the universal promise, the criterion of a real Christian."[15] Indeed, denying that believers receive, feel, or are sensible of the Spirit is equated with denying "the whole Scriptures, the whole truth and promise and testimony of God."[16]

It is characteristic of Wesley's pneumatology that grace is considered synonymous with the empowering presence and work of the Spirit. He recognized that grace involves the free pardoning love and unmerited reconciling mercy of God in Jesus Christ which is shed abroad by the Spirit in our heart. But he also identified grace with "that power of God the Holy Ghost which 'worketh in us both to will and to do of his good pleasure'."[17] As Maddox rightly pointed out, Wesley's understanding of the Spirit in this respect is similar to Eastern Orthodoxy, with its emphasis on the enabling, vivifying, and restoring—*therapeutic*—power (energies) of the Spirit. So grace (as the Holy Spirit working in us) can be explained as "the power that enables our recovery of Christ-likeness—an expression of God's renewed presence in our life."[18]

One of the most prominent features of Wesley's pneumatology is his insistence that the Spirit's gracious work in our lives is perceptible. He explained the possibility of such perception with an empiricist account of the *sensus spiritualis*.[19] He suggested that part of the great change that comes with the "new birth" is the impartation to the believer of "spiritual senses" that enable them to be sensible of

Divine Presence. Analogous to physical senses, these spiritual senses become the means to our communion with God and the spiritual world. The one born of the Spirit "is now sensible of God, and he [or she] can now say by sure experience, 'Thou art about my bed, and about my path'; I feel thee in 'all my ways'."[20]

Wesley connected his emphasis on the perceptibility of grace to his affirmation of the *synergy* (or co-operation) of divine grace and human response in work of the Spirit. He was clear that human salvation depends not only on the initiating activity of God but also on the responsive activity of believers. Importantly, his accounts of this cooperation are not merely abstract or intellectual, they render the spiritual life as dynamic reciprocal breathing between God and the believer:

> The Spirit or breath of God is immediately inspired, breathed into the new-born soul; and the same breath which comes from, returns to God. As it is continually received by faith, so it is continually rendered back by love, by prayer, and praise, and thanksgiving—love and praise and prayer being the breath of every soul which is truly born of God.[21]

Note the role of *experiencing* the Spirit's inspiration in this relationship. Only with the experienced action of the Spirit can true divine/human, synergic fellowship and communion exist.

Characteristically, Wesley teamed *action* with *re-action* in describing the divine-human relationship in the spiritual life. He insisted that without continual human re-action our spiritual life cannot be sustained, let alone grow.

> And hence, we may . . . infer the absolute necessity of this re-action of the soul (whatsoever it be called) in order to the continuance of the divine life therein. For it plainly appears God does not continue to act upon the soul unless the soul re-acts upon God. . . . He first loves us, and manifests himself unto us . . . But if we do not then love him who first loved us; . . . his Spirit will not always strive; he will gradually withdraw, and leave us to the darkness of our own hearts. He will not continue to breathe into our soul unless our soul breathes toward him again.[22]

It is in the role of such re-action that Wesley discusses the proper place for fear, humility, and watchfulness in unceasing prayer, as guards against complacency or deception in our gradual progress of sanctification.

Wesley's doctrine of assurance is much more well known than such discussions of fear. He used the terms "witness" and "testimony" for this important aspect of the Spirit's perceptible work. His various claims about assurance over the course of his ministry have occasioned a lot of scholarly debate.[23] I will limit attention to three central aspects of his mature view.

First, the direct witness or testimony of the Holy Spirit was important for Wesley because of the deep, unspeakable *mystery* of the Spirit's workings. He allowed that human language cannot adequately express what the children of God experience. So we might only say that "the testimony of the Spirit is an inward impression on the soul, whereby the Spirit of God directly 'witnesses to my spirit that I am a child of God'."[24] And even in this claim Wesley was not trying to explain the *manner* in which this Divine testimony is manifested to the heart. He was only insisting that there *is* a direct witness and intimate perception of the Spirit's work.[25]

Second, Wesley considered it inadequate to rest our confidence in the Spirit's work merely on reflection or argumentation. This led him to emphasize the priority of the Spirit's act of bearing witness (the "witness of the Spirit") to our response of conscious assurance (the "witness of our spirit"). He often stressed this point in relation to the final goal of Christian experience—the life of holiness: "we must be holy in heart and life before we can be conscious that we are so. But we must love God before we can be holy at all, this being the root of all holiness. Now we cannot love God till we know he loves us."[26] The witness of the Spirit was for Wesley precisely the way we "experience" God's love for us.

Third, Wesley was convinced that love, joy, peace, and the full range of the fruit of the Spirit emerge responsively from our experience of the love of God shed abroad in our hearts by the witness of the Spirit. But he stressed that these fruits are not mere passing emotions, they should become habitual affections and holy tempers. In this connection, he emphasized the need to purify the heart's inordinate affections. Thereby love could become the ruling disposition, directing the whole heart and life of believers.[27]

This takes us from Wesley's stress on the witness of the Spirit to his other well-known emphasis: the centrality of sanctification to the Christian life. The first thing to note in this regard is the realistic, "experienced" wisdom evident in Wesley's mature stress on the gradual process of maturing sanctification. As we observed at the

beginning of this essay, Wesley's mature spiritual guidance acknowledged the remaining presence of sin in believers. While the new birth
bestows true spiritual life, new believers are not altogether cleansed
or sanctified. Their hearts are truly, yet *not entirely* renewed.[28] The
remaining sin, however, no longer has dominion over them. In Wesley's
view, when believers walk after the Spirit and the Spirit dwells in
them, they are delivered from the guilt and power of sin. But the *being*
of sin still exists, and consequently believers feel the flesh lusting
against the Spirit.[29] This means believers will have an inevitable need
for continual repentance and perpetual spiritual growth.

This growth is not something we should (or can) attempt in our
own power. For Wesley, sanctification is instead the real, transforming process of our deepened participation in Divine life, power, and
presence of the Spirit.[30] The Holy Spirit is the immediate cause of our
holiness. Sanctification is the gradual, maturing transformation
"from grace to grace." As Maddox says, Wesley's spirituality of
sanctification stressed the centrality of *gradual growth in grace* to
Christian life.[31] Through the Spirit's gracious workings the inner human is transformed, renewed, and restored to the image and likeness
of God. As was mentioned earlier, this central theme of sanctification in
Wesley is related to the profound theme of deification—*theosis*—in
Eastern orthodox spirituality. Thus Wesley can describe sanctification as the "life of God in the [human] soul, a participation of the
divine nature, the mind that was in Christ, or the renewal of our heart
after the image of [God] who created us."[32]

However, it is important to note that Wesley did not restrict
sanctification to believers' hearts; it should be expressed in their
character and life as well. Out of the holy tempers, dispositions, and
affections of the heart should flow holy actions, which holistically
determine the ethical life-style of true Christians. Virtuous character
and lives of Christ-like holiness were characteristic of genuine Christianity for Wesley. At the center of such lives would be the universal,
disinterested love of God and neighbors.[33] From this center would
flow all right affections and actions which form genuine Christian
character. Since Wesley coupled happiness with virtue, his spirituality of sanctification aimed ultimately at a harmonious, desirable
character which reflects and conforms to the true image of God
manifested in the character of Christ. His vision of true religion can
be summarized as providing for the "gradual, graciously empow-
ered formation of Christ-like character."[34]

Perfection is the dynamic goal (*telos*) of this process of sanctification. Since the main work of the Spirit includes sanctifying and perfecting the creation, Christian perfection cannot be attained without the all-transforming experience of the Holy Spirit. For Wesley, perfection meant above all to be filled with pure, perfect Love of God governing the whole being—heart, character, and life—of the human person. As this holy, pure love increases to the fullest, the contrary affections and sinful passions decrease and are gradually rooted out. Perfection is the dynamic goal in which this fullness of love is attained, we become full of God, wholly directed by love.

As Outler has emphasized, Wesley did not understand perfection in a static sense. Rather, it was a dynamic goal for the ongoing Christian journey of sanctification in our responsive cooperation with Divine empowering grace. Even if the possibility of *entire sanctification* is always there, Wesley was more concerned about *perpetual growth* in grace and love toward the fullness of salvation. Like the Eastern Christian Fathers, Wesley seems to admit the ever-increasing possibilities of infinite love. His statements on sanctification affirm strongly the temporal, human dimension of "not as though I had already attained." And he allows that the perfect can continue to grow in perfection "not only while they are in the body, but to all eternity."[35] On the other side of the coin, Wesley was experientially assured that those who have claimed perfection can fall from their responsive relationship with God, and recover it again.

The core of Wesley's spirituality of perfection lies in purified, perfect love in heart and life. Like early monastic Fathers, Wesley emphasized the purification of heart from all sinful passions by Divine love—*apatheia*. In *The Character of a Methodist* he described a true Methodist as one whose heart was purified throughout by the perfect Love of God.[36] Fixed upon God alone, all of his/her desires are conformed to the will of God. All of God's commandments and the law of Christ—that is love—are wholly kept. After all, Love reigns alone in their lives. Since this love was perfectly manifested by Christ, Wesley described perfection as perfect conformity to and union with the holy Jesus in heart and life. Sanctified throughout by the Spirit, the perfect are to "have 'the mind which was in Christ,' and to 'walk as He walked'; to have all the mind that was in Him, and always to walk as He walked: in other words, to be inwardly and outwardly devoted to God; all devoted in heart and life."[37]

Our consideration of Wesley's emphasis on the renewing impact of experience of the Spirit has focused so far on the renewal of human believers. Present in his writings (most emphatically in his later sermons) is another dimension of this impact, the *renewal of the whole creation*.[38] As Ted Runyon has elaborated, the theme of *new creation* in its holistic scope is one of the most distinctive motifs in Wesley's theology and spirituality.[39] Focused initially in the renewal of persons, this goal-oriented *leit-motif* of new creation is widened to salvation history in the economy of the Trinity. For Wesley, the new creation or grand renovation is not just a restoration of things to their original condition. It produces something far superior to the original creation. Once again, stasis is not the norm! Runyon clarifies that "this is the pattern followed by the Eastern Fathers whom Wesley admired, linking cosmic redemption to human salvation."[40] Thus, the transforming experience of the Spirit for Wesley is to be applied to the whole creation, renewing not only the hearts and lives of persons, but society, history, and the whole created universe.

Spirit-filled Experience in Macarius

There has been active scholarly debate in recent decades over the *Homilies* that Wesley attributed to Macarius, questioning the real identity of the author, his relationship to Gregory of Nyssa, whether he represents Messalianism, and so on.[41] Without going into details, suffice it to say that it is now generally agreed that the milieu presupposed in the *Homilies* is Syriac, even though their language is Greek. Consequently, they contain highly distinctive themes, vocabularies, and imageries that are Syriac. Written out of profound personal experience, the *Homilies* provide an existential, intuitive approach to dealing with concrete spiritual problems encountered in the Christian life. As an experienced spiritual master, the author offers "inspiration and practical advice to particular groups of ascetics; and so the teaching is tailored to their circumstances."[42]

George A. Maloney has argued that the spirituality of Macarius is distinctively *Semitic*, thanks to his Syriac background.[43] This designation is offered in specific contrast to the *Hellenistic* spirituality of the Greek Fathers of Alexandria. Maloney's point is that we find in Macarius not just the characteristic differences of Eastern Christian theology from that of the Western church, but also specific emphases that are distinctive within the Eastern Christian family. In particular, the Semitic influence of his Syriac setting inclined Macarius to stress "the dynamic, the voluntaristic, the existential and psychological, the process of continued growth in the interpersonal relations between God and human beings."[44] Free from polemical philosophical under-pinnings, his spirituality was more oriented towards the holistic understanding of the human person and the Christian life.

Spiritual experience of God for Macarius is placed in the "heart," which is the center and ground of our entire being. In its biblical, comprehensive sense, the heart here means more than mere emo-tions and affections; it is the moral, spiritual core of our whole person, directing and governing all the other organs of the body.[45] There is no dichotomy between head and heart, between soul and body. With this unified understanding of human nature, Macarius stressed "the total encountering in ever-increasing awareness and even 'feeling' of the presence of the Trinity through the power of the Holy Spirit."[46] Through the indwelling grace of the Spirit in our heart, we meet God in our whole person.

Macarius' holistic assumptions about human nature are reflected in the very vocabulary of his writings. Indeed, Columba Stewart has used the distinctiveness of the spiritual vocabulary and metaphors in the *Homilies* to demonstrate their Syriac milieu. Part of his case is the unique Macarian usage of Greek words that are particularly expressive of vivid Christian experience.[47] This is buttressed by the distinctive prominence of metaphors of spiritual experience such as mixing and blending, or being filled with sin or the Spirit.[48] Out of this linguistic inquiry, Macarius emerges as a Syriac spiritual master who emphasized above all direct, personal experience of the Holy Spirit.

Linguistic investigation also reveals that Macarius used the expe-riences of everyday life for symbolic, metaphoric comparison to spiritual experiences. The distinctiveness of this is caught in Vincent Desprez' insistence that "the two worlds of the visible and the invisible according to the Greek tradition, are here brought together by the Syriac sense of symbolism, inspired by the gospel parables."[49] Thus, Macarius was faithful to the Semitic orientation that sees more continuity (than a Hellenistic orientation) between nature and grace, creation and re-creation. He allowed the experience of transforming grace to embrace the whole of reality in a symbolic way.

The direct, conscious experience of God's Holy Spirit is the central theme of the Macarian *Homilies*. Within a paranetic context of a spiritual elder's sayings to his disciples, they describe with the wisdom of experience the reality of the Christian's ascetic struggle between sin and grace. The Christian life is presented as a progressive journey in which the experience of the Spirit and of opposing Evil is quite real. Numerous metaphors and images are used to describe the inexpressible, mystical experience of the Holy Spirit; particularly the language of participation, communion, and indwelling. The goal of Christian life is termed the fullness of the Spirit and complete freedom from evil passions—*apatheia*. By being mingled and drenched with the Spirit, the soul becomes one Spirit and changed into Spirit.[50] This thorough union and communion is described as being made Christ-like, or coming to the perfection of the fullness of Christ.

Macarius also stressed *spiritual sensibility* in relation to the workings of the Spirit. Drawing an analogy with the disciples who journeyed toward Emmaus with the resurrected Savior, he claimed that the experience of the Holy Spirit inflames the heart of the believers and opens their inward, spiritual eyes that they may behold the wonders of God.[51] These eyes are to see Divine beauty and to sense the love of our Lord. Here we find in Macarius a continuity and possible interpenetration between the visible and invisible. The transformed spiritual senses provide the sacramental means to see the eternal through the ordinary.

As a master spiritual director, Macarius was concerned about the experiential progress, growth, or improvement of life in the Spirit.[52] He made clear that such progress involved not only the increase of the Spirit's grace but also responsive human striving for perfection. He placed a particular value on the cooperative human longing, seeking, and desire for holiness: "We must therefore strive, and with the utmost prudence take care to 'work out our salvation with fear and trembling'."[53] God responds with further grace as we show our willingness to grow, and *vice versa*. Our response includes toil and labor, perseverance, and cultivation of virtues in the spiritual combat. We should see trials, suffering, and affliction as given by God for the purpose of furthering our serious pursuit of perfection.[54] And we must be ever aware of the possibility of falling. Reflecting his distinctive conviction about divine-human synergy, Macarius insisted that the Spirit's gracious empowerment is not irresistible.[55] Even the perfect can lose Divine grace and turn to evil; Christian perfection is not absolute and unshakable. So every Christian should take continual care to respond to and work with Divine grace.

The spiritual vision of Christian perfection in the *Homilies* is inseparable from the continual emphasis on life-long progress and growth in grace. For Macarius, the very term "perfection" (*teleios*) connotes maturity or completion. So the "perfect" Christian is the mature spiritual adult—one who, after being born by the Spirit, grew through spiritual responsiveness and discipline into the perfect measure and fullness of our Lord.[56] In the progress of sanctification, believers attain by degrees to the likeness of God envisioned in the true image of Christ, that is the heavenly Adam. This dynamic understanding of perfection reflects the practical, realistic wisdom of the spiritually "experienced." Such experience led Macarius to show special concern "for those who think that they are perfect while in fact sin remains present in their inner selves."[57]

In Macarius' view, the goal of perfection can only be reached by entire liberation from the sinful, inordinate passions or old affections.[58] This desired final freedom is described as *apatheia* (dispassion), and is characterized in terms of the purification/sanctification of the heart, with a resulting release from the tyranny of sin. For Macarius, "*apatheia* or release from sin is the hallmark of the love of God, and makes possible the perfect observance of the commandments."[59] Observance of God's will now comes without strain or effort. This spiritual one (*pneumatikos*) has received the Spirit entirely and perfectly, and has attained perfect rest, tranquility, and peace. Most importantly, *apatheia* has made room for the perfect, pure love of God to rule the heart. But Macarius knew that such perfect love derives itself from our experience of the infinite, inconceivable love, mercy, and compassion of the Holy Trinity.[60] Thus, "if any one comes to perfect love, he is for ever after bound and captivated by *grace*."[61]

As a typical Eastern spiritual writer, Macarius used "deification" (*theosis* or *apotheosis*) to refer to Christian perfection. Drawn from the biblical image of partaking of the Divine nature (2 Peter 1:4), deification (sometimes also translated "divinization") means being entirely transformed into or filled with the Spirit or Godhead.[62] By entering into the Lord, or having Christ dwell in them through the Spirit, believers become true children of God. In some contexts Macarius presents divinization as a recovery of the original pure nature of Adam.[63] This sets the goal of renewal or restoration over against the Fall within the economy of salvation history. Fallen humanity is aimed at the restoration of the lost or wounded image of God. In Macarius' Syriac Christianity the return to Paradise was a characteristic image for this important theme.[64] But drawing on the typology between Adam and Christ (the second Adam), Macarius also argues that Christians—as children of the Spirit—are deemed *greater* than the first Adam. In answer to the question whether the natural concupiscence is rooted out by the coming of the Holy Spirit, Macarius said that "sin is rooted out, and man receives the original formation of Adam in his purity. Through the power of the Spirit, he comes up to the first Adam; yea, is made greater than him."[65] Here we sense the important motif that the new creation is more than a restoration, or a simple return to the starting point.

"New creation" is the goal of all God's gracious work for Macarius.[66] At the human level this involves the renewal of the person in Christ, achieving a transformed humanity far superior to the first Adam.[67] This new creation of humanity was made possible by Christ's "recapitulation" of Adam. In his Incarnation, Christ the true Shepherd and Physician came to reclaim humanity, to heal them, and to make it possible for them to be created anew. As Macarius explains, the actual new creation of humanity in this life is then effected by Christ through the Spirit:

> He that cometh to God, and desires to be the person that *sitteth with Christ upon his throne* ought to come to him upon this very view, that he may be changed from his former state and conversation, . . . For our Lord Jesus Christ came for this very reason, that he might change, and renew, and *create afresh* this soul that had been perverted by vile affections, tempering it with his own Divine Spirit. He came to work a new mind, and a new soul, and new eyes, new ears, a new spiritual tongue; . . . that he might *pour* into them the *new wine*, which is his Spirit.[68]

Macarius embraced a holistic vision of the eschatological transforming experience of the Spirit. His Semitic-influenced anthropology stressed the resurrection of the body. In the last day, we will be reintegrated as whole beings—body and soul—to inherit the eternal glory in God. But the incorruptible glory of the body we will be clothed with is foreshadowed now in the Christian life (a reality expressed typologically by Moses at Mount Sinai and by Jesus Christ in his transfiguration). In the present life true Christians have a foretaste of the future glory in the enlightened experience of the Spirit; in the age to come, the children of the Spirit will be entirely glorified.[69]

Macarius often invoked imagery from nature to depict the new creation. A favorite image was depicting the eschatological experience as something like the springing to life of trees and flowers once winter has passed. He equated the day of resurrection with *Xanthicus* (April), the first month of the Persian/Syrian year. On this day the Spirit of resurrection will pour out life-giving power and joy over the whole creation:

> This brings joy to every creature. It clothes the naked trees; it opens the earth. This produces joy in all animals. It brings mirth to all. This is for Christians *Xanthicus*, the first month, the time of the resurrection in which their bodies will be glorified by means of the light which even now is in them hiddenly, this is the power of the Spirit who will then be their clothing, food, drink, exultation, gladness, peace, adornment, and eternal life. For the Divine Spirit, whom they were considered worthy even now to possess, will then bring about in them every beauty of radiance and heavenly splendor.[70]

In this powerful imagery Macarius makes clear that the resurrection and transfiguration of the whole creation is one of the central messages of Christianity. The experience of the Spirit is destined to transform the whole of reality in its new creation.

Conclusion

The numerous parallels in the understanding of the experience of the Holy Spirit in Wesley and Macarius should be obvious to readers by now. These parallels underscore my contention that Macarius the *Syriac* Father should be regarded as the major patristic source for Wesley's unique understanding in our subject. They also provide warrant for the current attempts to break out of the confines of the Western theology and re-read Wesley as a promising ecumenical theologian. Finally, they set the stage for asking how a creative synthesis of Macarius' spirituality with that of Wesley might provide a helpful resource for global Methodism.

I would suggest three areas where the Syriac emphases of Macarius can enrich current Methodist theology and spirituality. First, his beautiful style of metaphor, symbolism, parables, and stories could serve to help us shift from the dominant focus on the conceptual (even as "plain truth to plain people") to the imaginative and colorful in our theology and spirituality. A more sense-oriented, experiential way of approaching religion is likely to be very desirable in the next era of worldwide Christianity.

Second, the holistic emphasis of Macarius' Semitic orientation provides a helpful corrective to the more dualistic or "spiritualized" understandings of salvation evident in much of the West (including Wesley at times). A theology and spirituality that promises the proleptic, eschatological transformation of the whole creation will be very important to Christians around the world as we face the issues of global ecology.

Finally, Macarius' ascetic spirituality can be instructive to contemporary Methodists. As Ted Campbell rightly suggests, it was the model of spirituality embodied in their actual living out of a virtuous life of Christ-like holiness that Wesley himself primarily valued in Macarius and other ancient monastics.[71] While Wesley adopted some of the ascetic practices involved in Macarius' model, later Methodists have tended to abandon them. As an Asian Methodist, I believe a reappropriation of such practices is quite desirable. The recent flourishing of interreligious dialogues in Asia has given us a new appreciation for the spiritual resources in Christian ascetic/monastic traditions. Macarius offers an attractive model of Christian asceticism as the cultivation of sanctified, Christ-like virtue and character through life-long, religious discipline. It is a model that values the experienced wisdom and discernment of spiritual masters. In an age when too much information and technology flood over humanity, a recovery of deeper dimensions of religious practice and wisdom out of life-long experience in the Spirit could help restore human, spiritual value. I believe Asian Christians will be drawn more and more to something like Macarius' model of spirituality, as they find the inherited Western models inadequate. In today's spiritually impoverished world, there is no greater need that to rediscover together the gospel message of holiness and conformity to the image of Christ.

CHAPTER 14

Reclaiming an Inheritance: Wesley as Theologian in the History of Methodist Theology

Randy L. Maddox

In 1960 Colin Williams published *John Wesley's Theology Today*, which was intended both to provide a much-needed survey of Wesley's theology and to suggest how his theology undergirded Methodism's unique contribution to the ecumenical movement. Harold Bosley's review of this book in the standard journal of theological reflection for the Methodist Church commended Williams for achieving a fine historical study (his first goal), but rejected the assumption behind Williams' second goal. For Bosley, the idea that Methodist pastors or theologians should look *backwards* to Wesley for theological guidance instead of looking to the *present* life of the church and its *future* possibilities was simply preposterous.[1]

This interchange provides a revealing glimpse into the larger setting against which the recent renewed consideration of Wesley by Methodist theologians should be understood. On the one hand it is noteworthy that it took over a century and a half after Wesley's death for a Methodist scholar to provide a fairly comprehensive survey of Wesley's theology. On the other hand it is striking how Bosley—a trained theologian, former seminary dean, and current pastor of a prominent Methodist congregation—scoffed at the suggested relevance of Wesley's theology for contemporary Methodist theological development.

This episode suggests that Wesley's significance *as a theologian* had been receiving little positive attention among his Methodist descendants up to 1960. Broader inspection reveals that this was indeed the case. The purpose of this essay is to sketch some of the evidence of this neglect of Wesley as a theologian and reflect on its causes. Then I will note how this situation has been changing since 1960.

Nineteenth-century Developments

Since John Wesley died in 1791 we can begin with nineteenth-century developments, recognizing that the roots of these trail back into the last decades of the previous century. In this time period it is particularly helpful to frame the investigation with two foci: one focus of interest being the kinds of things that were published specifically about Wesley (i.e., the area of Wesley Studies[2]); the other being how Methodist theologians were interacting with Wesley.

Wesley Studies: Hagiography and Theological Neglect

From the time of his death through the nineteenth century the vast majority of publications dealing with Wesley fit in the category of biography. Far from being detached scholarly accounts, these biographies were typically triumphalist panegyrics and/or defenses of Wesley—offering loving accounts of "Wesley the Dynamic Evangelist," "Wesley the Tireless Church Founder," "Wesley the Pious Christian," and so on. In short, they were hagiography.[3] This is not to say these biographies were devoid of convictions about Wesley as theologian. Quite the contrary! They generally operated with distinctive assumptions about this topic just below the narrative surface (where their particular model of Wesley could exercise powerful influence, without having to be defended).

What kinds of concerns about Wesley as theologian were involved? The most common was the attempt to disassociate Wesley from his Anglican past. This is quite ironic because Wesley had been concerned throughout his ministry to demonstrate that all of his distinctive doctrinal claims were supported in the Anglican standards of doctrine, and he had struggled until near the end of his life to keep Wesleyan Methodists within the Anglican communion. This struggle failed (for a variety of reasons), and shortly after Wesley's death British Methodists followed the earlier example of their American counterparts in separating officially from the Church of England. In publications like these biographies, both groups then began the task of legitimating that move by obscuring the most explicit evidences of Wesley's Anglican loyalties and by stressing those aspects of his life or work that favored the dissenting traditions.

The most glaring example of obscuring Wesley's explicitly Anglican side is Thomas Jackson's omission of Wesley's extract of the *Homilies* of the Church of England from what became the standard edition of Wesley's works. This exclusion is indefensible, given the fact that Wesley published at least twenty editions of the extract during his lifetime and included it in his own edition of collected works in 1771–74.[4] What the exclusion demonstrates is that while Wesley considered the *Homilies* authoritative, Jackson (and most other nineteenth-century Methodists) did not.

Such "de-Anglicanization" is also obvious, if more subtle, in many of the biographies. They provide only cursory treatment of Anglican elements of Wesley's life (such as his ordination), while dealing at length with his contacts with Moravians and other dissenting traditions. They express regret over any censure Wesley might bestow on Lutheran, Calvinist, or mystic writers, while ignoring his frequent defenses of Anglican standards.[5] Most of all, they tend to construe Aldersgate as Wesley's "conversion" *from* high-church bigotry and intolerance, *to* the true (i.e., low-church) faith.[6]

The other major theological trend evident in the nineteenth-century biographies of Wesley was a growing contrast between doctrinal convictions and personal religious experience, with the resulting tendency to portray Wesley as one concerned with experience, *rather than* doctrinal convictions. In other words, the caricatures developed by the least-nuanced participants in the Scholasticism/Pietism debates among Protestants were adopted, and Wesley was portrayed as one who—at Aldersgate—was liberated from dry orthodoxy and discovered that the essence of Christianity was *experience* (as contrasted with church membership, ritualistic observances, or doctrinal convictions).[7] As a result, Wesley's nineteenth-century descendants, becoming ever-more acclimated to the model of him as a warm-hearted (low-church) evangelist, found any reference to Wesley as a theologian to be increasingly foreign and inappropriate.

This helps explain why the only published monographs specifically on Wesley's theology in the nineteenth century were apparently written by non-Methodists! I have been able to locate two such studies. In 1857 Michel Haemmerlin, a Lutheran pastor involved in the *Société évangélique* at Strasbourg, published an *Essai Dogmatique sur John Wesley,* which presented an introductory summary of

Wesley's doctrines (particularly soteriology, but branching wider) as found in his full collected sermons.[8] The other study was more ambitious. Robert Brown, apparently an "evangelical" dissenter, published *John Wesley's Theology* in London in 1865, where he used Wesley's theology as a test case to prove that one could remain within evangelical orthodoxy while embracing the current philosophical focus on conscience as the essence of the human (and thus of religion). In making this case Brown explicitly contrasted Wesley with Protestant Scholasticism. He set this contrast up as a difference between a theology that was based merely on the intellect (Scholasticism) and one that was grounded intuitively in the conscience or human heart (Wesley). He argued that Wesley derived his creed from his experience of conscience—which Brown understood to be an immediate voice of God within us, a faculty *distinct from* our understanding.[9] While this argument recognized the importance of the affections and the presence of ethical/praxis dimensions in Wesley's theology, its near dichotomy between the heart and the mind implied that careful intellectual consideration of doctrines played little role in Wesley's thought. His creed was seen as that of a man of obedience and action, *rather than* education and reflection. Whatever questions one might have about the accuracy of this characterization, the ironic point (given Brown's intention) is that for most Methodist theologians of the time it would only have served to justify further their devaluation of Wesley as a theologian!

Methodist Theology: Increasing Marginalization of Wesley as Theologian

To understand this effect we need to appreciate the changes in the style and self-understanding of Methodist theology as it moved outside the Anglican context of its origin. Due to its unique history of development, the Anglican tradition understood the standard forms and practice of theology differently from their continental counterparts (both Roman Catholic and Protestant). Instead of identifying "serious" theological activity with the production of scholastic summaries/defenses of doctrine, Anglicans followed the example of the early church in focusing this activity on the production of such formative materials as creeds, collections of catechetical homilies, and liturgies. Thus, John Wesley was functioning as a typical serious

216

Anglican "divine" (i.e., a theologian) when he devoted the bulk of his theological activity to these forms.[10]

But as Methodists distanced themselves from their Anglican past their default location became in the midst of continental-based Protestant movements (particularly the Reformed tradition). In this new context they were quickly reminded that they lacked a "real" theology. In one of the most vivid examples, E. P.Humphrey argued that Methodist theology was unworthy of serious consideration because it:

> . . . has yet to be reduced to a systematic and logical form. . . . We have its brief and informal creed in some five and twenty articles; but where is its complete confession of faith, in thirty or forty chapters? . . . Where is its whole body of divinity, from under the hand of a master, sharply defining its terms, accurately stating its belief, laying down the conclusions logically involved therein, trying these conclusions, no less than their premises, by the Word of God, refuting objections, and adjusting all its parts into a consistent and systematical whole?[11]

What Humphrey was here assuming as the standard against which Methodist theology came up short is a scholastic theology—i.e., a textbook that provides a comprehensive and carefully organized survey of a tradition's truth claims, defending any controverted claims polemically, and providing rational grounding for the whole. Rather than taking Wesley's failure to provide such a work as warrant to question the preeminence being given this form of theological activity by their critics, his descendants set out to fill this perceived deficiency in Wesley's bequest.

The first attempt was the 1825 publication of *Wesleyana: A Selection of the Most Important Passages in the Writings of the Late Rev. John Wesley, A.M. Arranged to form a Complete Body of Divinity.*[12] This publication serves well to represent the transition from Wesley being valued *as a theologian* (i.e., as a model of serious theological activity) to him becoming simply a scholastic authority to be quoted on select theological claims.

An after-the-fact collection of excerpts from Wesley could obviously not satisfy the challenge issued by critics like Humphrey. So Wesley's descendants rapidly moved on to producing full-fledged original scholastic theologies. The trailblazer was Richard Watson, who published his multivolume *Theological Institutes* in 1825–28.[13] Several others would broaden and pave the path he blazed through the remainder of the century.[14] Thus, at the same time that Brown was registering a protest (in Wesley's name) against the scholastic style of theology, the majority of Methodist theologians were seeking to "advance" to this style!

But as they advanced, the status of Wesley as a theologian declined yet further. This is because his adequacy as a scholastic source was increasingly called into question. One dimension of the issue of adequacy was comprehensiveness. Since their primary interest in Wesley was his articulation and defense of contested Methodist distinctives, most of which fell in the classic locus of soteriology, Methodist scholastic theologians ended up developing large sections of their theology with little dependence on Wesley. Watson set the precedent for the later scholastic compendiums in referring to Wesley only about a dozen times in his two-volume work, with almost all of these citations confined to the section on soteriology.[15] Thus emerged the common (mis)impression that Wesley's theological concern was limited to a few matters of soteriology.

The second dimension of the issue of Wesley's adequacy as a scholastic source concerned consistency. This dimension came into play precisely in those areas where Wesley was typically cited as an authority in scholastic texts. The best example is the argument over Wesley's teachings on entire sanctification that erupted in nineteenth-century American Methodism.[16] On one side of this debate was a "holiness" camp that consolidated at mid-century, who gathered every instance that they could find where Wesley suggested that entire sanctification was an instantaneous gift available *now* to even the most recent convert. In response, a series of authors demonstrated that there were apparent inconsistencies or temporal transitions in the comments on entire sanctification that Wesley made over the long course of his ministry, and contended that the most balanced reading of Wesley's mature thought would put the emphasis on a slow process of growth toward entire sanctification. These proposals sparked blistering rebuttals that touted Wesley's consistency and intellect over that of the "revisionists."[17] The eventual response of the latter party to such rebuttals was to affirm a general commitment to Wesley while insisting that he was not inerrant. As James Mudge put it, "It is more important to be well-reasoned, self-consistent, and wholly scriptural than to accord in every smallest phrase with Wesley."[18] In other words, Wesley should not be treated as an unquestioned scholastic source even in those limited areas that he frequently addressed.

If Wesley's role was reduced to providing an occasional questionably authoritative dictum within the scholastic theologies that dominated the nineteenth century, it was further marginalized by the Methodist transition to systematic theologies toward the end of the century. This transition took place more rapidly in America (and Germany) than in Britain as the emerging Methodist Episcopal seminaries adopted with little question the fourfold curriculum being championed in the continental European discussion of "theological encyclopedia" (i.e., Biblical Theology, Historical Theology, Systematic Theology, and Practical Theology).[19] This model stressed the need to maintain clear borders between each of the disciplines and tended to call into question the theological nature of the first three disciplines, because theology "proper" was usually equated with Systematics. Thus, the "true" theologian was now the systematic theologian.

It is small wonder that the new Methodist systematic theologians hardly knew what to make of Wesley as a theologian. On the fourfold model most of Wesley's theological productions would fall within the "application" discipline of Practical Theology, which is precisely the realm to which a few restricted his interest and abilities.[20] Others rejected this narrow classification, allowing that Wesley combined aspects of a professional theologian with those of a practical Christian teacher.[21] But this concession only heightened the problem. What serious theologian would overlook these boundaries? And why did Wesley never undertake the central theological task of a Systematic Theology? Some of his academic descendants were inclined to excuse Wesley on the basis of his "misfortune" of training in the methodological backwaters of Anglican theology.[22] Others appealed to a supposed principle of historical development—that revivals of Christian life inevitably focus on immediate ministry, while creative epochs of theological science necessarily follow and consolidate these revivals.[23] In either case, the departure of later Methodist theologians from Wesley's model of theological activity was neatly justified; after all, he had not been a *real* theologian![24]

As most nineteenth-century Methodist theologians lost touch with Wesley's Anglican roots, they also lost their awareness of the early Christian setting of his understanding of Christian life. By default, they found themselves trying to articulate Wesley's distinctive soteriological concerns (responsible grace and therapeutic salvation) within the categories of guilt and merit that had come to dominate later Western theology. This proved to be an impossible blend. The most common result was a shift of emphasis from Divine grace and empowerment to human initiative and ability, with a theology of "gracious ability" being proclaimed in Wesley's name—a theology that he would have rejected vehemently.[25] Thus, the nineteenth-century Methodist neglect (or dismissal!) of Wesley as a model of theological activity eventually resulted in the obscuring of his distinctive theological convictions.

Early Twentieth Century: Wesley as Partisan Theological Hero

With the transition to the twentieth century, biographical and historical studies of Wesley tended to become a little more critical, moving beyond mere pious recountings of the founder's life. Moreover, while remaining largely in-house studies for Wesleyan traditions, they began to view Wesley within the larger context of Christian history. This stage of biographical studies is exemplified by the five-volume work of John S. Simon.[26]

Meanwhile most Methodist academic theologians continued to show little interest in Wesley through the first half of the century.[27] They were more interested in coming to terms with the modern intellectual trends that their predecessors had avoided. For many of them it appears that concern about similarities with Wesley was considered a shackle that had to be broken in order to embrace new theological agendas. Randolph Sinks Foster set the tone when he began a multivolume series of Studies in Theology in 1891 with the vigorous insistence that "We know more today than our fathers a hundred years ago [the year of Wesley's death!]. We have truer beliefs than they had." Predictably, Foster almost never interacts with Wesley in his series.[28] His precedent was widely emulated in twentieth-century Methodist theology.

This backdrop makes the cases where Methodist participants in the various theological agendas of the twentieth century do appeal to Wesley all the more striking. Investigation shows that their appeal was typically limited to claiming Wesleyan warrant for their particular revisionist theological agenda. As one proponent put it, "Back to Wesley is forward into the spirit of what is best in the twentieth century!"[29]

By this claim, Frank Collier was suggesting that Wesley rejected all merely traditional dogma, opting for Scripture, reason, and love (*sic*) as the only standards of truth; and that Wesley viewed Scripture as speaking solely on religious topics, not scientific ones. While this is not a complete misreading of Wesley, it is surely a partial and partisan one. Indeed, Collier epitomizes what must be considered the general tendency of the specific theological studies of Wesley that emerged during this period: the appeal to Wesley as a hero, in defense of one's particular theological agenda.[30]

The first examples of such an appeal to Wesley as partisan theological hero were associated with liberal theological agendas. The move from the "pietist Wesley" common in nineteenth-century studies of Wesley to such a "liberal Wesley" was not as far as it might seem. Indeed, Schleiermacher—the founder of modern liberal theology—had himself come from a pietist background. His primary reformulation of this pietist heritage had been to shift the focus of attention from specific religious or conversion experiences to the more general human experience of dependence upon the Mysterious Other (God). He then argued that the only legitimate Christian doctrines were those which were *derived* from this experience.

Thus, when some early twentieth-century studies identified Wesley as a "proto-Schleiermacher," they were not abandoning the contrast between experience and doctrine common in nineteenth-century studies of Wesley; they were refocusing the type of experience to which one appealed. For them it was less a conversion experience than a general sense of assurance (an *optimistic* form of dependence!). They were also assuming that Wesley shared Schleiermacher's agenda of reducing authoritative Christian doctrine to that which could be grounded in or derived from such experience.[31]

For some other early twentieth-century Methodist theologians this romantic version of the appeal to experience was still too narrow. They were more inclined toward the empirical language of the burgeoning natural sciences. To them Wesley was the model of a scientific mind that insisted that the test of truth was verifiability in *general* human experience (not just the "feeling" of assurance).[32] While the experience they appealed to might have been different, the reason for the appeal was the same—to reject sole reliance on traditional authorities.

Besides the subordination of traditional authorities to present experience, another typical agenda of early twentieth-century liberal theology was the critique of an exclusively conversionist model of

Christian initiation. Most liberals found William James' argument that "once-born" persons could develop just as authentic of a spirituality as "twice-born" to be persuasive. This fostered a renewed appreciation of the role of nurture and religious education in Christian life. As Methodist liberals struggled to moderate the conversionist model of Christian life inherited from their immediate predecessors, they discerned a champion in Wesley with his intense concern for catechisms and schools for Methodist children.[33]

One other classic concern of early twentieth-century liberal theology was the Social Gospel, with its emphasis on the *present* reality of Christian salvation—in the form of social and economic improvement. As this movement grew in public awareness, Methodist scholars were quick to remind themselves and others of Wesley's social concern and ministries.[34] Some early contributors held Wesley up as an example of philanthropic ministry.[35] For others, he was a prototype of Christian socialism.[36] The latter suggestion sparked vigorous counterarguments that Wesley instead supported the emerging capitalism of his day.[37] The ensuing debate proved to be very difficult to resolve. As a result, the main focus of scholarly study gradually turned from Wesley's explicit socioeconomic *claims* to the theological *grounds* for his claims and the *effects* of his revival on British culture.[38] While this nuanced the discussion significantly, the conflict over appeals to Wesley as theological warrant has continued.

A reaction to the various liberal appeals to Wesley arose as neo-Orthodoxy gained influence between the World Wars. This movement emphatically rejected the experientialism of liberal theology and called for a return to the biblical and doctrinal foundations of the Christian Church. It particularly sought a reappropriation of the Reformation insights of Luther and Calvin. It was not long before a parallel "neo-Wesleyanism" could be detected, which laid claim to Wesley in its criticism of the subjectivism and overemphasis on experience in liberal Methodist theology.[39] This neo-Wesleyanism demonstrated convincingly the limitations of many of the liberal appropriations of Wesley. However, it had its own problems. In particular, neo-Orthodoxy tended towards a one-sided emphasis on human incapacities and forensic justification—emphases that could not do justice to the Catholic side of Wesley's Anglican theology.[40]

Closely following the neo-Orthodox shift in twentieth-century Western Christian theology (*or*, existing with some tension within it) was the articulation of an existentialist approach to Christian faith and life. The major concern of theological existentialism was to argue that Christian doctrinal affirmations were not primarily objective attempts to describe metaphysical reality but subjective articulations of human anxiety and hope. As with neo-Orthodoxy, some scholars found this approach to be distinctively appropriate to Wesley.[41] This sense was particularly prominent in the renewed interest in Wesley among Japanese Methodist theologians.[42] But others vigorously rejected such an "existentialist Wesley."[43]

The middle of the twentieth century witnessed the burgeoning of ecumenical concern and dialogue in theological circles. By this point, one is hardly surprised by the emergence of advocates of an "ecumenical Wesley," who drew attention to his explicit irenic spirit and his distinctive blending of emphases from various Christian traditions.[44]

In general then, the first half of the twentieth century witnessed far more appeals to and interest in Wesley's theology than its predecessor. However, this interest was typically partisan and partial, focusing on Wesley's validation of desired theological agendas. While a wealth of insights into Wesley's theology were uncovered in these studies, several crucial limitations became increasingly evident. First, Wesley was often read too directly in terms of contemporary issues, without sufficient sensitivity to the debates and presuppositions of his original context. Second, attention was typically devoted to individual aspects of Wesley's thought or practice that were of interest, ignoring his larger doctrinal concerns and the perspective that these might provide for such individual issues. Comprehensive treatments of his theology continued to be exceedingly rare.[45] Finally, these studies retained the nineteenth-century assumption that Wesley may be of importance as a *warrant* in theological argument, but not as a *model* of theological activity. Whatever their particular theological agenda, they typically began with an apology for the fact that Wesley was not really a theologian![46]

After 1960: Recovering Wesley as a Theological Mentor

Such was the state of the argument when Colin Williams offered his survey of Wesley's theology as a resource for contemporary Methodism and Harold Bosley scoffed at the suggestion of Wesley's relevance. Developments since 1960 have shown Williams to be more the "son of a prophet" than Bosley. While there is plenty of reason to question how widely Wesley is known or appreciated in Methodist churches at large, he has certainly received more attention from Methodist scholars in the last four decades than at any time previously. Due in large part to the leadership of tireless advocates like Frank Baker and Albert Outler, the study of Wesley has grown from an occasional avocation of a few scholars to an academic subject in its own right, with scholarly societies, research specializations, and the rest.[47]

One major expression of this increased scholarly interest has been the undertaking of the first truly critical edition of Wesley's works: the Bicentennial Edition.[48] This textual work has been complemented by a proliferation of detailed secondary studies which bring to their investigation a broad knowledge of Wesley's context and a historical-critical realism about his unique stance or contribution. These studies have provided the basis for a revised comprehensive understanding of Wesley that is less partisan and triumphalist than previous examples.[49]

The recent increased sophistication of Wesley scholarship has been as evident in theological studies as in biographical ones. For example, while there has been continued interest in the relationship of Wesley to contemporary theological trends (in particular, liberation,[50] feminist,[51] and process[52] theologies), it has generally taken the form of tentative suggestions of affinities rather than appeals to a partisan theological hero.

More to the point, the majority of recent theological studies have been devoted to detailed comparative investigations of various individual aspects of Wesley's theology, such as his doctrine of assurance, his epistemology, or his social ethics.[53] These detailed studies have dramatically increased our knowledge of the sources, precedents, and implications of many of his central theological convictions. Thereby, they have contributed important insights to the continuing debate over Wesley's place within the Christian theological traditions. They have also deepened our awareness of developments (or shifts?) in some of Wesley's central convictions during his lifetime and escalated debate over the significance of these changes.[54]

What is most striking about recent theological studies of Wesley, however, is the degree to which Wesley's *model* of theological activity has become a focus of consideration and—increasingly—of positive reevaluation. Throughout the last thirty years Wesley scholars have protested the ease with which previous treatments dismissed any suggestion that Wesley was a serious theologian. And yet, they have had to admit that Wesley did not exemplify the model of serious theology assumed as normative in academic theological circles. So, how *should* Wesley be viewed?

No one can represent better, or has contributed more to, the changing evaluation of Wesley's model of theological activity than Albert Outler. In 1961, moving very much against the stream, he began to argue that Wesley should be valued as a major theologian.[55] To make this case, he found it necessary to distinguish between academic theology and Wesley's "folk theology." That is, he argued that Wesley's value as a major theologian lay in his ability to simplify, synthesize, and communicate the essential teachings of the Christian gospel to laity, not in contributions to speculative academic theology.[56] This characterization of Wesley as a "folk theologian" remained constant throughout Outler's studies. However, the relative valuation of such folk theology in comparison with academic theology underwent a very important shift. In the early 1960s Outler simply assumed that folk theologians did not belong in the front rank with speculative theologians. By the mid-1980s he was arguing that Wesley's theological model was an authentic and creative form in its own right. It need no longer be compared negatively with academic theology.[57]

It is important to recognize that the current reevaluation of Wesley's model of theological activity, which Outler exemplifies, has not been motivated solely by new insights into Wesley. It also reflects a growing uneasiness with the reigning academic model of theology against which Wesley was previously being measured and found wanting. In contemporary academic theological circles there has been a mounting call for recovering an understanding and practice of serious theological reflection that is more closely connected to Christian life and worship. As Outler came to realize, this move goes far beyond simply valuing "folk theology" alongside academic theology; it recasts the dominant model of theology itself. Along with Outler, several other Wesleyan theologians have begun to suggest that when Wesley is judged in terms of such a practical discipline of theology, he not only receives more favorable evaluation, he emerges as an exemplary model.[58]

The importance of such a renewed appreciation of Wesley's model of practical theological activity should not be underestimated. It was noted earlier that the dismissal of Wesley's model of theological activity was accompanied by an obscuring of some of his most distinctive theological convictions. This would suggest that a recovered understanding of his model of theological activity could help significantly in the current attempts to clarify the concerns and implications of Wesley's theological convictions. It could also facilitate the current effort to reclaim Wesley as *a theological mentor* for his contemporary descendants (and the larger Christian community), as opposed to reducing his importance to that of historical originator or enshrining him as a scholastic authority.

Abbreviations

Chr. Library
A Christian Library: Consisting of Extracts from, and Abridgements of, the Choicest Pieces of Practical Divinity which have been Published in the English Tongue, 50 vols. (Bristol: F. Farley, 1749–55).

John Wesley
John Wesley, ed. Albert C. Outler (New York: Oxford University Press, 1964).

Letters (Telford)
The Letters of the Rev. John Wesley, A.M., ed. John Telford, 8 vols. (London: Epworth, 1931).

Minutes (Mason)
Minutes of the Methodist Conferences, from the First, held in London, by the Late Rev. John Wesley, A.M., in the Year 1744, vol. 1 (London: John Mason, 1862).

NT Notes
Explanatory Notes Upon the New Testament, 3rd. corrected edition (Bristol: Graham & Pine, 1760–62; many reprint editions since).

OT Notes
Explanatory Notes upon the Old Testament, 3 vols. (Bristol: Pine, 1765; reprinted Salem, OH: Schmul, 1975).

Works
The Works of John Wesley, begun as "The Oxford Edition of the Works of John Wesley (Oxford: Clarendon Press, 1975–83); continued as "The Bicentennial Edition of the Works of John Wesley" (Nashville: Abingdon Press, 1984—); 15 of 35 volumes published to date.

Works (Jackson)
The Works of John Wesley, ed. Thomas Jackson, 3rd edition, 14 vols. (London: Wesleyan Methodist Book Room, 1872; reprinted Grand Rapids: Baker, 1979).

Notes

Notes to Introduction

1. John B. Cobb Jr., *Grace and Responsibility: A Wesleyan Theology for Today* (Nashville: Abingdon Press, 1995), 8–9.

2. Hildebrandt's major publications were *From Luther to Wesley* (London: Lutterworth Press, 1951); *Christianity According to the Wesleys* (London: Epworth Press, 1956); and "Introduction," §I, *Works* 7:1–22. His influence went beyond these publications. For example, he was the instigator in founding in 1955 a "Wesley Society" dedicated to recovering Wesleyan tradition for contemporary Methodism (the society faded quickly when he returned to Europe in 1968).

3. To mention just a few publications: "Religion: An Anachronism in a Secularized World?" in *Old Myths and New Realities* (Munich: U.S. Cultural Affairs Office, 1965), 8–11; "Thomas Altizer and the Future of Theology," in *The Death of God Debate*, ed. J. L. Ice & J. J. Carey (Philadelphia: Westminster Press, 1967), 56–59; "Secularization and Sacrament," in *The Spirit and the Power of Secularity*, ed. Albert Schlitzer (Notre Dame: University of Notre Dame Press, 1969), 123–55; and (editor), *What the Spirit Is Saying to the Churches* (New York: Hawthorne Books, 1975).

4. See esp. "How Can We Do Theology in the South Today?" *Perkins School of Theology Journal* 29.4 (1976):1–6; (editor), *Hope for the Church: Moltmann in Dialogue with Pratical Theology* (Nashville: Abingdon Press, 1979); "The World as the Original Sacrament," *Worship* 54 (1980):495–511; and (editor), *Theology, Politics, and Peace* (Maryknoll, NY: Orbis Books, 1989).

5. Ted first attended the Fourth Institute in 1969, delivering the paper "Conflicting Theological Models for God," later published in *The Living God*, ed. Dow Kirkpatrick (Nashville: Abingdon Press, 1971), 22–47. Note that there are no Wesley references in this paper!

6. *Sanctification and Liberation: Liberation Theologies in Light of the Wesleyan Tradition,* ed. Theodore Runyon (Nashville: Abingdon Press, 1981). Ted's essay, "Wesley and the Theologies of Liberation," is found on pp. 9–48.

7. The papers are collected in *Wesleyan Theology Today: A Bicentennial Theological Consultation,* ed. Theodore Runyon (Nashville: Kingswood Books, 1985). Ted's opening address, "What is Methodism's Theological Contribution Today?" is on pp. 7–13.

8. *The New Creation: John Wesley's Theology Today* (Nashville: Abingdon Press, 1998). See also his 1995 keynote address to the Wesleyan Theological Society: "The New Creation: The Wesleyan Distinctive," *Wesleyan Theological Journal* 31.2 (1996):5–19.

Notes to Chapter 1 (Carder)

1. See especially Theodore Runyon, *The New Creation: John Wesley's Theology Today* (Nashville: Abingdon Press, 1998).

2. Richard P. Heitzenrater, *Wesley and the People Called Methodists* (Nashville: Abingdon Press, 1995), 308.

3. See vols. 1–4 of *Works*. Albert Outler's notes in these volumes make clear Wesley's extensive use of Scripture for the insights, language, and style of his preaching.

4. The initial design of these conferences was to focus on three issues: What to teach, how to teach, and how to regulate Methodist doctrine, discipline, and practice. Cf. *Minutes* (25 June 1744), *Minutes* (Mason) 1:1 (or *John Wesley*, 136). The discussion of justification and sanctification occurred on 25–26 June 1744, *Minutes* (Mason) 1:1–6 (or *John Wesley*, 136–41).

5. Sermon 130, "On Living Without God," §15, *Works* 4:175. Editor Note: In quotes from Wesley throughout this book we will render references to humanity inclusive, in light of Wesley's own precedent in this direction; cf. Randy L. Maddox, "Wesley and Inclusive Grammar: A Note for Reflection," *Sacramental Life* 4.4 (1991):40–43.

6. Sermon 120, "The Unity of the Divine Being," §25, *Works* 4:71.

7. Theodore Runyon, "What is Methodism's Theological Contribution Today?" in *Wesleyan Theology Today*, ed. Theodore Runyon (Nashville: Kingswood Books, 1985), 11–12.

8. Ibid., p. 11.

9. Ibid., p. 12.

10. M. Douglas Meeks' provocative book *God the Economist* (Minneapolis: Augsburg/Fortress, 1989) provides a clear description of the pervasive nature of the consumerist market logic and its challenge to biblical and historic faith. *Selling Out the Church: The Dangers of Church Marketing* (Nashville: Abingdon Press, 1997), by Philip Kenneson and James Sweet offers a needed corrective to the marketing strategies on which much of "church growth" strategy is based. Kenneson and Sweet illustrate that all methods and tools have theological implications and that the market logic is changing the church's self-understanding and its evangelical and missional vision.

11. See especially the writings of Stanley Hauerwas, who argues that much of the activity of the modern United Methodist Church renders God unnecessary. Wesley's description of *practical atheism* in his sermon "On Living without God" is applicable to much of the church's activity.

12. Sermon 120, "The Unity of the Divine Being," §25, *Works* 4:71.

13. I am especially indebted to Ted Jennings for his frequent emphasis that the God we are to imitate is no generic deity, but a specific God made known in Jesus Christ who hears the cries of the poor, defends "orphans, the widows, and the immigrants," and comes in weakness and vulnerability. See especially his essay in this volume [Chapter 4].

14. Ted Jennings' book *Good News to the Poor: John Wesley's Evangelical Economics* (Nashville: Abingdon Press, 1990) brought this critical component of our Wesleyan heritage to the forefront. The 1992 Oxford Institute of Methodist Theological Studies was devoted to the theme, "Good News to the Poor," and major lectures from this Institute have been published in *The*

Portion of the Poor: Good News to the Poor in the Wesleyan Tradition, ed. M. Douglas Meeks (Nashville: Kingswood Books, 1994).

15. *Journal* (25 May 1764), *Works* 21:466.

16. "Thoughts upon Methodism" (4 August 1786), *Works* 9:527–30. This same concern is expressed in Wesley's Sermon 107, "On God's Vineyard" (*Works* 3:503–17), which was written a year later, after a visit of the Methodist work across Britain.

17. See "Children and Poverty: An Episcopal Initiative, Biblical and Theological Foundations" (Nashville: The United Methodist Publishing House, 1996).

18. The work of David Lowes Watson has been especially helpful in understanding this component of our Wesleyan tradition and appropriating the tradition of the contemporary church.

19. I am especially indebted to Dr. Watson for this insight which he presented at my first meeting as a member of the Council of Bishops in the Fall 1992. In a lecture presented to the Council, Dr. Watson made a compelling case that the role of clergy and laity changed significantly as the result of a subtle power struggle that developed between clergy and laity when the circuit riders become stationed pastors. It laid the groundwork, according to Dr. Watson, for the creation of a passive laity who receive ministry dispensed by the ordained.

Notes to Chapter 2 (Langford)

1. Robert E. Cushman, *John Wesley's Experimental Divinity* (Nashville: Kingswood Books, 1989), 62–3. In this book, especially in chapters 2 and 3, Cushman illustrates how Wesley's understanding of the way of salvation is a restatement of doctrine as shaped by experience and experience as shaped by doctrine. With Luke Tyerman, Cushman asks, why was the doctrine of justification by faith not known to Wesley? He answers that in Wesley's time the doctrine was understood as wholly contingent upon God's predestination, it was imputed, not claimed, and it implied a final vindication of the elect only at the last judgment not as a present assurance (51). Wesley rediscovered the vitality of this doctrine and its theological attachments because of the authentication which his experience gave to the doctrine expounded by Peter Böhler. Through this combining of experience and doctrine Wesley developed his "scripture way of salvation," which included the attendant doctrines of the immediate working of the Holy Spirit, the reality of original sin and the requirement of repentance, justification and new birth, the gift of saving faith and assurance, prevenient and saving grace, and fulfillment in holiness of heart and life (35–44). This relating of doctrine to faith is the "distinctive contribution of Wesley to Protestant theology" (47).

2. Richard Watson, *Theological Institutes: or, A View of the Evidences, Doctrines, Morals, and Institutions of Christianity*, 3 vols. (London: John Mason, 1825–28).

3. William Burt Pope, *A Compendium of Christian Theology: Being Analytical Outlines of a Course of Theological Study, Biblical, Dogmatic, Historical*, 3 vols. (London: Wesleyan Book Room, 1880).

4. Schubert M. Ogden, *The Reality of God, and other Essays* (New York: Harper & Row, 1966).

5. Schubert M. Ogden, *Faith and Freedom: Toward a Theology of Liberation* (Nashville: Abingdon Press, 1979).

6. Schubert M. Ogden, *The Point of Christology* (San Francisco: Harper & Row, 1982).

7. Robert Cushman, "The Shape of the Christian Faith: A Platform," *The Iliff Review* 13 (March, 1956):31–40; reprinted in *Wesleyan Theology: A Sourcebook*, ed. Thomas Langford (Durham, NC: Labyrinth Press, 1984), 250–58.

8. Robert E. Cushman, *Therapeia: Plato's Conception of Philosophy* (Chapel Hill: University of North Carolina Press, 1958).

Notes to Chapter 3 (Suchocki)

1. My reflections on Wesley's theology of prayer began when I wrote a chapter called "How United Methodism Must Change" for *Unity, Liberty, and Charity: Building Bridges Under Icy Waters*, eds. Donald E. Messer and William J. Abraham (Nashville: Abingdon Press, 1996). The three pages in that chapter dealing with prayer are greatly expanded in this present essay, but echoes of that earlier work are seen especially in section III, and to a lesser extent in section I. Abingdon Press graciously permits this use.

2. *A Plain Account of Christian Perfection*, ¶25, Q. 38, §5, *Works* (Jackson) 11:437.

3. Ibid., Q. 38, §1, *Works* (Jackson) 11:435.

4. Ibid., Q. 32, *Works* (Jackson) 11:428.

5. Ibid., Q. 38, §2, *Works* (Jackson) 11:436.

6. Ibid.

7. Ibid., Q. 38, §4, *Works* (Jackson) 11:437.

8. Ibid., Q. 38, §5, *Works* (Jackson) 11:438.

9. Ibid., Q. 34, *Works* (Jackson) 11:431.

10. Ibid., Q. 38, §6, *Works* (Jackson) 11:438.

11. Ibid., Q. 38, §7, *Works* (Jackson) 11:439.

12. Ibid., Q. 38, §8, *Works* (Jackson) 11:440–41.

13. Ibid., Q. 38, §8, *Works* (Jackson) 11:440.

14. Ibid., Q. 38, §1, *Works* (Jackson) 11:435.

15. Ibid., Q. 38, §8, *Works* (Jackson) 11:441.

Notes to Chapter 4 (Jennings)

1. "Thoughts Upon Divine Sovereignty," *Works* (Jackson) 10:361–63.

2. For a fine study of this connection see Victorio Araya, *God of the Poor: The Mystery of God in Latin American Liberation Theology* (Maryknoll, NY: Orbis, 1987).

3. Psalm 82 from *The New Testament and Psalms: An Inclusive Version* (New York and Oxford: Oxford University Press, 1995).

4. Thus Thomas Aquinas takes this disclosure of the divine name to establish that God's essence is God's being in *Summa Contra Gentiles* I, 22, 9–10. See also *Summa Theologica* I, Q. 2, art 3. In this he is preceded by Origen (*On First Principles*, Book 1, ch. 3) and by Augustine (*On the Trinity*, Book 5, ch. 2).

5. José Porfirio Miranda, *Marx and the Bible: A Critique of the Philosophy of Oppression* (Maryknoll, NY: Orbis, 1974), 89–93.

6. Ibid., 49.

7. Karl Barth, *The Epistle to the Romans* (New York: Oxford University Press, 1933), 44.

8. Emmanuel Levinas, *Ethics and Infinity* (Pittsburgh, PA: Duquesne University Press, 1985), 76, 57.

9. Ibid., 86.

10. Ibid., 87.

11. Cf. Steven G. Smith, *The Argument to the Other: Reason Beyond Reason in the Thought of Karl Barth and Emmanuel Levinas* (Chico, CA: Scholars Press, 1983).

12. Emmanuel Levinas, *Totality and Infinity: An Essay on Exteriority* (Pittsburgh, PA: Duquesne University Press, 1969), 78.

13. Levinas, *Ethics and Infinity*, 92.

14. Levinas, *Totality and Infinity*, 39.

15. See Jacques Derrida, *The Gift of Death* (Chicago: University of Chicago Press, 1995), 68, 77–78, 82–115.

16. John D. Caputo, *The Prayers and Tears of Jacques Derrida: Religion Without Religion* (Bloomington, IN: Indiana University Press, 1997), 52–53.

17. Ibid., 68.

18. Miranda, *Marx and the Bible*, 48.

19. See Benjamin Weems, *Reform, Rebellion and the Heavenly Way* (Tucson, AZ: University of Arizona Press, 1964). As yet unexplored, but of particular interest, is the connection between this movement and the "Tai Ping" movement in China which also freely adapted elements of folk Christianity into a distinctively "eastern way." See Jonathan D. Spence, *God's Chinese Son: The Taiping Heavenly Kingdom of Hong Xiuquan* (New York: W. W. Norton, 1996).

20. Sermon 24, "Sermon on the Mount, IV," §3.7, *Works* 1:546.

21. Note that in Wesley's earlier cited remarks on sovereignty it was precisely the idea of judge that came to the fore.

22. For further reflection on the "Son of Man" as the human one see my essay "The Martyrdom of the Son of Man," in *Text and Logos: The Humanistic Interpretation of the New Testament*, ed. Theodore W. Jennings (Atlanta, GA: Scholars Press, 1990), 229–43.

Notes to Chapter 5 (Meeks)

1. See esp. Theodore H. Runyon, *The New Creation: John Wesley's Theology Today* (Nashville: Abingdon Press, 1998).

2. For biblical and Hellenistic usages of *oikonomia* see John Reumann, *The Use of Oikonomia and Related Terms in Greek Sources to about A.D. 100 as a Background for Patristic Applications* (Ann Arbor, MI: University Microfilms, 1957); and John H. Elliott, *A Home for the Homeless: A Sociological Exegesis of 1 Peter, Its Situation and Strategy* (Philadelphia: Fortress Press, 1981).

3. See M. Douglas Meeks, *God the Economist: The Doctrine of God and Political Economy* (Minneapolis: Fortress Press, 1989), 29–45.

4. See Aristotle, *Politics*, Book II.

5. Cf. Jonathan J. Bonk, *Mission and Money: Affluence as a Western Missionary Problem* (Maryknoll, NY: Orbis Books, 1991).

6. These household rules are found in the Covenant Code (Exod. 20:22-23:33), the Deuteronomic Code (Deut. 12–26), and the Holiness Code (Lev. 17–26).

7. The opposition to the Old Testament Torah, to Jesus' Jewishness, and to the reign of God promised in the prophets has not a little to do with antisemitism, even when it has been unconscious. When the church leaves proximity to the synagogue, it becomes biblically heretical. The so-called Jesus Seminar has recently given us another Jesus devoid of Israel's history of promises. Jesus is reduced to a Hellenistic peasant cynic. See, e.g., John Dominic Crossan, *The Historical Jesus: The Life of a Mediterranean Jewish Peasant* (San Francisco: HarperSanFrancisco, 1991) and the critique by Luke Timothy Johnson, *The Real Jesus: The Misguided Quest for the Historical Jesus and the Truth of the Traditional Gospels* (San Francisco: HarperSanFrancisco, 1996).

8. Cf. Wesley's insistence that holiness "is neither 'circumcision', the attending on all the Christian ordinances, 'nor uncircumcision', the fulfilling of all heathen morality, but 'the keeping of the commandments of God'; particularly those, 'Thou shalt love the Lord thy God with all thy heart, and thy neighbor as thyself.' In a word, holiness is the having 'the mind that was in Christ', and the 'walking as Christ walked'." Sermon 127, "On the Wedding Garment," §17, *Works* 4:147.

9. Sermon 127, "On the Wedding Garment," §18, *Works* 4:148.

10. See Theodore W. Jennings Jr., *Good News to the Poor: John Wesley's Evangelical Economics* (Nashville: Abingdon Press, 1990), 139–56; and Jennings, "Wesley and the Poor: An Agenda for Wesleyans," in *The Portion of the Poor*, ed. M. Douglas Meeks (Nashville: Kingswood Books, 1995).

11. Lev. 25:35-38; Exod. 22:26-27. Cf. Deut. 24:6, 10-13; Deut. 15:7-11.

12. A collect of the Anglican Book of Common Prayers says: Jesus Christ "in whose service is perfect freedom."

13. Lev. 19:9-10. Cf. Deut. 24:19-22; Lev. 23:22; Ruth 2.

14. Sermon 87, "The Danger of Riches," §1.1, *Works* 3:230.

15. Ibid.," §1.4, *Works* 3:231.

16. This point is developed in Robert Gnuse, *You Shall Not Steal: Community and Property in the Biblical Tradition* (Maryknoll, NY: Orbis Books, 1985).

17. Sermon 87, "The Danger of Riches," §1.5, *Works* 3:231–32.

18. See Sermon 122, "Causes of the Inefficacy of Christianity," *Works* 4:86–96.

19. We have yet to benefit from a full-scale study of ways in which Wesley's great appreciation for the community of goods in Acts 2 might have found expression in Wesley's ministry. At crucial junctures he maintained the Anglican dismissal of common goods as "Anabaptist." Despite the fact that "almsgiving" is usually set over against "common good," it is also a kind of commons. In what other ways did Wesley seek to create commons?

20. Sermon 51, "The Good Steward," §3.5, *Works* 2:295.

21. Sermon 131, "The Danger of Increasing Riches," §3.12, *Works* 4:183–84.

22. Deut. 15:7-11; Isa. 58:6-9. Cf. Isa. 1:12-17; Amos 2:6-7; 5:21-24.

23. Isa. 58:6-9. Cf. Isa. 1:12-17; Amos 2:6-7; 5:21-24.

24. See Jennings' fine description of Wesley's life with the poor in *Good News to the Poor*, 47–69.

25. Cf. my forthcoming essay, "Trinity, Community and Power," in *Trin-*

ity, Community and Power: Mapping Trajectories in Wesleyan Theology, ed. M. Douglas Meeks (Nashville: Kingswood Books, 1998).

26. This theme of "cooperant" or "responsible grace" is definitively developed by Randy L. Maddox, *Responsible Grace: John Wesley's Practical Theology* (Nashville: Kingswood Books, 1994).

27. For a discussion of this question see Michael Walzer, *Spheres of Justice: A Defense of Pluralism and Equality* (New York: Basic Books, 1983).

Notes to Chapter 6 (Marquardt)

1. See Theodore H. Runyon, *The New Creation: John Wesley's Theology Today* (Nashville: Abingdon Press, 1998).

2. *Qui creavit nos sine nobis, non salvabit nos sine nobis* (Augustine).

3. Cf. Colin W. Williams, *John Wesley's Theology Today* (Nashville: Abingdon Press, 1960), 101.

4. An introduction to these debates can be gained from *Aldersgate Reconsidered*, ed. Randy L. Maddox (Nashville: Kingswood Books, 1990).

5. Helmut Burkhardt, *Die biblische Lehre von der Bekehrung* (Giessen: Brunnen, 1978), 78, defines conversion as "a one-time event with eternal significance." For an overview of biblical uses, see Paul Löffler, "Bekehrung," *Evangelisches Kirchenlexikon*, 3rd ed. (1986), 1:404–5.

6. Runyon, *New Creation*, 60.

7. A caveat against any misleading synergism is found in Jeremiah 31:18: "I have surely heard Ephraim bemoaning himself *thus*; Thou hast chastised me, and I was chastised, as a bullock unaccustomed *to the yoke*: turn thou me, and I shall be turned; for thou *art* the LORD my God" (KJV, which is closer to the Hebrew text than other translations). This prophetic word should not be understood in the sense of the old Protestant concept of *truncus et lapis*, a misleading attempt of describing the role of the believer in the process of salvation.

8. Cf. William J. Abraham's contrasting description of "the advocates of conversion [who] insist on some favored pattern of experience that everyone must undergo if he or she is to be counted among the elect"; *The Logic of Evangelism* (Grand Rapids: Wm. B. Eerdmans, 1989), 122.

9. See among others Isaiah 44:22: "I have swept away your transgressions like a cloud, and your sins like mist; return to me (*šûbāh ʾēlay*), for I have redeemed you."

10. "The OT history is the history of the unfaithfulness of human beings and of God's faithfulness" (Johannes Schniewind, *Das biblische Wort von der Bekehrung* [Berlin, 1948], 4). A similar metaphor is that of the good shepherd, which in the NT is extended to Jesus, the Son of God. Because of limited space I will not discuss the biblical texts that use this metaphor.

11. For the following quotes see Dietrich Bonhoeffer, *The Cost of Discipleship*, 2nd ed. (New York: Macmillan, 1963), 45–48.

12. *The United Methodist Book of Worship*, 1992, 291ff. Compare Charles Wesley's: "O that I could repent! / With all my idols part, / And to thy gracious eye present / An humble, contrite heart!" *Hymns*, #99, *Works* 7:205.

13. José Míguez Bonino, "Conversion, New Creature and Commitment," *International Review of Missions* 72 (1983):330.

14. Abraham, *Logic of Evangelism*, 129.

15. John B. Cobb Jr., *Grace and Responsibility: A Wesleyan Theology for Today* (Nashville: Abingdon Press, 1995), 99.

16. See Walter Klaiber, *Call and Response: Biblical Foundations for a Theology of Evangelism* (Nashville: Abingdon Press, 1997), 181.

17. See respectively, Gerhard Lohfink, *Jesus and Community: The Social Dimension of the Christian Faith* (Philadelphia: Fortress Press, 1984); and Walter Klaiber, "Proexistenz und Kontrastverhalten," *Jahrbuch für biblische Theologie* 7 (1992):125ff.

18. See e.g. 1 Cor. 4:10: "We are fools for the sake of Christ, but you are wise in Christ. We are weak, but you are strong. You are held in honor, but we in disrepute."

19. As far as I have been able to determine, this term was forged by Christians in the former German Democratic Republic in the early 1950s. See Elisabeth Adler, *Pro-Existence: Christian Voices in East Germany* (London: SCM, 1964). Elisabeth Adler was Secretary and Vice President of the World Student Christian Fellowship.

20. John 3:16; 8:12; 2 Cor. 5:18; 1 John 4:14.

Notes to Chapter 7 (Logan)

1. Michael Marshall, *The Gospel Connection: A Study in Evangelism for the 90s* (Harrisburg, PA: Morehouse Publishing, 1990), 2.

2. Loren B. Mead, *The Once and Future Church* (Washington, DC: The Alban Institute, 1991), 8–29.

3. See Rodney Clapp, *A Peculiar People: The Church as Culture in a Post-Christian Society* (Downers Grove, IL: InterVarsity Press, 1996).

4. *General Minutes of The Annual Conferences of The United Methodist Church* (Evanston, IL: General Council on Finance and Administration, 1969–84).

5. Cf. Philip Kenneson and James Sweet, *Selling Out the Church: The Dangers of Church Marketing* (Nashville: Abingdon Press, 1997).

6. Nathan O. Hatch, *The Democratization of American Christianity* (New Haven: Yale University Press, 1989), 3.

7. Albert C. Outler, *Evangelism and Theology in the Wesleyan Spirit* (Nashville: Discipleship Resources, 1996), 45.

8. Ibid.

9. Gerald Cragg, "Introduction," in *Works* 11:15.

10. Sermon 107, "On God's Vineyard," §1.8, *Works* 3:507.

11. George A. Lindbeck, *The Nature of Doctrine: Religion and Theology in a Postliberal Age* (Philadelphia, PA: Westminster Press, 1984), 33.

12. See *Minutes* (2 Aug. 1745), Q. 15, *John Wesley*, 151; and "Large Minutes," Q. 38, *Works* (Jackson) 8:318. Cf. Sermon 36, "The Law Established by Faith, II," §1.6, *Works* 2:37–38.

13. Charles Wesley, "Come, Sinners, to the Gospel Feast," *The United Methodist Hymnal* (Nashville: The United Methodist Publishing House, 1989), #339 (cf. *Works* 7:81–82).

14. Sermon 20, "The Lord Our Righteousness," *Works* 1:449–65.

15. Martin E. Marty, "Albert C. Outler: United Methodist Ecumenist," *Christian Century* 105 (12 Feb. 1988):221.

16. Cf. Albert C. Outler, "Introduction," *Works* 1:18–29.

17. Sermon 107, "On God's Vinyard," *Works* 3:503–17.

18. Cf. *Journal* (13 March 1743), *Works* 19:318; Letter to Christopher Hopper (31 July 1773), *Letters* (Telford) 6:36; and Letter to Joseph Benson (4 March 1774), *Letters* (Telford) 6:77.

19. "Rules of the Band Societies," *Works* 9:77–78.

20. See letter to Thomas Maxfield (2 Nov. 1762), §3, *Letters* (Telford) 4:194; and *Plain Account of Christian Perfection*, ¶25, Q. 37, *Works* (Jackson) 11:433.

21. David Lowes Watson, *The Early Methodist Class Meeting* (Nashville: Discipleship Resources, 1992), 84.

22. Peter Berger, *The Sacred Canopy: Elements of a Sociological Theory of Religion* (Garden City, NY: Anchor Books, 1969).

23. Jürgen Moltmann, "Is 'Pluralistic Theology' Useful for the Dialogue of World Religions," in *Christian Uniqueness Reconsidered*, ed. Gavin D'Costa (Maryknoll, NY: Orbis Books, 1990), 152.

24. Robert W. Jenson, "How the World Lost Its Story," *First Things* (October 1993):21.

25. Letter to Miss March (9 June 1775), *Letters* (Telford) 6:153.

26. Sermon 122,"Causes of the Inefficacy of Christianity," *Works* 4:86–96.

27. "Thoughts on the Present Scarcity of Provisions," §7, *Works* (Jackson) 11:57.

28. "Thoughts Upon Slavery," §4.2, *Works* (Jackson) 11:70.

Notes to Chapter 8 (Beck)

1. See *The Book of Discipline of The United Methodist Church* (1988), ¶112 (pp. 116–18). The paragraph continues in a revised and much abridged form in *The Book of Discipline of The United Methodist Church* (1996), ¶109 (p. 109).

2. 1766 *Minutes*, *Minutes* (Mason), 61 (also as "Large Minutes," Q. 27, *Works* [Jackson] 8:312).

3. 1769 *Minutes*, *Minutes* (Mason), 87–88 (also as "Address to the Traveling Preachers" [4 August 1769], §2, *Works* [Jackson] 13:242).

4. Letter to Ezekiel Cooper (1 February 1791), *Letters* (Telford) 8:260.

5. "Large Minutes," Q. 3, *Minutes* (Mason), 447 (or *Works* [Jackson] 8:299).

6. Sermon 24, "Sermon on the Mount IV," §1.1, *Works* 1:533–34.

7. *Minutes* (25 June 1744), *Minutes* (Mason) 1:1 (or *John Wesley*, 136).

8. Cf. Wesley's comment "I sent for them to *advise*, not to *govern* me," in 1766 *Minutes*, *Minutes* (Mason) 1:61 (also as "Large Minutes," Q. 27, *Works* [Jackson] 8:312).

9. *The Book of Discipline of the United Methodist Church* (1988), ¶112 (p. 116). While the specific analogy with covenant is missing from the abridged form of this paragraph in the 1996 *Book of Discipline* (¶109, p. 109), the construal of connexion totally in terms of its horizontal dimension remains the same.

10. "Costly Unity," ¶25, available in *Costly Obedience*, eds. T. F. Best & M. Robra (Geneva: World Council of Churches, 1997).

11. Included with responses in *The Unity of the Church as Koinonia*, eds. G. Gassmann & J. A. Radano (Geneva: World Council of Churches, 1993).

12. *Fifth World Conference on Faith and Order: Message, Section Reports and Discussion Paper* (Geneva: World Council of Churches, 1993), Discussion Paper, p. 12.

13. Ibid., Report of Section I, pp. 6–8.

14. J. H. Rigg, *A Comparative View of Church Organizations, Primitive and Protestant*, 3rd. ed. (London: Charles H. Kelly, 1897), 11.

15. "Costly Unity," ¶31.

16. Letter to "Our Brethren in America" (10 September 1784), §6, *Letters* (Telford) 7:239.

17. *Letter to a Roman Catholic*, §§16–17, *Works* (Jackson), 10:85–86.

18. Sermon 39, "Catholic Spirit," *Works* 2:81–95.

Notes to Chapter 9 (Moore)

1. Two exceptions to this generalization are the succession of ministry studies in many communions of the Wesleyan family and the ecumenical bilateral dialogues. Both have involved considerable theological reflection, though in the context of denominational or ecumenical decision-making.

2. Cf. Theodore Runyon, ed., *What the Spirit Is Saying to the Churches* (New York: Hawthorn Books, 1975); Runyon, ed., *Sanctification and Liberation: Liberation Theologies in Light of the Wesleyan Tradition* (Nashville: Abingdon Press, 1981); and Runyon, ed., *Theology, Politics, and Peace* (Maryknoll, NY: Orbis Books, 1989).

3. As Runyon reflected on the charismatic movement, he urged people to give attention both to the Spirit and to Christ, and to heed both the internal witness and external witness of God in our lives; likewise, he appealed to Paul's first letter to the Corinthians, urging that enthusiasm be combined with understanding, and religious experience be combined with transformed living (*Spirit to the Churches*, 11–15, 109–14). In this book and others, he urged that personal religious experience and social responsibility be held together (ibid., 121–23; *Sanctification and Liberation*, 39–48). Likewise, he drew upon the Wesleyan tradition in holding the unity of justification and sanctification, sanctification and liberation, grace and works (*Sanctification and Liberation*, 9–11, 30–39). At times, Runyon also spoke of the need to engage diverse theological views to supplement and correct one another (*Theology, Politics, and Peace*, esp. the Preface, p. xx).

4. I fully recognize the limits of my focus. My goal is to analyze one context in some depth. Similar localized studies of Methodist movements in the Philippines, Western and Central Europe, Sierra Leone, and other parts of the United Methodist Church, as well as other branches of the Wesleyan family in the United States and throughout the world are very desirable for enriching the initial account of the textures of Methodist ministry that I offer here.

5. Paul S. Sanders, "The Sacraments in Early American Methodism," in *Perspectives on American Methodism: Interpretive Essays* (hereafter, *Perspectives*), eds. Russell E. Richey, Kenneth E. Rowe, and Jean Miller Schmidt (Nashville: Kingswood Books, 1993), 82.

6. Ibid., 90. Cf. Jeffrey P. Mickle, "A Comparison of the Doctrines of Ministry of Francis Asbury and Philip William Otterbein," in *Perspectives*, 96. The situation led to a clear distinction between those local preachers who

were located and those who were members of the conference and appointed by the bishop. Mickle points out that primary ministerial identity was actually established by membership in the annual conference. A more comprehensive discussion of the early decades of conferences is found in Russell E. Richey, *The Methodist Conference in America: A History* (Nashville: Kingswood Books, 1996).

7. Mickle, "Comparison of Doctrines," 103. According to Mickle, "The governing authority of elders and deacons depended on their conference membership." Mickle also explains that the administration of sacraments was not the primary distinction of ordained ministry, but conference membership and itinerancy (96).

8. Ibid., 101–3, 96.

9. Ibid., 99.

10. Ibid., 103. The distinctive role of elders was to ordain other elders, thus insuring continuity (104). The ordinations took place in local churches rather than in the conference.

11. Will B. Gravely, "African Methodisms and the Rise of Black Denominationalism," in *Perspectives*, 111–13. The phrase "for the time being" in these 1796 "Articles of Association of the African Methodist Episcopal Church" was in continuity with the 1794 Bethel proclamation, which had "asserted the goal of the Bethel founders to push for ordination of black 'persons endowed with gifts and graces to speak for God'" (112).

12. Ibid., 114.

13. Ibid., 125. Gravely adds, "Without full ordination, there was no chance for direct denominational representation and participation in governance" (125). He attributes the emergence of black denominationalism to the failure of the church to grant conference membership to ministers, direct representation within the denomination, and full ordination (126).

14. See Kenneth E. Rowe, "The Ordination of Women: Round One; Anna Oliver and the General Conference of 1880," in *Perspectives*, 302.

15. "Report of the Committee on Itinerancy No. X," as quoted in Rowe, "Ordination of Women," 306. Specific reference was made in the announcement of the 1880 decision that women, though not licensed as local preachers or ordained, could still serve as Sunday school superintendents, class leaders, and stewards; cf. Rosemary Skinner Keller, "Creating a Sphere for Women: The Methodist Episcopal Church, 1869–1906," in *Perspectives*, 332; see also 333–34.

16. Donald K. Gorrell, "'A New Impulse': Progress in Lay Leadership and Service by Women of the United Brethren in Christ and the Evangelical Association, 1870–1910," in *Perspectives*, 329.

17. Ibid., 330.

18. Keller, "Creating a Sphere," 333. Keller argues that the formation of Woman's Societies was actually an attempt to create a woman's sphere of service within a context where many areas of service were not permitted to women.

19. Gorrell, "New Impulse," 323.

20. Ibid., 322–27.

21. They waited fourteen years, for example, to get approval for publishing a journal (Gorrell, "New Impulse," 325). In all of the predecessor bodies of the UMC, initial efforts were made to form an auxiliary relationship

between the women's societies and the denominational mission boards, but these efforts were resisted in the Methodist Episcopal and United Brethren Churches; see Keller, "Creating a Sphere," 338–39; and Gorrell, "New Impulse," 324–25.

22. Val Plumwood, *Feminism and the Mastery of Nature* (London: Routledge, 1993). In developing her ideas, she explains how dualisms are often part of the assumptive structures even of liberation movements, thus undercutting the fullest possible liberation.

23. Plumwood, *Feminism*, 31–33. She says, "Dualism is the process by which contrasting concepts (for example, masculine and feminine gender identities) are formed by domination and subordination and constructed as oppositional and exclusive" (31).

24. Plumwood, *Feminism*, 47.

25. Ibid., 48–55, summarized and paraphrased.

26. Ibid., 55; see also 3–5.

27. Study committees on ministry have actually been formed every quadrennium since 1944 until the present one. A description and commentary on this process is offered by Richard Heitzenrater, and since his presentation offers different perspectives on the issues than I present in this paper, it is valuable to read as amplification and contrast to this presentation; Richard P. Heitzenrater, "A Critical Analysis of the Ministry Studies Since 1948," in *Perspectives*, 431–47.

28. John Wesley, "A Treatise on Baptism," intro., *John Wesley*, 318. His intent in naming the first of the three essentials (episcopal administrator) is complex, as Wesley was seeking to make a distinction from the Anabaptist practice of baptism.

29. Ibid., §1.1, §2.2–5, *John Wesley*, 319, 322–23.

30. Sermon 45, "Of the Church,"§§3–6, *Works* 3:47–8.

31. Ibid., §§8–13, *Works* 3:48–50.

32. "A Letter to a Roman Catholic," §§6–11, *Works* (Jackson) 10:81–82.

33. To be sure, Wesley often critiqued Roman Catholic doctrines and practices, as he did the Reformed, Moravian, Dissenting, Anabaptist, and other traditions; but he also engaged frequently in seeking relationships and points of correspondence, as in this letter to a Roman Catholic. For a thorough study of Wesley and the Roman Catholic Church, see David Butler, *Methodists and Papists: John Wesley and the Catholic Church in the Eighteenth Church* (London: Darton, Longman and Todd, 1995).

34. Sermon 16, "The Means of Grace," *Works* 1:378–97; quote in §2.1 (381). For a list that previews this sermon, see *Journal* (25 June 1740), *Works* 19:157.

35. This particular list of the means of grace is found in Wesley's *Journal* (31 December 1739), *Works* 19:133.

36. See esp. Sermon 16, "The Means of Grace," §5.4, *Works* 1:396. The power to save is "in the Spirit of God," and the merit is "in the blood of Christ." Thus, we see that the Trinitarian themes are visible in Wesley's descriptions of the work of God in human lives, as well as in summaries of Christian doctrine. This interplay between Trinitarian themes and spiritual-ethical issues in people's lives is well developed by Manfred Marquardt in *John Wesley's Social Ethics: Praxis and Principles* (Nashville: Abingdon Press, 1992), esp. 105–14.

37. "Ought We to Separate from the Church of England?" §2.1, *Works* 9:568.

38. Ibid., §3.1, *Works* 9:572.

39. Ibid., §3.2, *Works* 9:573.

40. Cf. Frank Baker, *John Wesley and the Church of England* (London: Epworth Press, 1970), 256–82.

41. Ibid., 324.

42. Quoted in Richard P. Heitzenrater, *The Elusive Mr. Wesley* (Nashville: Abingdon Press, 1984) 2:147.

43. One sign of this yearning is a recent book by the bishop who chaired the Study of Ministry in the last quadrennium (1992–96): David J. Lawson, *Hungering for the Future: Whispers of Hope for a Church in Mission* (Nashville: Abingdon Press, 1996).

44. Note the description of *new* flexible structures of organization and administration for the local church; the purpose of the organization is "so that [the local church] can pursue its primary task and mission in the context of its own community." *The Book of Discipline of the United Methodist Church* (Nashville: United Methodist Publishing House, 1996), ¶245 (p. 136); see ¶¶245–62.

45. *Discipline*, ¶60 (p. 39); the entire statement covers ¶¶60–63.

46. *Discipline*, ¶63 (pp. 72–83).

47. *By Water and the Spirit: A United Methodist Understanding of Baptism* (Nashville: The General Board of Discipleship, 1996).

48. Ibid. The same themes are found in the *Discipline*, as in the introduction to the section on "Clergy Orders": "Baptism is God's gift of unmerited grace through the Holy Spirit. It is an incorporation into Christ which marks the entrance of persons into the church and its ministry (Romans 6:3, 4, 18)"; *Discipline*, ¶310 (p. 178).

49. Council of Bishops, "Study of Ministry," a report to the General Conference of The United Methodist Church, 1996, 1.

50. *Discipline*, ¶101 (p. 107); the full statement runs ¶¶101–9.

51. *Discipline*, ¶303.3 (p. 171).

Notes to Chaper 10 (González)

1. Cf. Theodore Runyon, ed., *Sanctification and Liberation: Liberation Theologies in Light of the Wesleyan Tradition* (Nashville: Abingdon Press, 1981).

2. See Edwin Sylvest, "Wesley desde el margen hispano," *Apuntes* 1.2 (1981):14–19. While Sylvest deals with Wesley's early studies of Spanish, he does not follow this subject throughout Wesley's later career.

3. MS Diary (28 June 1736), *Works* 18:398.

4. *Journal* (4 April 1737), *Works* 18:178.

5. *Journal* (11 October 1756), *Works* 21:79.

6. See *Journal* (4 December 1762) & (5 January 1763), *Works* 21:399, 401–2.

7. Marcelino Menéndez Pelayo, *Historia de los heterodoxos españoles* (reprint, Madrid: Biblioteca de Autores Cristianos, 1956), 2:210.

8. In *Works* 25:487 n.4, Frank Baker says that the teachings of Molinos "brought him to death at the hands of the Inquisition." This seems to imply that the Inquisition condemned him to death. In truth, perhaps because of

his friendship with Innocent XI, the Inquisition only forced him to recant and spend the rest of his life (eleven years) in confinement.

9. Letter to Samuel Wesley Jr. (23 Nov. 1736), *Works* 25:487–88.

10. *Chr. Library*, Volume 38 (1754).

11. Cf. John Wesley, *Primitive Physick: Or an Easy and Natural Method of Curing Most Diseases*, 22nd ed. (Philadelphia: Hall, 1791).

12. For instance, León Lopetegui and Félix Zubillaga, *Historia de la Iglesia en América española*, vol. 1 (Madrid: Biblioteca de Autores Cristianos, 1965) ignores his contribution at least in two sections where he should be mentioned. He does not appear among the mystics of New Spain whom this otherwise very thorough work discusses. Nor is he mentioned among commentators of the Bible, although he wrote a *Commentary on the Apocalypse*. On his life, see Francis Cuthbert Doyle, *The Life of Gregory Lopez* (London: R. Washbourne, 1876).

13. *Journal* (31 August 1742), *Works* 19:294.

14. *Journal* (31 August 1754), *Works* 20:490.

15. *Journal* (15 October 1755), *Works* 21:32.

16. Sermon 55, "On the Trinity," §1, *Works* 2:375: "And on the other hand persons may be truly religious and hold many wrong opinions. Can anyone possibly doubt of this while there are Romanists in the world? For who can deny, not only that many of them formerly were religious (as à Kempis, Gregory Lopez, and the Marquis de Renty), but that many of them at this day are real, inward Christians?"

17. Sermon 114, "On the Death of John Fletcher," §3.12, *Works* 3:627.

18. Letter to Lady Maxwell (22 Sept. 1764), *Letters* (Telford) 4:264.

19. Letter to Philothea Briggs (16 Oct. 1771), *Letters* (Telford) 5:283.

20. Letter to Miss March (10 Dec. 1777), *Letters* (Telford) 6:293.

21. *The Life of Gregory Lopez*, written originally in Spanish, abridged by the Rev. John Wesley, in *Chr. Library*, Volume 50 (1755). Wesley's abridgement was based on the translation published by Abraham Woodhead in 1675: *The holy life, pilgrimage and blessed death of Gregory Lopez, a Spanish hermit in the West Indies*.

22. The title itself is a reprise of the title of a chapter in an earlier book I wrote, "Reading the Bible in Spanish," *Mañana: Christian Theology from a Hispanic Perspective* (Nashville: Abingdon Press, 1990), pp. 75–87. Much to my surprise, this title is the most often quoted phrase in that book.

Notes to Chapter 11 (Míguez Bonino)

1. See the discussion of this dimension of Wesley's contact with Hispanic culture in the essay by Justo González in this volume (chapter 10).

2. For the history of Protestantism in Latin America, see Pierre Bastian, *Historia del Protestantismo en América Latina* (1990); and Pablo A. Deiros, *Historia del Cristianismo en América Latina* (Buenos Aires: Fraternidad Teologica Latinoamericana, 1992).

3. I have attempted to characterize the theological trends in Latin American Protestantism in *Faces of Latin American Protestantism* (Grand Rapids: Wm. B. Eerdmans, 1997).

4. David O. Moberg, *The Great Reversal: Evangelism versus Social Concern* (Philadelphia: J. B. Lippincott, 1972).

5. Signs of this interest include the growing participation of Latin Americans in the work of the Oxford Institute; the appearance of books like *La tradición protestante en la teología latinoamericana: Primer intento— lectura de la tradición metodista*, ed. José Duque (San José, Costa Rica: DEI, 1983) edited by an ecumenical center and with the participation of several non-Methodist authors; and the great interest and cooperation by Latin American theologians and ministers (not only Methodists!) in the Spanish translation of Wesley's works now in process.

6. Parts of the following were presented at the Oxford Institute, August 1997, as the Kirkpatrick Lectureship, under the title: "Salvation as the Work of the Trinity: An Attempt at a Holistic Understanding from a Latin American Perspective." This lecture will be included in *Trinity, Community, and Power: Mapping Trajectories in Wesleyan Theology*, ed. M. Douglas Meeks (Nashville: Kingswood Books, 1998).

7. Juan Luis Segundo had already pointed in this direction in *Our Idea of God* (Maryknoll, NY: Orbis Books, 1974; original edition 1968). More recent work would include Leonardo Boff, *Trinity and Society* (Maryknoll, NY: Orbis Books, 1988); Ronaldo Muñoz, *The God of Christians* (Maryknoll, NY: Orbis Books, 1990); Gustavo Gutiérrez, *The God of Life* (Maryknoll, NY: Orbis Books, 1991); Míguez Bonino, *Faces of Latin American Protestantism*; and Guillermo Hansen, "Trinity and Liberation Theology: a Study of the Trinitarian Doctrine in Latin American Liberation Theology" (Chicago Theological Seminary, Ph.D. thesis, 1995).

8. Walter Klaiber and Manfred Marquardt, *Gelebte Gnade: Grundriss einer Theologie der Evangelisch-methodistischen Kirche* (Stuttgart: Christliches Verlagshaus, 1993), 223: "In a certain direction, these dimensions of grace correspond to the trinitarian revelation of God: prevenient grace to the work of God as Creator, redemptive grace to the redeeming action in Jesus Christ, and sanctifying grace to the work of the Holy Spirit."

9. Ibid., pp. 49–50.

10. Pope's argument is developed in different sections of his three volume *Compendium of Christian Theology* (London: Wesleyan Conference Office, 1880). Two brief quotations may help to display the passion that lies behind the insistence on this theme: "Certainly, there is nothing in the condition of human nature that shuts out the possibility of redemption. Its depravity, taken at the worst, is not a total extinction of every element that grace might hold on: the voice of conscience speaking in every language under heaven, in the accents both of fear and of hope; the irrepressible yearnings after some great Deliverer . . . all proclaim that there may be redemption. . . ." (2:46). "The preliminary grace which we regard as the firstfruits of the Redeemer's intervention for the race explains the secret desire of man to be restored; *and thus lights up the whole sphere of ethics*" (3:158, emphasis added). The fuller development of the doctrine of prevenient grace will be found in 2:358–90. It is no wonder that William Townsend says that the emphasis on prevenient grace was perhaps Pope's most lasting contribution to Methodist theology, in *New History of Methodism* (London: Hodder & Stoughton, 1909), 1:25.

11. For my earlier comments on this topic, see "Wesley's Doctrine of Sanctification From a Liberationist Perspective," in *Sanctification and Liberation*, ed, Theodore Runyon (Nashville: Abingdon Press, 1981), 49–63; and "Sanctification: A Latin American Rereading," in *Faith Born in the Struggle for Life*, ed. Dow Kirkpatrick (Grand Rapids: Wm. B. Eerdmans, 1988), 15–25.

12. Theodore H. Runyon, *The New Creation: John Wesley's Theology Today* (Nashville: Abingdon Press, 1998).

13. Hugo Assmann, *Opresión-Liberación: Desafío a los cristianos* (Montevideo, Uruguay: Tierra Nueva, 1971), 96.

14. Albert Outler, "Methodism's Theological Heritage: A Study in Perspective," in *Methodism's Destiny in an Ecumenical Age*, ed. Paul M. Minus Jr. (Nashville: Abingdon Press, 1969), 59.

15. Hansen, "Trinity and Liberation Theology," 868.

16. This last point might raise the vexed debate on *sola gratia-sola fides*. Wesley has not infrequently been questioned as to his Protestant purity in this respect. It seems to me that, placed in these terms, the discussion is not too fruitful. It is the result of the absolutization of an "extrincesism" of grace—the classical *extra nos*—which had a necessary polemical function in the struggle against "works righteousness" but which, out of that context, and used as the theological touchstone to understand the operation of grace, risks issuing in the "cheap grace" that Bonhoeffer denounced.

Notes to Chapter 12 (Grassow)

1. Theodore Runyon, "Wesley and the Theologies of Liberation," in *Sanctification and Liberation* (Nashville: Abingdon Press, 1981), 17.

2. Letter to Lord North (15 June 1775), *Letters* (Telford) 6:161.

3. "Observations on Liberty," §39, *Works* (Jackson) 11:108.

4. Eric Hobsbawm, "Capitalist Crisis in Historical Perspective," in *The Capitalist System*, eds. R. C. Edwards, M. Reich, & T. Weisskopf (Englewood Cliffs, NJ: Prentice-Hall, 1978), 434.

5. "Thoughts on the Present Scarcity of Provisions," *Works* (Jackson) 11:53–59.

6. Robert G. Tuttle, *John Wesley: His Life and Theology* (Grand Rapids: Zondervan, 1978), 334 n.10.

7. *Plain Account of Christian Perfection*, ¶2, *Works* (Jackson) 11:366.

8. For a survey of Wesley's shifting views on whether Christian perfection is normally obtained gradually, or at any instant, see Randy L. Maddox, *Responsible Grace: John Wesley's Practical Theology* (Nashville: Kingswood Books, 1994), 180–87.

9. Runyon, "Theologies of Liberation," 17.

10. "Free Thoughts on the Present State of Public Affairs," *Works* (Jackson) 11:24.

11. See his Letter to the American Preachers (1 March 1775), *Letters* (Telford) 6:142–43.

12. *A Calm Address to the Inhabitants of England*, §21, *Works* (Jackson) 11:137.

13. *Some Observations on Liberty*, §5, *Works* (Jackson) 11:92.

14. *Thoughts Concerning the Origin of Power*, §7, *Works* (Jackson) 11:47.

15. Ibid., p. 48.

16. *OT Notes*, Gen. 1:26–28. This idea is also found in Sermon 29, "Sermon on the Mount, IX," §6, *Works* 1:635, where Wesley quotes approvingly a maxim of the desert fathers: *Optimus Dei cultus, imitari quem colis*—"It is the best worship or service to God, to imitate Him you worship."

17. *Some Observations on Liberty*, §32, *Works* (Jackson) 11:104.

18. Ibid., §34, *Works* (Jackson) 11:105.

19. Ibid., §32, *Works* (Jackson) 11:104.

20. *A Word to a Freeholder*, *Works* (Jackson) 11:197.

21. *Some Observation on Liberty*, §5, *Works* (Jackson) 11:92.

22. *A Calm Address to Our American Colonies*, §14, *Works* (Jackson) 11:88.

23. *A Calm Address to the Inhabitants of England*, §16 *Works* (Jackson) 11:134.

24. For a discussion on the dynamics of civil religion see Robert Bellah, *Beyond Belief* (New York: Harper and Row, 1970); and R. N. Bellah & P. E. Hammond, eds., *Varieties of Civil Religion* (San Francisco, CA: Harper and Row, 1980).

25. See Gustavo Gutiérrez, *A Theology of Liberation* (Maryknoll, NY: Orbis Books, 1973), 300.

26. *Word in Season; or, Advice to an Englishman*, §7, *Works* (Jackson) 11:184.

27. Letter to "Our Brethren in America" (10 September 1784), §6, *Letters* (Telford) 7:239.

28. Letter to John Mason (13 January 1790), *Letters* (Telford) 8:196.

29. *A Plain Account of Christian Perfection*, §5, *Works* (Jackson) 11:367.

30. Albert Outler, "Introduction," *John Wesley*, 28.

31. Sermon 36, "The Law Established by Faith II," §§2.1, 3.3, *Works* 2:38, 41–42.

32. Richard P. Heitzenrater, *The Elusive Mr Wesley* (Nashville: Abingdon Press, 1984) 1:32, 198.

33. Heitzenrater, *Elusive Mr Wesley*, 1:32, 101, 198. See also Outler, *John Wesley*, 28; Tuttle, *John Wesley*, 335; and Jean Orcibal, "The Theological Originality of John Wesley and Continental Spirituality," in *A History of the Methodist Church in Great Britain*, eds. Rupert Davies & Gordon Rupp (London: Epworth Press, 1965) 1:83–111, esp. 95.

34. *Hymns and Sacred Poems* (1739), Preface, §§4–5, *Works* (Jackson), 14:321.

35. Runyon, "Theologies of Liberation," 42. See also Rupert Davies "Justification, Sanctification, and the Liberation of the Person," in *Sanctification and Liberation*, 80; and José Míguez Bonino, "Wesley's Doctrine of Sanctification from a Liberationist Perspective" in *Sanctification and Liberation*, 57–58.

36. Editor's note: The reader may want to compare the somewhat more positive assessment of Wesley on these two points in Manfred Marquardt, *John Wesley's Social Ethics: Praxis and Principles* (Nashville: Abingdon Press, 1992).

37. See Wellman Warner, *The Wesleyan Movement in the Industrial Revolution* (New York: Russell and Russell, 1930), 254.

38. Reinhold Niebuhr, *Moral Man and Immoral Society* (New York: Scribner, 1960), chapters 5 & 6.

39. Sermon 20, "The Lord Our Righteousness," §2.20, *Works* 1:464.

Notes to Chapter 13 (Lee)

1. Sermon 43, "The Scripture Way of Salvation," §1.7, *Works* 2:159.

2. Outler, Introduction, *Works* 1:40.

3. Note that Wesley also published "Extracts from the *Homilies* of Macarius" in *Chr. Library* 1:81–153.

4. Outler, Introduction, *Works* 1:74. For related suggestions, see also his introduction to *John Wesley*, pp. 9–15; and "John Wesley's Interest in the Early Fathers of the Church," *Bulletin of the United Church of Canada Committee on Archives and History* 29 (1980–2):5–17.

5. Ibid., 1:75.

6. Ibid.

7. Hoo-Jung Lee, "The Doctrine of New Creation in the Theology of John Wesley" (Emory University Ph.D. thesis, 1992). See esp. the chapter on "Influences on Wesley of the Eastern Fathers," which deals with Macarius and Ephrem Syrus (pp. 154–245). For related discussions of Wesley and Eastern Orthodoxy, see Randy Maddox, "John Wesley and Eastern Orthodoxy: Influences, Convergences and Differences," *Asbury Theological Journal* 45:2 (1990):28–59; Ted A. Campbell, "Wesley's Use of the Church Fathers," *Asbury Theological Journal* 50:1–2 (1995–6):57–70; and Campbell, "Wesleyan Quest for Ancient Roots: The 1980s," *Wesleyan Theological Journal* 32:1 (1997):5–16.

8. Ibid., 254–56.

9. Kallistos Ware, "Preface," *Pseudo-Macarius, The Fifty Spiritual Homilies and the Great Letter*, tr. & ed. George A. Maloney (New York: Paulist Press, 1992), xiv. This work will be cited hereafter as *Macarius*.

10. I have drawn on Randy L. Maddox, *Responsible Grace: John Wesley's Practical Theology* (Nashville: Kingswood Books, 1994) for helpful guidance in this section.

11. Sermon 3, "Awake, Thou That Sleepest," §2.8, *Works* 1:149.

12. Sermon 24, "Sermon on the Mount IV," §3.1, *Works* 1:541.

13. Sermon 3, "Awake, Thou That Sleepest," §2.10, *Works* 1:150.

14. *NT Notes*, 2 Peter 1:4.

15. Sermon 3, "Awake, Thou That Sleepest," §3.7, *Works* 1:155.

16. Ibid., §3.8, *Works* 1:155.

17. Sermon 12, "The Witness of Our Spirit," §§15–16, *Works* 1:309–10.

18. Maddox, *Responsible Grace*, 86.

19. Cf. Lee, "Doctrine of New Creation," chapter 4; Rex D. Matthews, "'Religion and Reason Joined': A Study in the Theology of John Wesley" (Harvard Divinity School Th.D. thesis, 1986); and Maddox, *Responsible Grace*, 127ff.

20. Sermon 19, "The Great Privilege of Those that are Born of God," §1.7, *Works* 1:434. Cf. Sermon 45, "The New Birth," §2.4, *Works* 2:192–93.

21. Ibid., §1.8, *Works* 1:434.

22. Ibid., §3.3, *Works* 1:442. See also Sermon 85, "On Working Out Our Own Salvation," §3.1–2, *Works* 3:206ff.

23. For a useful survey about this issue see Maddox, *Responsible Grace*, 125ff.

24. Sermon 10, "The Witness of the Spirit I," §1.7, *Works* 1:274.

25. See Sermon 11, "The Witness of the Spirit II," §3.3, *Works* 1:289.

26. Ibid., §3.5, *Works* 1:290.

27. See Sermon 8, "The First-fruits of the Spirit," §1.4, *Works* 1:236.

28. Sermon 13, "On Sin in Believers," §4.1–3, *Works* 1:325–27.

29. Ibid., §4.4–7, *Works* 1:328–29.

30. Cf. Maddox, *Responsible Grace*, 121–23.

31. Ibid., 177–78.

32. *Journal* (13 Sep. 1739), *Works* 19:97.

33. *A Plain Account of Genuine Christianity*, §1:1–9, *John Wesley*, 183–85.

34. Maddox, *Responsible Grace*, 179.

35. *Plain Account of Christian Perfection*, ¶25, Q. 29, *Works* (Jackson) 11:426.

36. *The Character of a Methodist*, *Works* 9:32–42.

37. *Plain Account of Christian Perfection*,¶15, *Works* (Jackson) 11:385.

38. Cf. Lee, "Doctrine of New Creation," chapters 2–3.

39. See esp. Theodore Runyon, "The New Creation: A Wesleyan Distinctive," *Wesleyan Theological Journal* 31.2 (1996):5–19; and Runyon, *The New Creation: John Wesley's Theology Today* (Nashville: Abingdon Press, 1998).

40. Runyon, "New Creation," 7.

41. See Lee, "Doctrine of New Creation," chapter 5 for the relationship between Wesley and the Macarian *Homilies*. A recent detailed study of the issues related to Macarius can be found in Columba Stewart, *"Working the Earth of the Heart": The Messalian Controversy in History, Texts, and Language to AD 431* (Oxford: Clarendon Press, 1991).

42. Ware, "Preface," xii.

43. Maloney, "Introduction," *Macarius*, 2.

44. Ibid.

45. Cf. *Macarius*, Homily 15, §20.

46. Maloney, "Introduction," 3.

47. Stewart, *Working the Earth of the Heart*, chapter 4.

48. Ibid., chapter 5.

49. Vincent Desprez, "Pseudo-Macarius, II: Spiritual Combat, Prayer, and Experience," *American Benedictine Review* 46.2 (1995):220.

50. Stewart, *Working the Earth of the Heart*, 75.

51. *Macarius*, H 25.10 (Wesley, H 13.4, *Chr. Library*, 1:126). References here and following are to the Homily number, then the paragraph number. I include reference to Wesley's edited edition whenever possible to reinforce his agreement with Macarius.

52. Cf. *Macarius*, H 10.1, 5; H 47.5–7 (Wesley, H 6.1, 4; H 21.7, *Chr. Library*, 1:105, 107, 150).

53. *Macarius*, H 15.4 (Wesley, H 7.2, *Chr. Library*, 1:109).

54. *Macarius*, H 15.53, H 16.3–4, H 29.3–5 (Wesley, H 7.5, H 8.1–2, H 17.3–5, *Chr. Library*, 1:110–11, 137–8).

55. See *Macarius*, H 10.2, H 15.16–18, H 27.14 (Wesley, H 6.2, H 7.3–4, H 15.4, *Chr. Library*, 1:106, 109–10, 132).

56. Stewart, *Working the Earth of the Heart*, 81.

57. Ibid., 83; See also *Macarius*, H 15.18 (Wesley, H 7.4, *Chr. Library*, 1:126).

58. See *Macarius*, H 4.1–15, H 10.5 (Wesley, H 3.1–4, 6.4 *Chr. Library*, 1:93–4, 116).

59. Stewart, *Working the Earth of the Heart*, 79–80.

60. *Macarius*, H 19.5 (Wesley, H 10.5, *Chr. Library*, 1:120).

61. *Macarius*, H 26.15 (Wesley, H 14.5, *Chr. Library*, 1:130). Emphasis added.

62. *Macarius*, H 26.15, H 27.17, H 44.4, H 45.3 (Wesley, H 14.5, H 15.5, H 19.4, H 20.3, *Chr. Library*, 1:130, 133, 143–4, 146).

63. Stewart, *Working the Earth of the Heart*, 78.
64. Ibid., 77.
65. *Macarius*, H 26.2 (Wesley, 14.2 *Chr. Library*, 1:129); cf. *Macarius*, H 16.4 (Wesley, 8.3 *Chr. Library*, 1:111).
66. Cf. Stewart, *Working the Earth of the Heart*, 77.
67. See *Macarius*, H 16.8 (Wesley, H 8.4, *Chr. Library*, 1:111).
68. *Macarius*, 44.1 (Wesley, H 19.1, *Chr. Library* 1:142–3).
69. Cf. Ware, "Preface," xv.; and *Macarius*, H 5:8–9 (Wesley includes only §8 as H 4:7, *Chr. Library*, 1:101).
70. *Macarius*, H 5.9.
71. Campbell, "Wesley's Use of the Church Fathers," 63–66.

Notes to Chapter 14 (Maddox)

1. See Colin W. Williams, *John Wesley's Theology Today* (Nashville: Abingdon Press, 1960); and Harold Bosley, "Review of Colin Williams' *John Wesley's Theology Today*," *Religion in Life* 29 (1960):615–17.
2. Surveys of the history of Wesley Studies that I have found helpful in pursuing the focus of this investigation include Frank Baker, "Unfolding John Wesley: A Survey of Twenty Years' Studies in Wesley's Thought," *Quarterly Review* 1.1 (1980):44–58; Richard P. Heitzenrater, "The Present State of Wesley Studies," *Methodist History* 22 (1984):221–33; and Albert C. Outler, "A New Future for 'Wesley Studies': An Agenda for 'Phase III'," in *The Future of the Methodist Theological Traditions*, ed. M. Douglas Meeks (Nashville: Abingdon Press, 1985), 34–52.
3. The most notable exception—a biography still worth reading—is Robert Southey, *The Life of Wesley and the Rise and Progress of Methodism*, 2 vols. (New York: Gilley, 1820). For brief insightful characterizations of many of these early biographies, see Richard Heitzenrater, *The Elusive Mr. Wesley*, 2 vols. (Nashville: Abingdon Press, 1984) 2:174–79.
4. This point has been noted in Kenneth E. Rowe, "The Search for the Historical Wesley," in *The Place of Wesley in the Christian Tradition*, ed. K. E. Rowe (Metuchen, NJ: Scarecrow, 1976), 1–10, p. 1. The extract from the *Homilies* is available in *John Wesley*, 123–33.
5. Cf. John Whitehead, *The Life of the Reverend John Wesley* (New York: R. Worthington, 1881 [original, 1793–96]), 318.
6. The best examples are Luke Tyerman, *The Life and Times of the Reverend John Wesley, M.A.* (London: Hodder & Stoughton, 1871); and James Harrison Rigg, *The Living Wesley* (New York: Nelson & Phillips, 1874). See also Rigg, *The Relations of John Wesley and Wesleyan Methodism to the Church of England* (London: Longmans, Green & Co, 1868), esp. p. 41.
7. A classic example is, again, Rigg, *The Living Wesley*. See also: Cyrus D. Foss, "Wesley and Personal Religious Experience," in *The Wesley Memorial Volume*, ed. J. O. A. Clark (New York: Phillips & Hunt, 1880), 128–48; and B. P. Raymond, "Wesley's Religious Experience," *Methodist Review* 86 (1904):28–35.
8. Michel Haemmerlin, *Essai Dogmatique sur John Wesley, D'Après ses Sermons* (Colmar: Camille Decker, 1857). This was originally a thesis for the bachelor of theology at the Protestant faculty at Strasbourg. Haemmerlin

used *Sermons on Several Occasions* (London: Mason, 1847), which contained 137 sermons. I am indebted to Michel Weyer for tracking down biographical information on Haemmerlin.

9. Cf. Robert Brown, *John Wesley's Theology: The Principle of its Vitality and its Progressive Stages of Development* (London: Jackson, Walford, & Hodder, 1865), 7, 23–25. This work was reprinted with a new preface (which makes his agenda clearer) as *John Wesley; or, The Theology of Conscience* (London: E. Stock, 1868). See also his *The Philosophy of Evangelicalism* (London, 1857); *The Gospel of Common Sense; or, Mental, Moral, and Social Science in Harmony with Scriptural Christianity*; and *The Fear of God in Relation to Religion, Theology, and Reason* (Edinburgh: A. Elliott, 1876). Kenneth Rowe suggests in the *Methodist Union Catalog* (Metuchen, NJ: Scarecrow, 1975ff.) that this Robert Brown is the Wesleyan Methodist minister who published *Membership of Class, a Condition of Membership in the Wesleyan Society* (Manchester, England, 1874), but there is no evidence in the latter's obituary of these other works (I am indebted for this information to John Vickers). He identifies himself only as an "evangelical."

10. For more on both the Anglican precedent and Wesley's practice, see Randy L. Maddox, "John Wesley—Practical Theologian?" *Wesleyan Theological Journal* 23 (1988):122–47.

11. E. P. Humphrey, *Our Theology and Its Development* (Philadelphia, PA: Presbyterian Board of Publication, 1857), 68–69. Note his rejection of even Watson's *Institutes* as adequate in the footnote on p. 69!

12. (London: W. Booth, 1825). This collection was apparently prepared by William Carpenter.

13. Richard Watson, *Theological Institutes: or, A View of the Evidences, Doctrines, Morals, and Institutions of Christianity*, 3 vols. (London: John Mason, 1825–28).

14. For the transition to Methodist scholasticism in British Methodism see Langford's chapter in this volume (chapter 2); and Thomas Langford, *Practical Divinity: Theology in the Wesleyan Tradition* (Nashville: Abingdon Press, 1983), 49–77. For an analysis of specific movement away from Wesley's model in American Methodism see Randy L. Maddox, "An Untapped Inheritance: American Methodism and Wesley's Practical Theology," in *Doctrines and Disciplines: Methodist Theology and Practice*, ed. Dennis Campbell, et al. (Nashville: Abingdon Press, 1998).

15. Watson's precedent is noted by Thomas Langford in *Doctrine and Theology in the United Methodist Church* (Nashville: Kingswood Books, 1991), 13. Martin Wellings has provided a similar analysis of continuing British Methodism in "'Throttled by a Dead Hand'? The 'Wesleyan Standard' in Nineteenth- and Early Twentieth-Century British Methodism," a paper presented at the Tenth Oxford Institute of Methodist Theological Studies (August 1997) and forthcoming in *Methodist History* (1999). For a detailed analysis of American Methodism, see Randy L. Maddox, "Respected Founder/Neglected Guide: The Role of Wesley in American Methodist Theology," forthcoming in *Methodist History* 37.2 (Jan. 1999).

16. For a survey of these debates see Randy L. Maddox, "Holiness of Heart and Life: Lessons from North American Methodism," *Asbury Theological Journal* 51.1 (1996):151–72.

17. The most vigorous examples are Asbury Lowrey, "Dr. Mudge and

His Book," *Methodist Review* 77 (1895):954–9; and William McDonald, *John Wesley and His Doctrine* (Chicago: Christian Witness, 1904), 107ff.

18. James Mudge, "A Friendly Word with my Critics," *Methodist Review* 78 (1896):125–30, here, 129.

19. On American developments see Maddox, "Untapped Inheritance." For emerging Methodist theology in Germany, see Karl Steckel, "Zur Theologie der Evangelisch-Methodistischen Kirche," in *Geschichte der Evangelisch-Methodistischen Kirche*, ed. K. Steckel & C. E. Sommer (Stuttgart: Christliches Verlagshaus, 1982), 243–76.

20. See the extended argument that Wesley should be valued as a preacher but not as a model theologian in Wilbur Fisk Tillett, *Personal Salvation* (Nashville: Cokesbury, 1902), 510–14.

21. The best example is George Richard Crooks & John F. Hurst, *Theological Encyclopedia and Methodology* (New York: Phillips & Hunt, 1884), 47.

22. Note how Anglican theological activity is specifically dismissed in William F. Warren, *Systematische Theologie, einheitliche behandelt, Erste Lieferung*: Allgemeine Einleitung (Bremen: Verlag der Tractathauses H. Neulsen, 1865), 87 n.1. It is striking that Warren never directly discusses Wesley in this book!

23. The suggestion of John McClintock in "Warren's Introduction to Systematic Theology," *Methodist Review* 48 (1866):100–24, pp. 102–4.

24. For some examples of how standard this concession had become, see F. W. MacDonald, "Wesley as a Theologian," *Methodist Recorder* 31 (1891):257; T. R. Pierce, *The Intellectual Side of John Wesley* (Nashville: MECS Publishing House, 1897); James W. Bashford, *Wesley and Goethe* (Cincinnati, OH: Jennings & Pye, 1903), 85–86; and Harris Franklin Rall, "Do We Need a Methodist Creed?" *Methodist Review* 89 (1907):221–30, pp. 222–23.

25. Cf. Elden Dale Dunlap, "Methodist Theology in Great Britain in the Nineteenth Century" (Yale University Ph.D. thesis, 1956), 133–38, 213–14, 286; and Robert Eugene Chiles, *Theological Transition in American Methodism: 1790–1935* (New York: Abingdon Press, 1965), 49. "Gracious ability" places the primary stress on our human *ability*, rather than God's grace. For more on Wesley's alternative see Randy L. Maddox, *Responsible Grace: John Wesley's Practical Theology* (Nashville: Kingswood Books, 1994).

26. *John Wesley and the Religious Societies* (1921); *John Wesley and the Methodist Societies* (1923); *John Wesley and the Advance of Methodism* (1925); *John Wesley, The Master Builder, 1757–72* (1927); and *John Wesley, the Last Phase* (1934) (all, London: Epworth Press).

27. For American Methodism see the analysis in Maddox, "Respected Founder." For British Methodism see the discussion of J. Robinson Gregory and John Shaw Banks in Wellings, "'Throttled by a Dead Hand'." A cursory survey of German Methodist theology of the time shows a similar dearth of interaction with Wesley.

28. The quote is from Foster, *Studies in Theology*, Vol. 1: *Prolegomena: Philosophic Basis of Theology; or, Rational Principles of Religious Faith* (New York: Hunt & Eaton, 1891), vi–vii. The only passing reference to Wesley I have found is in Vol. 6: *Sin* (New York: Hunt & Eaton, 1899), 179–81.

29. Frank Wilbur Collier, *Back to Wesley* (New York: Methodist Book Concern, 1924), 5.

30. Cf. George Eayrs' description of Wesley as his "human hero," in *John*

Wesley, Christian Philosopher and Church Founder (London: Epworth Press, 1926), 50.

31. E.g., John C. Granbery, "Method in Methodist Theology," *Methodist Quarterly Review* 58 (1909):230–43, p. 235; Herbert B. Workman, *The Place of Methodism in the Catholic Church* (New York: Methodist Book Concern, 1921), 23–6; and George Croft Cell, *The Rediscovery of John Wesley* (New York: Henry Holt, 1935) esp. 46–51.

32. E.g., Eayrs, *John Wesley*, 58–59; Frank Wilbur Collier, *John Wesley Among the Scientists* (New York: Abingdon Press, 1928) 49, 61; and Paul Waitman Hoon, "The Soteriology of John Wesley" (Edinburgh University Ph.D. thesis, 1936), 342ff.

33. Note especially John Wesley Prince, *Wesley on Religious Education* (New York: Methodist Book Concern, 1926); and Alfred Harris Body, *John Wesley and Education* (London: Epworth Press, 1936).

34. Note how this issue predominates in Francis J. McConnell, "New Interest in John Wesley," *Journal of Religion* 20 (1940):340–58.

35. E.g., David Decamp Thompson, *John Wesley as a Social Reformer* (New York: Eaton & Mains, 1898); John Alfred Faulkner, *The Socialism of John Wesley* (London: Charles Kelley, 1908); and Eric McCoy North, *Early Methodist Philanthropy* (New York: Methodist Book Concern, 1914).

36. E.g., W. H. Meredith, "John Wesley, Christian Socialist," *Methodist Review* 83 (1901):426–39; and Kathleen Walker MacArthur, *The Economic Ethics of John Wesley* (New York: Abingdon-Cokesbury Press, 1936).

37. E.g., Ernst Cahn, "John Wesley als Vorkämpfer einer christlichen Sozialethik," *Die Christliche Welt* 46 (1932):208–12.

38. For summaries of this debate see Vilém D. Schneeberger *Theologische Wurzeln des Sozialen Akzents bei John Wesley* (Zürich: Gotthelf, 1974), 25–29; and Luke Keefer Jr., "John Wesley, The Methodists, and Social Reform in England," *Wesleyan Theological Journal* 25.1 (1990):7–20.

39. Note in particular the entire issue of *Religion in Life* 29.4 (1960), which was devoted to the topic of "Neo-Wesleyanism." Significant representatives of essentially neo-Orthodox construals of Wesley include William Cannon, *The Theology of John Wesley, with Special Reference to the Doctrine of Justification* (New York: Abingdon-Cokesbury Press, 1946); John Deschner, *Wesley's Christology: An Interpretation* (Dallas, TX: Southern Methodist University Press, 1960); Franz Hildebrandt, *From Luther to Wesley* (London: Lutterworth Press, 1951); Harald Lindström, *Wesley and Sanctification* (Stockholm: Nya Bokförlags Aktiebolaget, 1946); and E. Gordon Rupp, *Methodism in Relation to Protestant Tradition* (London: Epworth Press, 1954).

40. This point was made in Lycurgus Starkey, *The Work of the Holy Spirit: A Study in Wesleyan Theology* (New York: Abingdon Press, 1962), 162; and Claude Thompson, "Aldersgate and the New Reformers," *Christian Advocate* 6.10 (1962):7–8.

41. The best example would be Carl Michalson, though his published works do not show how much he felt a Wesleyan identity; cf. Theodore H. Runyon, "Carl Michalson as a Wesleyan Theologian," *Drew Gateway* 51.2 (1980):1–13. For a more recent existentialist reading, see Schubert Ogden, "Process Theology and the Wesleyan Witness," *Perkins School of Theology Journal* 37.3 (1984):18–33, esp. 25.

42. See esp. Yoshio Noro, "The Character of John Wesley's Faith," and Hiroaki Matsumoto, "John Wesley's Understanding of Man," in *Japanese Contributions to the Study of John Wesley*, ed. Clifford Edwards (Macon, GA: Wesleyan College, 1967), 6–22, 79–98. For an account of the resurgence of Wesley studies in Japan which started in 1959 see John W. Krummel, "Wesley Studies in Japan," *Northeast Asia Journal of Theology* 2 (1969):135–40. See also the bibliography of "Japan Wesley Studies: 1959–1972" in *Wesley and Methodism* (Tokyo: John Wesley Association) 6 (1972): 20–23. It is not clear whether this attraction to existentialism was due to cultural factors or simply a result of the fact that most of the scholars involved studied at Drew under Carl Michalson.

43. E.g., E. Herbert Nygren, "Wesley's Answer to Existentialism," *Christian Advocate* 9.3 (1965):7–8.

44. The best examples are J. Ernest Rattenbury, *Wesley's Legacy to the World* (London: Epworth, 1928); Williams, *Wesley's Theology Today*; and Michael Hurley, "Introduction," in *John Wesley's Letter to a Roman Catholic* (Nashville: Abingdon Press, 1968), 22–47. This interest was also central to the emerging work of Albert C. Outler. Cf. Leicester R. Longden, "To Recover a Christian Sense of History: The Theological Vision of Albert Cook Outler" (Drew University Ph.D. thesis, 1992).

45. Paul Hoon appears correct in identifying his 1936 study as the first relatively comprehensive survey of Wesley's theology; Hoon, "Soteriology of John Wesley," 6.

46. For a few examples see John A. Faulkner, *Wesley as Sociologist, Theologian, Churchman* (New York: Methodist Book Concern, 1918), 38; Prince, *Wesley on Religious Education*, 11–12; William Henri Guiton, *John Wesley: Esquisse de sa Vie et de son Oevre* (Neuilly, Seine: Depot de Publications Methodistes, 1920), 64–7; and Johannes Schempp, *Seelsorge und Seelenführung bei John Wesley* (Stuttgart: Christliches Verlagshaus, 1949), 9.

47. In addition to the continuing Wesley Historical Society, The Oxford Institute of Methodist Theological Studies began meeting in 1958, the Wesleyan Theological Society was formed in 1965, and a Wesleyan Studies Group was organized at the American Academy of Religion in 1982. Chairs of Wesley Studies have also been established at such universities as Duke and Southern Methodist.

48. For a description, see Frank Baker, "The Oxford Edition of Wesley's Works and Its Text," in *Place of Wesley*, 117–33.

49. Cf. the survey of this period in Heitzenrater, "Present State," and Thor Hall, "Tradition Criticism: A New View of Wesley," in *Inaugurating the Leroy A. Martin Distinguished Professorship of Religious Studies* (Chattanooga, TN: The University of Tennessee at Chattanooga, 1987), 6–23, p. 7.

50. For a few representative comparisons (positive and negative) of Wesley and Latin American liberation theology see the articles by Rupert Davies, José Míguez Bonino, and Theodore Runyon in *Sanctification and Liberation*, ed. Theodore Runyon (Nashville: Abingdon Press, 1981); the articles by Mortimer Arias and Hugo Assman in *Faith Born in the Struggle for Life*, ed. Dow Kirkpatrick (Grand Rapids: Wm. B. Eerdmans, 1988); Theodore W. Jennings Jr., *Good News to the Poor: John Wesley's Evangelical Economics* (Nashville: Abingdon Press, 1990); and Kenneth Collins, "John Wesley and Liberation Theology," *Asbury Theological Journal* 42.1 (1987):85–90.

51. E.g., Earl Kent Brown, "Feminist Theology and the Women of Mr. Wesley's Methodism," in *Wesleyan Theology Today*, ed. Theodore Runyon (Nashville: Kingswood Books, 1985), 143–50; Sheila Davaney, "Feminism, Process Thought and the Wesleyan Tradition," in *Wesleyan Theology Today*, 105–16; Randy L. Maddox, "Wesleyan Theology and the Christian Feminist Critique," *Wesleyan Theological Journal* 22 (1987):101–11; and Marjorie Suchocki, "Coming Home: Wesley, Whitehead, and Women," *Drew Gateway* 57.3 (1987):31–43.

52. See John Culp, "A Dialogue with the Process Theology of John B. Cobb Jr.," *Wesleyan Theological Journal* 15.2 (1980):33–44; Davaney, "Feminism"; Ogden, "Process Theology"; Michael Peterson, "Orthodox Christianity, Wesleyanism, and Process Theology," *Wesleyan Theological Journal* 15.2 (1980):45–58; and Suchocki, "Coming Home."

53. Cf. the Select Bibliography in Maddox, *Responsible Grace* (375–408), which includes over one hundred book-length studies on aspects of Wesley's theology between 1960 and 1994.

54. For a survey of these debates see Randy L. Maddox, "Reading Wesley as Theologian," *Wesleyan Theological Journal* 30.1 (1995):7–54. A good introduction to resulting readings of Wesley's theology can be gained by comparing Maddox, *Responsible Grace*; Kenneth Collins, *The Scripture Way of Salvation: The Heart of John Wesley's Theology* (Nashville: Abingdon Press, 1997); and Theodore Runyon, *The New Creation: John Wesley's Theology Today* (Nashville: Abingdon Press, 1998).

55. Albert C. Outler, "Towards a Re-appraisal of John Wesley as a Theologian," *Perkins School of Theology Journal* 14 (1961):5–14.

56. See Outler, "Introduction," *John Wesley*, vii; Outler, "John Wesley as Theologian—Then and Now," *Methodist History* 12.4 (1974):63–82, esp. 65; Outler, "John Wesley: Folk Theologian," *Theology Today* 34 (1977): 150–60; Outler, "John Wesley's Interests in the Early Fathers of the Church," *Bulletin of the United Church of Canada Committee on Archives and History* 29 (1980–82):5–17, esp. 6–7; and Outler, "Introduction," *Works* 1:67.

57. Contrast Outler, *John Wesley*, 119; with Outler, "A New Future," 48.

58. E.g., M. Douglas Meeks, "The Future of the Methodist Theological Traditions," in *Future of Methodist Theological Traditions*, 13–33; Meeks, "John Wesley's Heritage and the Future of Systematic Theology," in *Wesleyan Theology Today*, 8–46; Maddox, "John Wesley—Practical Theologian?"; and Gregory Clapper, *John Wesley on Religious Affections: His Views on Experience and Emotion and Their Role in the Christian Life and Theology* (Metuchen, NJ: Scarecrow Press, 1989), 169–71.

Contributors

Brian E. Beck, Secretary of the British Methodist Conference 1984–98; Co-chair of the Oxford Institute of Methodist Theological Studies.

Kenneth L. Carder, Resident Bishop, Nashville Area, The United Methodist Church.

Justo L. González, Executive Director, Hispanic Theological Initiative, Emory University, Atlanta, Georgia.

Peter Grassow, Minister, Methodist Church, Lyttleton, South Africa; Tutor of Methodist Ordinance and Part-Time Lecturer, John Wesley College, Pretoria, South Africa.

Theodore W. Jennings Jr., Professor of Biblical and Constructive Theology, The Chicago Theological Seminary, Chicago, Illinois.

Thomas A. Langford, William Kellon Quick Professor of Theology and Methodist Studies, Emeritus, The Divinity School, Duke University, Durham, North Carolina.

Hoo-Jung Lee, Associate Professor of Historical Theology, Methodist Theological Seminary, Seoul, Korea.

James C. Logan, E. Stanley Jones Professor of Evangelism, Wesley Theological Seminary, Washington, D.C.

Randy L. Maddox, Paul T. Walls Professor of Wesleyan Theology, Seattle Pacific University, Seattle, Washington.

Manfred Marquardt, Dean and Professor of Systematic Theology, Theologische Seminar der Evangelische-methodistischen Kirche, Reutlingen, Germany.

M. Douglas Meeks, Academic Dean and Professor of Systematic Theology, Wesley Theological Seminary, Washington, D.C.

José Míguez Bonino, Professor of Systematic Theology and Ethics, Emeritus, Facultad Evangélica de Teología, ISEDET, Buenos Aires, Argentina.

Jürgen Moltmann, Professor of Systematic Theology, Emeritus, University of Tübingen, Germany.

Mary Elizabeth Mullino Moore, Professor of Theology and Christian Education, Claremont School of Theology, Claremont, California.

Marjorie Suchocki, Ingraham Professor of Theology and Vice President for Academic Affairs, Claremont School of Theology, Claremont, California.